The Writer's Guide to Self-Editing

The Writer's Guide to Self-Editing

Essential Tips for Online and Print Publication

NAVEED SALEH

McFarland & Company, Inc., Publishers
Jefferson, North Carolina

Library of Congress Cataloguing-in-Publication Data

Names: Saleh, Naveed, author.
Title: The writer's guide to self-editing : essential tips for online and print publication / Naveed Saleh.
Description: Jefferson, North Carolina : McFarland & Company, Inc., Publishers, 2019 | Includes bibliographical references and index.
Identifiers: LCCN 2018046338 | ISBN 9781476671598 (paperback : acid free paper) ∞
Subjects: LCSH: Editing—Handbooks, manuals, etc. | Online authorship—Handbooks, manuals, etc.
Classification: LCC PN162 .S15 2019 | DDC 808.02/7—dc23
LC record available at https://lccn.loc.gov/2018046338

British Library cataloguing data are available

ISBN (print) 978-1-4766-7159-8
ISBN (ebook) 978-1-4766-3404-3

Front cover photograph by SI Photography/IStock

Printed in the United States of America

McFarland & Company, Inc., Publishers
Box 611, Jefferson, North Carolina 28640
www.mcfarlandpub.com

For Maliheh, Saeed, Fareed, Zain, Zaid,
Zachary, Zavier, Dokhi, Emily, Charlie,
Dr. Gastel, Mrs. Robichaud, Dr. Trunsky,
Dr. Balon, Dr. Christensen, Madame Corcos,
and Mrs. Witucki. It takes a village…

Table of Contents

Part V: Organization

Part VI: Online Publication

Part VII: Global Considerations

Preface

We live in marvelous times where the Internet has changed so much so fast—most notably publication.

With the immediacy of online content, media coverage has transformed. We no longer have to wait for the morning newspaper to find out about an event that occurred half a world away. Nowadays, news is instant, and there's a premium for timely copy that's clean and well written.

Sheer volume and rapid turnover limit editorial oversight at even the biggest online publications. Many successful professional writers who routinely attract tens or even hundreds of thousands of readers a month must turn in publishable content without the benefit of a dedicated editor who will provide comprehensive feedback.

The Internet has also provided so many more writers access to publication. Nowadays, anybody can set up a website or WordPress blog and attract a following. These writers are one-person shows who act as their own fact checkers, editors, and publishers. That being said, nothing beats having a knowledgeable and experienced editor review your work. Unfortunately, in the current media milieu, many writers lack this luxury. Instead, writers must become *self-editors.*

The principles presented in this guide will help you become a successful self-editor who is capable of producing publishable nonfiction autonomously. Moreover, even if you have the benefit of an editor who will analyze your work before publication—such as, for example, at a reputable print publication—the principles contained herein will help you present crisp copy, which will no doubt please.

This book grew out of my own study of style guides and editing treatises representing various publishers and organizations. As a professional writer and editor, I learned to use such style guidance to not only edit articles and other documents for clients but also to benefit my own practice of writing. By self-editing my own work, my writing improved greatly. I hope to share this knowledge and success with others interested in becoming self-editors.

When writing any style, writing, or editing guide, one obvious concern is how to distinguish the new guide from what is already out there. This book is different from other books in two notable ways. First, this book looks at online publishing practices in detail—using the most current knowledge of search engine optimization (SEO) to help guide the writing and self-editing process. Second, this book endeavors to take an evidence-based approach to writing and self-editing. This book extends past the prescriptive guidance of ordinary stylebooks, and it incorporates empirical, corpus-based research from prominent linguists including Geoffrey Leech, Douglas Biber, and Pam Peters.

One limitation of corpus-based research is that closed corpora become dated. Much of the data presented here dates back to corpora from the late twentieth century. Moreover, with the advent of the Google and sophisticated search tools, the field of corpus linguistics will likely soon evolve to include web-based approaches.

Introduction

This book is intended for anybody who wants to create clean copy that is ready for publication. To apply the principles described in this guide, a person need only a curious mind and a critical and introspective eye. Ultimately, I see this self-editing guide proving of value to aspiring and professional writers of nonfiction alike.

I suggest using this book in the following fashion. First, read the book in its entirety. Second, write your own articles and other nonfiction documents with these principles in mind. Third, edit your work using these principles. In sum, I want you to *write* as best you can and then *self-edit* using these principles. If done well, after you *write* and *self-edit*, you can *publish* your work: *write, self-edit, publish.*

After reading this book once through, I hope that it remains a lifelong reference that will aid in all your online and print publication efforts. For ease of reference, this book is divided into seven parts: Style, Diction, Mechanics, Punctuation, Organization, Online Publication and Global Considerations. The part on style provides guidance that is well accepted by many experts and publications. The part on diction, however, goes much deeper to explain how to use words in a clear, correct, and effective manner.

Much of the guidance in this book is intended for every writer at any skill level. Some of the guidance in this book is more nuanced and intended for those who pay close attention to the craft. Often, it's small differences that distinguish the work of a professional writer.

Each of the 75 chapters (tips) is structured so that it can stand alone. In order for each tip to stand alone, key concepts are occasionally repeated. Because some points are covered from different vantage points in different parts of this book, I encourage you to use the index to further explore each topic.

If you want to learn more about where I gleaned the information found in this book, please take a closer look at the bibliography. When structured well, a bibliography can serve as a road map that indicates where a writer has been during the writing process.

Part I: Style

1. Adverb Placement

Tip: In general, place an adverb closest to what it modifies.

Key Points

- With transitive verbs, adverbs are placed before the verb.
- With intransitive verbs, adverbs are placed after the verb.
- In a verb phrase that consists of an auxiliary verb and a principal (main) verb, an adverb that modifies this phrase is naturally placed between the auxiliary verb and the principal verb.
- Splitting infinitives is okay.
- Watch your placement of *only.*
- Copulative verbs take adjectives, not adverbs.

Generally, you want to place an adverb closest to what it modifies. Doing so limits confusion. You also want to make sure that your use of adverbs is idiomatic and sounds right.

This general guidance, however, belies how nuanced the proper placement of adverbs can be. It also fails to address issues of contention, such as split infinitives and splitting verb phrases.

Unfortunately, many writing and editing texts provide only cursory guidance with regard to adverb placement. Two guides that provide more robust guidance regarding adverb placement are *The Chicago Manual of Style* and *Fowler's Dictionary of Modern English Usage.*

It's impossible to provide guidance that addresses every thorny case of adverb placement. Sometimes the placement of an adverb depends on the writer's choice and intention to stress or modify certain elements of a sentence. Nevertheless, we can take a look at certain scenarios that are representative of constructions that you'll commonly encounter in your writing. We'll also look at a related concept: copulative verbs.

Transitive Verbs

Transitive verbs require an object to make sense and can take direct objects, indirect objects, or both. Most verbs are transitive. With transitive verbs, the adverb should be placed before the verb so as not to split the verb from the object.

EXAMPLE: Sonny gleefully ate the entire bag of chips.

EXAMPLE: Rocco couldn't really hear her.

EXAMPLE Zavier begrudgingly handed him the tube of shaving cream.

Intransitive Verbs

Intransitive verbs are verbs that don't need a direct object to make sense. However, other phrases can follow an intransitive verb, including a prepositional phrase with an object, or a modifying phrase. More typical examples of intransitive verbs include *pray*, *arrive*, *sit*, *laugh*, and *talk*.

Adverbs are usually placed directly following an intransitive verb.

EXAMPLE: Klaus sat quietly.

EXAMPLE: Klaus sat quietly on the bench.

EXAMPLE: Klaus sat quietly while his girlfriend cried.

On a related note, certain verbs, such as *leave*, can be either transitive or intransitive.

TRANSITIVE: The client quickly left the building.

INTRANSITIVE: You must leave quickly.

Verb Phrases

In a verb phrase that consists of an auxiliary verb and a principal (main) verb, an adverb that modifies this phrase is naturally placed between the auxiliary verb and the principal verb.

EXAMPLE: Many universities are completely opposed to Trump's executive order limiting immigration.

If there are two auxiliary verbs followed by a principle verb, an adverb modifying this verb phrase can be placed between the two auxiliary verbs.

EXAMPLE: President Obama predicted that had he run against Trump for a third term, he would definitely have defeated him.

On a more minute point, when a compound transitive verb is written in the passive voice, the adverb follows the auxiliary elements. Of note, all passive constructions are transitive because they begin with the object.

EXAMPLE: The fugitive will be swiftly apprehended.

Split Infinitives

Unlike English, in which an infinitive comprises *to* followed by the base form of the verb, in Latin, the infinitive form is one word. For example, in Latin, *to run* is *currere,* and *to climb* is *ascendere.* Because in Latin these infinitive forms are one word, they can't be split. Consequently, English grammarians and style mavens alike have historically advocated that infinitives never be split, and between 1850 and 1925, many declared splitting infinitives a solecism. (In case you're wondering, *solecism* is a big word for a mistake in speech or grammar.) However, views on splitting adverbs—and more generally verb phrases—have softened. Nowadays, it's totally acceptable to *split infinitives* when doing so sounds right.

Curiously, the splitting of infinitives has a long history. Split infinitives began to pop up in the English language in the thirteenth century and were occasionally used between the thirteenth and the fifteenth centuries. For instance, in the works of Chaucer, there are two instances when infinitives are split. Between the sixteenth and eighteenth centuries, however, the practice of splitting infinitives fell out of favor.

Toward the beginning of the nineteenth century, the practice of splitting infinitives reemerged. Nowadays, splitting infinitives is acceptable. Of interest, *The Associated Press Stylebook* and *The Chicago Manual of Style* also recommend splitting infinitives when prudent and idiomatic.

Star Trek fans (Trekkies) will instantly recognize the following example of a split infinitive from the opening credits of the original series: "To boldly go where no man has gone before." Now, imagine if this line were recast to avoid a split infinitive: "To go where no man has gone before boldly." Sounds super weird, right?

Here is an example where the infinitive needs to be split to retain meaning. Recasting this sentence to avoid the split infinitive (in other words, placing "quickly" anywhere else) would alter meaning.

EXAMPLE: Jeff plans to quickly eat his sandwich before running to class.

DIFFERENT MEANING: Jeff quickly plans to eat his sandwich before running to class.

DIFFERENT MEANING: Jeff plans to eat his sandwich before quickly running to class.

Special Cases

Overall, there are many reasons to change the placement of an adverb, including meaning, rhythm, and emphasis.

EXAMPLE: Increasingly, people are using smartphones.

Here the adverb "increasingly" doesn't split the verb phrase.

Certain adverbs should be placed gingerly to minimize confusion. These adverbs include the following:

- always
- never
- often
- only
- rarely
- seldom

Now, let's consider these examples where placement affects meaning.

EXAMPLE: Jane only buys the best speakers.

DIFFERENT MEANING: Jane buys only the best speakers.

In the first example, the implied meaning is that all Jane does is buy speakers and nothing else, which is nonsense. (Jane could also work, eat meals, exercise, raise her kids, and so forth.) Whereas, in the second example, the meaning is that when Jane buys speakers, she buys the best ones available. In other words, the second example makes sense and the first is most likely wrong.

EXAMPLE: Juan rarely sells items listed on eBay.

DIFFERENT MEANING: Juan sells items rarely listed on eBay.

When self-editing your own work, identify all adverbs used and check their placement with the preceding guidance in mind. When in doubt, follow your ear and think about what the adverb is modifying.

Copulative or Linking Verbs

There are three kinds of verbs: transitive verbs, intransitive verbs, and copulative, or linking, verbs. Transitive verbs need objects to make sense. Intransitive verbs make sense without objects. Copulative (copular) verbs link subject and complement.

The word *copula* is a grammatical term referring to linking words. This word is derived from the prefix *co-*, which means together, and the Latin *apere,* meaning *fasten.*

Copular verbs refer to states of being. The most commonly used copular form is *be*. Here are other copular verbs:

- appear
- become
- feel
- look
- seem
- smell
- taste

The thing about copulative verbs is that they don't take adverbs. Instead, they link subjects to adjectives.

WRONG: These flowers smell ~~well~~.

RIGHT: These flowers smell good.

WRONG: After eating too much, Greg felt ~~terribly~~.

RIGHT: After eating too much, Greg felt terrible.

2. Articles

TIP: Check your writing for dropped articles.

Key Points

- The definite article *the* introduces specific nouns or noun phrases.
- The indefinite articles, *a* or *an,* introduce nonspecific nouns or noun phrases.
- Proper nouns typically don't take an article.
- Keep an eye out for dropped articles and when warranted, try to stick them back in.

Although we use articles countless times each day, proper usage of articles can be confusing. In fact, professional editors spend a lot of time sticking dropped articles back into the text of documents, and otherwise fixing article usage.

Before we examine more specific usages, let's take a more general look at the definite article, *the,* and indefinite articles, *a* and *an.*

Definite Article

There's only one type of definite article: *the.* A definite article introduces a specific noun or noun phrase that has been previously defined, is already defined, is about to be defined, or has already been mentioned. Alternatively, a definite article is used to introduce something that exists only in one form. Definite articles are used to refer to something exact.

EXAMPLE: I know that humongous squirrel that ran across the yard. The squirrel was gray.

EXAMPLE: Herman went to the local movie theater.

Definite articles are used to introduce nouns or noun phrases that begin with adjectives or qualifying words and are thus specific. This guidance also applies to plural nouns, which in their bare form don't take a definite article, but when combined with a modifier refer to something specific.

EXAMPLE: The big explosion occurred two weeks ago.

EXAMPLE: Austin likes to watch the newest movies.

BUT: Austin likes to watch movies.

Indefinite Articles

Usually, the indefinite articles, *a* and *an,* are used to introduce new nouns or noun phrases into speech or writing. Indefinite articles are a type of *determiner* (also referred to as *noun markers*). Indefinite articles are used to introduce things that exist in more than one form or case.

Importantly, indefinite articles are nonspecific and thus don't refer to a specific or previously identified person or thing.

EXAMPLE: Alice never saw a narwhal before.

Use the indefinite article *a* before words that begin with a consonant sound and the indefinite article *an* before words that begin with a vowel sound. This guidance applies to abbreviations, too.

EXAMPLES: a cat, a dog, a year, a train, a hotel, a hypothesis, a CEO

EXAMPLES: an owl, an aardvark, an NAACP event, an FBI agent

According to Bryan A. Garner in *The Oxford Dictionary of American Usage and Style:* "The traditional rule is that if the *h-* is sounded, *a* is the proper form. Most people following that rule would say *a historian* and *a historic*.... The theory behind using *an* in such a context, however, is that the *h-* is very weak when the accent is on the second rather than the first syllable. Today, however, *an hypothesis* and *an historical* are likely to strike readers and listeners as affectations. As Mark Twain once wrote, referring to *humble, heroic* and *historical*: 'Correct writers of the American language do not put an *an* before these words.'"

Count Nouns

Count nouns refer to individual things that are countable, such as one car, three buildings and five computers. Generally, indefinite articles are used with singular count nouns.

EXAMPLE: Ari brought a mug to the office.

When referring to a specific count noun, use a definite article. Typically, specific count nouns are followed by modifiers, such as a prepositional phrase or *adjective clause* (relative clause). An adjective clause begins with *that, which, who,* or *whom.*

EXAMPLES The honey badger is a very aggressive animal.

EXAMPLE: Ari brought the coffee mug with the Hello Kitty face to the office.

EXAMPLE: Ari brought the coffee mug that he bought on eBay to the office.

Plural count nouns take no article when they refer to something generalized.

EXAMPLE: Computers are getting cheaper.

Specific plural count nouns take a definite article.

EXAMPLE: The computers sold at Walmart are meant for general consumers.

When plural count nouns are modified by an adjective, and are thus specific, they take a definite article.

EXAMPLE: The obnoxious children spoke throughout the movie.

Noncount Nouns

Noncount nouns (mass nouns) are abstractions or materials that can't be counted, such as wisdom, anger, love, homework, mail, milk, cheese, pasta, dirt, grain, or cement. Noncount nouns take either a definite article or no article. Noncount nouns never take an indefinite article.

EXAMPLE: Rose likes penne pasta.

EXAMPLE: Rose likes the penne pasta.

When referring to a specific noncount noun, use a definite article. Specific count nouns are followed by modifiers, such as a prepositional phrase or adjective clause. Once again, an adjective clause begins with *that*, *which*, *who*, or *whom*.

EXAMPLE: Wisdom comes from experience.

EXAMPLE: The wisdom that Walter seeks can't be learned in books.

EXAMPLE: Steel is made in the United States.

EXAMPLE: The steel made in the United States is more expensive than that made in China.

Proper Nouns

Singular proper nouns typically take no article.

EXAMPLE: LeBron James was chosen first in the 2003 NBA draft.

EXAMPLE: Everyone knows that Earth is the third planet from the sun.

Of interest, when the word *earth* is preceded by *the,* it's not capitalized because it's not a proper noun and is instead a noncount noun.

EXAMPLE: Sonic booms shake the earth.

When the first word of a singular proper noun acts as a modifier of the words that follow, a definite article is used. Furthermore, possessive "of" constructions in proper nouns act as modifiers and thus take a definite article even when singular.

EXAMPLE: The largest indoor aquarium in the world is the Shedd Aquarium in Chicago.

EXAMPLE: The Stockholm archipelago consists of 30,000 islands, skerries, and rocks.

EXAMPLE: The Indian subcontinent consists of India, Pakistan, and Bangladesh

EXAMPLE: American broadcaster Studs Terkel graduated from the University of Chicago.

EXAMPLE: Salazar Slytherin created the Chamber of Secrets.

EXAMPLE: Versailles is home to the Hall of Mirrors.

Example: In an editorial published in April 2017, the *Los Angeles Times* wrote the following about President Trump's presidency: "Still, nothing prepared us for the magnitude of this train wreck."

Note that in the preceding example, as recommended by *The Chicago Manual of Style* for periodical titles found in text—like newspapers—*the* is neither capitalized nor italicized.

Plural proper nouns take a definite article.

Example: The Grammys were first awarded in 1959.

Articles in Series

According to *The Chicago Manual of Style*, it's recommended that when an article is used before two or more coordinate nouns, if each noun is conceptualized individually, the article should be placed before each noun.

Example: Eli brought a calculator, a protractor, and a ruler to the test.

Example: The dog, the horse, and the chickens that belong to Eve live in the backyard.

When the coordinate nouns comprise one unit, however, use only one article.

Example: Norman owns a horse and buggy.

Example: The macaroni and cheese that Ella prepared was delicious.

Finally, *The Chicago Manual of Style* recommends that "if the named things are covered by one plural noun, the definite article should not be repeated with each modifier (in the first and second years of college)."

Dropped Articles

By the mid-twentieth century, writers and editors started publishing sentences in which the initial article was omitted.

Example: Japanese drove other forces out of Burma and began occupation.

Here, we're referring to the Japanese conquest of Burma during World War II in which British and Chinese forces were driven out. However, in this sentence, "Japanese" specifically refers to the Japanese military forces and thus should begin with a definite article.

Better: The Japanese drove other forces out of Burma and began occupation.

If we were to restructure this sentence, the decision to place definite article before "Japanese" will make more sense.

RESTRUCTURED: Chinese and British forces were driven out of Burma by the Japanese and occupation began.

In the classic text, *The Careful Writer,* Theodore M. Bernstein describes this phenomenon as follows: "Whence cometh this affectation? *Time* magazine had much to do with spreading it, but *Time* did not originate it. It may be surmised that once upon a time a newspaper editor looked over his paper as it came fresh from the press, noting to his horror that every story on the front page began with the word *the.* He acted decisively. He ordered that thereafter no story was to begin with *the*.... In any event, some of the mythical editor's disciples went out into the wide world. They carried his rule with them. Indeed, they went him one better. They decided that not only must no story begin with *the,* but in addition no sentence must begin with *the*.... Nor is the beginning of the sentence the only point attacked by this cancer; nouns in the middle of a sentence now occasionally suffer the loss of their articles, too: 'Borough lines, color lines should be invisible, nonexistent, when we are looking for a way to improve education of our children.' Why not 'the education'?"

Notably, the definite article "the" shouldn't be dropped before the word "police."

EXAMPLE: The door was battered down by police.

BETTER: The door was battered down by the police.

On a final note, articles are commonly dropped in the titles of papers, headings, or figure legends. For example, consider the title "Electric Field Effect in Atomically Thin Carbon Films."

3. Comparison-Formations

TIP: Refer to a dictionary when unsure about comparatives and superlatives.

Key Points

- Adjectives have three forms: the absolute, the comparative, and the superlative.
- Typically, one-syllable adjectives take suffixes (inflections) to form comparative and superlative forms.
- There are no hard and fast rules dictating comparison-formations of adjectives, and they change over time—a process linguists refer to as *analyticization.*
- Bases that are three or more syllables don't take suffixes and are instead *periphrastic,* which means that comparative-formations are formed with *more* or *most.*

Adjectives take one of three forms: the *absolute* (for example, *late*), the *comparative* (for example, *later*), and the *superlative* (for example, *latest*). When a suffix (*-er* or *–est*) is added to the absolute form, linguists refer to the new construction as either an *inflectional comparative* or an *inflectional superlative.* When extra words are added to an adjective to form a comparative or a superlative (*more* or *most*), linguists refer to this new construction as either a *periphrastic comparative* or a *periphrastic superlative.*

The adjectives *good* and *bad* have the following irregular forms:

- best
- better
- worse
- worst

People rarely make mistakes with irregular comparatives and superlatives. However, regular forms of superlatives and comparatives are a different story and can be confusing. Moreover, the choice of whether to go with an inflectional or periphrastic form is hard to prescribe, with choice changing over time.

One-Syllable Adjectives

Typically, one-syllable adjectives take suffixes unless the base is a participle.

EXAMPLE: slim, slimmer, slimmest

EXAMPLE: fast, faster, fastest

But: lit, better lit, best lit (*lit* is a participle)

EXAMPLE: stuck, more stuck, most stuck (*stuck* is a participle)

EXAMPLE: built, better built, best built (*built* is a participle)

NOTABLE EXCEPTION: fun, more fun, most fun

Two-Syllable Adjectives

When the base is two syllables and ends in an unstressed *–ow*, *–y*, or *–le*, the superlative and comparative forms are formed using suffixes, or inflections. This guidance also applies to forms taking the prefix *un-*.

EXAMPLE: slimy, slimier, slimiest

EXAMPLE: shallow, shallower, shallowest

EXAMPLE: unlucky, unluckier, unluckiest

EXAMPLE: humble, humbler, humblest

EXAMPLE: noble, nobler, noblest

Notably, the absolute adjective *gentle* can take either inflectional or periphrastic forms.

ABSOLUTE: gentle

COMPARATIVE: gentler or more gentle

SUPERLATIVE: gentlest or most gentle

Typically, the inflectional form of *gentle* is used in an attributive sense.

EXAMPLE: Gandhi was the gentlest person.

The periphrastic form is used for emphasis in the predicate.

EXAMPLE: Sue made sure that the most gentle detergent was used to clean the wedding dress.

Comparative forms of bases that are two syllables but don't end in *–ow*, *–y*, or *–le* are more complicated and can take either inflectional or periphrastic forms depending on whether you're using comparative or superlative forms.

For instance, let's consider two absolute adjectives ending in *–ly: costly* and *friendly*. The absolute adjective *costly* is *more costly* in the comparative and *costliest* in the superlative. Similarly, the absolute adjective *friendly* is *more friendly* in the comparative and *friendliest* in the superlative.

However, *likely* is usually *more likely* or *most likely*, and *early* is *earliest* and *earlier*.

Absolute adjectives ending in *–er* are typically periphrastic, such as *eager*, *more eager*, and *most eager*.

Base forms ending in *-ful*, *-less*, *-ous*, *-ing*, *-ed*, and *–ive* all take periphrastic forms.

EXAMPLE: furtive, more furtive, most furtive

EXAMPLE: careless, more careless, most careless

EXAMPLE: shameful, more shameful, most shameful

Here are a few more oddities:

- *cruel* is both inflected and periphrastic: *crueler* or *more cruel* and *cruelest* or *most cruel;*
- *handsome* is both inflected and periphrastic: *handsomer* or *more handsome* and *handsomest* or *most handsome;*
- *quiet* is inflected: *quieter* and *quietest.*

Sometimes, when an adjective vacillates between the inflectional and periphrastic, your choice of which form to use can be guided by parallelism.

NON-PARALLEL STRUCTURE: Although the curmudgeon often insults others, his recent diatribe was more distasteful and crueler than anything we expected.

PARALLEL STRUCTURE: Although the curmudgeon often insults others, his recent diatribe was more distasteful and more cruel than anything we expected.

Three-Syllable Adjectives

Bases that three or more syllables don't take suffixes and are instead periphrastic.

EXAMPLE: complicated, more complicated, most complicated

Analyticization

When Old English evolved to early Modern English, there was a move from synthetic to analytic structures, a process called *analyticization.* Haspelmath and Michaelis define analyticization as "the replacement of an earlier pattern by a new, more elaborate pattern based on lexical or concrete items." With respect to comparison-formation, corpus-based research suggests that analyticization is taking place.

Specifically, adjectives that once upon a time allowed for inflectional and periphrastic variants have now drifted to the periphrastic comparative. For example, *bitterer, severer,* and *pleasanter* have drifted toward *more bitter, more severe,* and *more pleasant,* respectively.

On a final note, with comparison-formations, it's often a good idea to let your ear guide you. What sounds right? When in doubt refer to a dictionary.

4. Personal Pronouns

TIP: Avoid only using *he, his,* and *him* to refer to both men and women.

Key Points

- Use of the generic *he* is biased.
- Instead of using the generic *he,* recast the sentence.
- Indefinite pronouns, such as *anyone* or *anybody,* can be paired with the plural possessive pronoun *their.*

For the longest time, people used the generic *he, his,* and *him* to refer to both men and women. When used in this fashion, these pronouns are referred to as *generic singular pronouns.*

EXAMPLE: Every boss should be nice to his employees.

EXAMPLE: A boss must make many important decisions, and he should make decisions that are sound.

EXAMPLE: A boss must make many important decisions, and employees should respect decisions made by him.

The generic *he,* however, has fallen out of favor. Nowadays, many editors and publishers prefer bias-free alternatives to this construction.

EXAMPLE: Every 10 years, an American must fill out his census form.

The best way to revise this statement is by getting rid of the pronoun *his.*

BEST: Every 10 years, an American must fill out *a* census form.

Depending on your audience—specifically, if your audience consists of Americans—you can also rewrite this sentence using the second person.

OKAY: Every 10 years, you must fill out your census form.

According to *The Chicago Manual of Style,* in speech and informal writing, you can also recast the sentence in third-person plural.

OKAY: Every 10 years, Americans must fill out their census forms.

Finally, the sentence can be recast using the passive voice. It's usually best to avoid the passive voice; however, use of the passive voice is probably better than using the generic *he*.

Okay: Every 10 years, a census from must be filled out by every American.

Some writers and publications will alternate usages of the generic *he* and generic *she*, so as to provide some gender balance. This approach can be used sparingly—especially when otherwise recasting sentences sounds weird or forced.

When taking this approach, it's a good idea to avoid strict alternation and instead clump your use of personal pronouns in a more aesthetic manner. In other words, perhaps in one paragraph you use the generic *he* and *his* a couple of times, and in a following paragraph—further along in the document—you use the generic *she* and *her* a couple of times.

When using both the generic *he* and the generic *she*, make sure that you don't consistently subordinate either gender role or use the generic *he* and generic *she* in stereotypical ways. For example, consistently casting surgeons and CEOs as men and secretaries and assistants as women is gender biased.

Two things you don't want to do when expressing a generic case is to use the *s/he* construction or use *he/she*.

Wrong: This cubicle belongs to the new employee, and he/she will be expected to keep it clean.

Better: This cubicle belongs to the new employee, and this person will be expected to keep it clean.

Using the generic *one* usually sounds overly formal.

Inadvisable: One should take time to read the instructions.

Better: Everyone should take time to read the instructions.

In the 1990s, many editors began to embrace pairing a compound indefinite pronoun, such as *everyone* or *anybody*, with the plural possessive pronoun *their*, and style guides followed suit. This construction can also be used to obviate gender bias.

Example: Everyone should take their notebook.

Example: Anyone who comes should bring their wallet.

You'll note that in each of these examples, a singular object ("notebook" and "wallet") follows a plural possessive pronoun. This convention is preferred by some experts when each person possesses only one of each item. In other words, each person has only one notebook and each person has only one wallet.

Here is a list of compound indefinite pronouns:

- anybody
- anyone
- everybody
- everyone
- no one
- nobody
- somebody
- someone

5. Plurals

TIP: Plural forms of nouns usually end in *–s* or *–es,* but there are other plural endings.

Key Points

- When a word that ends in *–o* is preceded by a consonant, it's becoming more common that the plural is formed with *–s* and not *–es.*
- Certain Latin and French words can be made plural in two ways.
- "Zero plurals" are spelled the same in singular and plural form.
- When in doubt about a plural ending, check the dictionary and go with the first option listed.

Most of the time, forming the plural of a noun is easy: All you need to do is add an *–s* to the end of the word (for example, *planes, trains,* and *automobiles*). Alternatively, if a word ends in *-sh,-ch,-x,-z,-j,* or *-s,* make the word plural by adding the inflection *–es* (for example, *torches* and *foxes*).

The following guidance is not definitive and taken from several style guides—some of which offer contradictory advice in certain instances. Nevertheless, this guidance is generally well accepted.

Common Endings

Here is some general guidance for pluralizing words with common endings.

Words Ending in -o

When a word ends in *-o*, the plural takes an *–s* when a vowel precedes the *-o* (for example, *stereos*). However, if a consonant precedes the *-o*, then you can add an *–es* (for example, *potatoes*). With respect to this latter bit of guidance, there are numerous exceptions—for example, *mosquitos* or *mosquitoes*, *flamingos* or *flamingoes*, *zeros* or *zeroes*—and this guidance is soft.

The results of the Langscape Survey, which tested the preferences of 1,100 English speakers between 1998 and 2001, indicate that although plurals in which a consonant precedes the *–o* can often be formed with *–s* or *–es*, there's a clear preference for *–s* among respondents—especially among young respondents from the Northern Hemisphere. Thus, among younger Americans and Canadians, *mosquitos*, *flamingos*, and *buffalos* are preferred to *mosquitoes*, *flamingoes*, and *buffaloes*, respectively. The only three exceptions to this preference are *echoes*, *heroes*, and *tomatoes*.

In the Langscape survey, preference for the plural form of *volcano* was split evenly between *volcanos* and *volcanoes*. Furthermore, the word *potato* was left out of the study—a conspicuous omission.

Words Ending in –f or -fe

When a word ends in *–f* or *–fe* and the letter preceding either of these endings is a single vowel or consonant, then the plural is formed as *–ves* (for example, *halves*, *knives*, *loaves*, and *wharves* but *dwarfs*). Nouns that end in two vowels followed by an *–f* or *–fe* take an *-s* in the plural (such as *chiefs*).

Words Ending in –y

With words that end in *–y* preceded by a consonant, the plural is formed by adding the *–ies* inflection (for example, *cherries*). However, when a vowel precedes the *–y* ending, an *–s* inflection is used (for example, *monkeys*).

Words Ending in -en

There are only three words in the English language that take the *–en* inflection in the plural form: *oxen*, *children*, and *brethren*.

Interestingly, until the late sixteenth century, *brethren* was the plural of *brothers.* Nowadays, *brethren* is mostly used only in the King James Bible and among certain Protestant evangelical groups as well as in conservative religious discourse. Catholic orders, however, prefer the modern term *brothers.*

Internal Vowel Changes

Some very old words in the English language form plurals by internal change of vowels (for example, *men*, *women*, and *teeth*).

Foreign Roots

With English words that are derived from Latin, plurals can either take a Latin infection or an English one.

Singular	*Latin plural*	*English plural*
cactus	cacti	cactuses
appendix	appendices	appendixes
millennium	millennia	millenniums
vortex	vortices	vortexes

Of note, the plural of "cactus" can also be "cactus."

Certain Latin-derived words take only Latin plurals.

alumnus ▶ alumni
criterion ▶ criteria
vertebra ▶ vertebrae

Certain words derived from French and ending in *-eau* can take either French or English inflections.

Singular	*French inflection*	*English inflection*
gateau	gateaux	gateaus
trousseau	trousseaux	trousseaus
chateau	chateaux	chateaus

Certain words that end in *-is* are derived from Greek and take the Greek inflection *-es.*

thesis ▶ theses
crisis ▶ crises
analysis ▶ analyses

Zero Plurals

Certain English nouns are the same in both singular and plural forms and, in their plural form, are referred to as *zero plurals*. For instance, certain loanwords from Latin and French don't change, including *series, species, status,* and *chassis*. Additionally, collective words for some animals don't change endings either, including *fish, deer,* and *sheep.*

Obviously, English words that already end in *–s* or *–es* don't change spelling in plural form, including *shears, scissors, news*, and *binoculars.*

On a related note, mass nouns such as *research* and *evidence* are not made plural.

Additional Guidance

Here is extra guidance regarding plurals presented in tabular format.

Type	***Notes***	***Examples***
Proper nouns	The plurals of proper nouns are usually formed using *–s* or *–es.*	Three Johnsons
	The plural of a proper noun ending in *–s* is formed by adding an *–es.*	Three Joneses
	The plural of a proper noun that ends in *–y* is formed by adding an *–s.*	Two Timmys
Compound nouns	Closed compounds are formed by adding *–s.*	throwbacks spoonfuls
	With hyphenated or open compounds, the plural can be formed using the key noun.	poets laureate mothers-in-law attorneys general men-of-war hors d'oeuvres also hors d'oeuvre romans à clef culs-de-sac also cul-de-sacs
Compounds in which both nouns are of equal importance	Make both nouns plural.	women leaders (not woman leaders)
Compounds that contain no nouns	Add *–s* to make plural.	follow-throughs

Type	*Notes*	*Examples*
Names ending in an unpronounced -*s* or -*x*	Leave unchanged in the plural form.	three Descartes
Italicized words	The plural inflection should not be italicized. For clarity, try rephrasing.	12 *Catcher in the Rye*s Better: 12 copies of *Catcher in the Rye*
Words or phrases in quotation marks	Add an 's before the closing quotation mark	Most people hate "I told you so's"
Noun coinages	Can take –*s*, -*es*, or sometimes *'s* for clarity.	ifs, ands, or buts dos and don'ts maybe's, yes's and no's
Letters, numerals, and abbreviations	Capital letters that represent words take –*s* when forming plurals. Numerals that are used as nouns take –*s* when forming the plural. Abbreviations that are written without periods take –*s* when forming the plural.	Bs and Cs elderly men in their 80s 1920s MBAs UFOs but: *x*'s, *y*'s, and *z*'s but: M.D.'s and D.O.'s
Tribal names and national groups	Certain Native American tribes prefer adding the –*s* inflection with plural forms; previously no –*s* inflection was added. Similarly, many other national groups now prefer adding –*s*, too, when forming plurals. The reason why tribal and national groups prefer the –*s* inflection to zero plurals is because using a zero plural is reminiscent of how animals are referred to.	Apaches (not Apache) Hopis (not Hopi) Uighers (not Uigher) Kurds (not Kurd)
Abbreviated units of measure	Don't add -*s*	5 kg (not 5 kgs) 1355 mL (not 1355 mLs)

This guidance on plurals is robust. Nevertheless, if you're unsure of how to form a plural noun, check the appropriate dictionary. If there are two alternatives, both alternatives are listed. When such a choice is presented, it's best to go with the first alternative. For instance, in *Webster's New World College Dictionary,* which is the preferred dictionary when writing in AP style, under the entry for *flamingo*, *flamingos* is given first and *flamingoes* is given second.

6. Prepositions

TIP: When in doubt about preposition use, refer to a dictionary.

Key Points

- Preposition use is idiomatic.
- For the most part, fluent speakers of English can discern which prepositional idioms apply.
- Some prepositional idioms are tricky, and must be looked up in a dictionary.

There's a book titled *Words into Type* by Marjorie E. Skillin and Robert M. Gay. This book has held up remarkably well over time. Even though it was last published in 1974, this guide is still used today by editors and instructors. Skillin and Gay devote an entire 15 pages to preposition choice, and even this list falls short of being exhaustive. (Something you'll learn if you ever try to use it.)

According to Skillin and Gay:

> The prepositional idiom—that is, a word and a particular preposition before a noun or after a verb or adjective—is the source of countless errors. Some are created through false analogy: although *forbid to* is correct, *forbid from* is often seen, because an analogy is made to *prohibit from*. Other errors arise through ignorance of nuance of meaning: *adapt for*, *adapt from*, *adapt to* have different uses. The idiom is subject to shifts, as a reading of Shakespeare shows. Correct current usages are simply idiomatic and must be learned or looked up.

The choice of which preposition to use—either after a verb or adjective, or before a noun—is often something that can't be reasoned through. Either you're familiar with the correct proper prepositional idiom because of previous experience, or you're not. If you're unsure about which preposition to use, then look up the word and accompanying preposition in the dictionary.

It's a good idea to memorize a few commonly used words and their associated prepositions.

EXAMPLE: Many people *died of* coal miner's lung.

Notice that it's *die of* and not *die from* when writing about diseases or disorders.

But: The crops died from the frost.

The preposition *in* can refer to the quality or aspect on which a decision is made.

Example: With diamonds, variations *in* clarity affect price.

The preposition *of* is used to indicate the relationship between a scale or measure and a value.

Example: We noticed an increase *of* 10 percent.

Here are some other useful preposition choices:

- accompanied by (not accompanied with)
- based on (not based upon)
- contingent on (not contingent upon)
- equivalent to, equivalent in (not equivalent with)
- independent of (not from)

Of note, the word *accompany* means "go somewhere with" so "accompany with" is redundant. Furthermore, in most instances, *on* is preferred to *upon* because *on* is shorter.

---

7. Present and Past Participles

Tip: When unsure of a past or present participle, check the dictionary.

Key Points

- The verb *lie* means to rest or recline on something.
- The verb *lay* means to put or place something.

A past participle is a verb form ending in *–ed, -en, -n, -t,* or *–d* (for example, *bitten, claimed,* and *seen*). Past participles are used with helping verbs to form the perfect tense. Past participles are also used to form the passive voice.

A present participle is a verb form ending in *–ing* (for example, *wanting, eating,* and *sitting*). Along with helping verbs, present participles constitute the progressive tense.

The verb *lie* means to rest or recline on something. (Hint: There's an "i" in the words "lie" and "recline").

PAST TENSE: Marlon lay on the carpet.

PAST PARTICIPLE: Marlon had lain on the carpet.

PRESENT PARTICIPLE: Marlon was lying on the carpet.

The verb *lay* means to put or place something.

PAST TENSE: The mason laid the brick.

PAST PARTICIPLE: The mason had laid the brick.

PRESENT PARTICIPLE: The mason was laying the brick.

For even native speakers of English, the past participles of irregular verbs can be confusing. Whenever you are unsure of what the proper past participle is, refer to a dictionary. Let's consider a few more tricky cases.

Infinitive	*Past Tense*	*Past Participle*
to awake	awoke, awaked	awaked, awoke
to beat	beat	beaten, beat
to bring	brought	brought
to build	built	built
to go	went	gone
to prove	proved	proved, proven
to show	showed	shown, showed

In this table, entry items are listed in order of preference. For instance, the preferred past participle of the base form *awake* is *awaked;* however, *awoke* is an acceptable alternative.

8. Subject-Verb Agreement

TIP: Identify the intended subject.

Key Points

- Discount word groups that separate the subject from the verb.
- A collective noun is a subject that acts as a unit and takes a singular verb.

- Not only must subjects and verbs agree with one another but they must also agree with corresponding pronouns.

With subject-verb agreement, it all boils down to intention. You look for the intended subject with which the verb agrees. For the most part, it's pretty easy to pick out the subject and figure out whether the corresponding verb agrees, because the subject and verb are next to each other. Sometimes, however, there are word groups—for instance, prepositional phrases or restrictive and nonrestrictive clauses—that separate the subject and verb. But when this happens, all you have to do is discount these word groups and then check for agreement between the subject and verb.

Continued misuse ~~of prescription painkillers~~ results in dependence.

The idea ~~that we opened the gates~~ is unsubstantiated.

The word group that separates the true subject from the verb that it agrees with can be tricky to identify. For example, phrases beginning with prepositions—*in addition to*, *together with*, *as well as,* and *accompanied by*—are discounted when determining whether the subject agrees with the verb.

My brother ~~in addition to Jason's sisters~~ is a supporter of the independent candidate.

Another tricky situation involves *or* or *nor.* When *or* or *nor* is used to connect a compound subject, the verb agrees with the subject closest to the verb.

EXAMPLE: Fareed or his friends use the toaster.

With quantifiers including *some of*, *most of*, *half of*, *a majority of*, or *a lot of*, the verb agrees with the object or the noun closest to the verb.

EXAMPLE: Half of the <u>students</u> have more than 10 apps loaded onto their smartphones.

Similarly, with the expressions *one of the people who* or *one of the things that,* the verb agrees with the object.

EXAMPLE: Zain is one of the <u>students</u> who take the ferry.

Nouns that refer to the subject or unit, or *collective nouns,* take singular verbs when the subject is intended to act as a single entity. For example, consider the following:

The jury delivers a guilty verdict.

The "jury" acts as a unit to deliver the verdict: a singular subject that takes a singular verb.

Although the collective nouns *data* (singular: datum) and *criteria* (singular: criterion) may sound like they would take singular verbs, in many instances of formal writing, these nouns, in fact, take plural verbs. (Some pundits accept the singular *data* in computing and general contexts.)

INADVISABLE: Although relevant data is limited, it seems that the findings are important.

BETTER: Although relevant data are limited, it seems that the findings are important.

WRONG: Stringent criteria is used to analyze academic performance.

BETTER: Stringent criteria are used to analyze academic performance.

Another more nuanced example of subject-verb agreement involves measurements. Remember that measurements act as collective nouns.

WRONG: The gold miners were disappointed because only 20 ounces were mined last week.

RIGHT: The gold miners were disappointed because only 20 ounces was mined last week.

WRONG: Eight thousand dollars are sitting on the night stand.

RIGHT: Eight thousand dollars is sitting on the night stand.

On a final note, remember that not only must subjects and verbs agree with one another, but they must also agree with corresponding pronouns. In other words, singular verbs take singular pronouns, and plural verbs take plural pronouns.

EXAMPLE: Each of the NFL football players takes his helmet.

EXAMPLE: Players in the NFL are generally happy with their salaries.

9. Tenses

TIP: Understand why you're using certain tenses.

Key Points

- The progressive tense is used with continuing action.
- The perfect tense is used to describe continuing action that has spanned some period of time and is either completed or will be completed.

The tenses that you use to recount a story or series of events must have the proper meaning. When self-editing your own work, ensure that the tenses that you use are appropriate and consistent.

The simple tenses are the *present tense*, *past tense*, and *future tense*. The present tense is used to describe actions that occur at one specific point of time or occur regularly. Additionally, the present tense is used either to express general truths or describe literature. The past tense is used to describe past actions. The future tense is used to describe events or actions that occur in the future.

In academic writing, the present tense is used for the following:

- to describe what is known about the topic
- to introduce evidence
- to make general conclusions
- to make general statements
- to make interpretations

In academic writing, in addition to the passive voice, the past tense is used to recount methods or data from an experiment. The past tense is also used to describe results of a study, with currently valid results written in the present tense. With respect to previously published results, the present tense can be used for currently valid results and the past tense used for dated (or historical) results. Moreover, the present perfect tense can be used to describe results connected to the present in some way (for example, *has demonstrated this correlation*).

Progressive Tense vs. Perfect Tense

The *progressive tense* is used when the continuing action is, was, or will be going on. In other words, the progressive tense indicates that the action of a verb is either in progress or ongoing at some moment in time.

According to *Merriam-Webster* the *perfect tense* is "a verb tense that is used to refer to an action or state that is completed at the time of speaking or at a time spoken of."

<u>Present progressive tense</u>: My friend is preparing dinner.

<u>Past progressive tense</u>: My friend was preparing dinner.

<u>Future progressive tense</u>: My friend will be preparing dinner.

Instantaneous actions don't take the progressive tense.

WRONG: The patient was swallowing the pill.

RIGHT: The patient swallowed the pill.

The perfect tense is derived from the Latin *per factus* meaning "completely finished." The perfect tense is used to describe continuing action that has spanned some period of time and is either completed or will be completed.

Present perfect tense: My friend has studied for the test.

Past perfect tense: My friend had studied for the test.

Future perfect tense: My friend will have studied for the test.

The perfect tense has many uses.

First, the perfect tense can be used for emphasis: to draw attention to an important or significant event that has occurred in the recent past—an event that still affects the present.

EXAMPLE: Andy has finally passed the California Bar Examination!

Although "Andy finally passed" would work here, by using the perfect tense we stress the significance of the hard-won accomplishment.

Second, the perfect tense is used by researchers or explorers differentiating their own discoveries from those of others. Consider the following hypothetical example.

Our research group has discovered a second earth-sized planet in a habitable zone near a distant star. In 2015, scientists working on NASA's Keppler mission discovered the first such planet.

Third, the present perfect tense is also used to bridge previous research with current research and describe results that are still valid.

EXAMPLE: Studies have shown that drugs that only reduce cholesterol levels don't prevent stroke or heart attack. Our research supports these previous findings.

Finally, the past perfect tense can be used with the past tense to indicate the order of events. In combination, the past perfect is used to indicate the first event to occur, and the past tense is used to indicate the second event to occur.

EXAMPLE: By the time her mother brought dinner, Adelina had already eaten.

Knowing the names of these tenses isn't that important. It is important, however, to recognize that the progressive and perfect tenses all have shades of meaning that revolve around continuing action. You should be using these tenses when whatever you're writing about extends for some—possibly unspecified—period of time.

Other Considerations

If you are using the present tense to record events—like with a fictional narrative—then complement this usage with the present perfect and present progressive tenses. Whereas, if you are using the past tense to record events—like with reportage—then use the *past perfect* and *past progressive tenses* to describe continuing actions.

Consider these last two tenses, which have nuanced meanings.

Past perfect progressive tense: The generator had been running for three days *when* the electrician arrived.

Future perfect progressive tense: The generator will have been running for three days *by the time* that the electrician arrives.

10. Who and Whom

TIP: When unsure, go with *who.*

Key Points

- The relative pronouns *who* and *whoever* act as subjects of verbs.
- The relative pronouns *whom* and *whomever* act as objects, and are acted on.
- Avoid hypercorrect uses of *whom*. In other words, don't use *whom* to sound fancy.

In technical terms, *who* and *whoever* are relative pronouns in the nominative case. This statement means that *who* and *whoever* are subjects of verbs.

EXAMPLE: Who wants ice cream?

EXAMPLE: Whoever wants ice cream should line up.

Technically, *whom* and *whomever* are relative pronouns in the objective case. In other words, *whom* and *whomever* are objects of the sentence or clause, and are *acted on* by verbs.

EXAMPLE: The applicant whom they choose.

EXAMPLE: The panel did not just choose whomever.

In both of these examples, "whom" and "whomever" are acted on by the verb "choose."

Things get tricky in sentences with a subordinate clause is involved. Subordinate clauses are dependent on main clauses.

EXAMPLE: Terry prefers an employee who has a college degree.

Here, "who has a college degree" is the subordinate (noun) clause and depends on the main clause "Terry prefers an employee." In this subordinate clause, "who" is the subject and "has" is the verb. Many writers will incorrectly write the following:

Terry prefers an employee ~~whom~~ has a college degree.

The reason many writers get confused has to do with the placement of a pronoun after the verb "prefers." Typically, people expect a pronoun following a subject and verb to be in the objective case (whom) no matter what. In other words, people expect subject-verb-object patterns. However, if the pronoun at the start of a subordinate clause serves as the subject of its own verb—in the preceding example, "who has"—then the nominative case is right.

Let's look at another example:

Terry prefers an employee whom we all like.

In this noun clause, "whom" serves as the object of "we all like."

Now, consider the following:

Terry prefers an employee <u>who</u> we think will do well.

By extension, the subordinate (noun) clause in this example, "who we think will do well," can be restructured as follows, with "he" substituted for "who": "we think *he* will do well." Here, "he"—ergo "who"—is the subject of the verb "will."

In addition to restructuring, sometimes merely substituting *he* or *him* when choosing between *who* or *whom,* respectively, will help you figure out whether you are supposed to use the nominative or objective case. For instance, if we substituted "him," the result would be clearly wrong: "we think ~~him~~ will do well."

(When substituting the relative pronouns *who* or *whom* with *he* or *him,* don't worry about gender bias. This substitution is a temporary mental exercise to help you figure things out. Alternatively if you prefer, you could substitute *she* or *her* for *who* or *whom,* respectively.)

Next, consider the following example:

Who do you think you are?

Although unnatural and unidiomatic, restructuring this question in the following fashion may make the point more clearly:

Do you think that you are who?

Here, we use “who” not “whom” because “who”’ follows a copulative verb (also called a linking verb). Some examples of copulative verbs are *be*, *appear*, and *seem*. Copulative verbs aren't active verbs, and pronouns that follow copulative verbs aren't objects. Instead, these pronouns take on a reflexive quality and thus rename subjects (you are who=who are you). Pronouns following copulative verbs are in the nominative case.

Similarly, we could have substituted “he”—not “him”—for “who.”

Do you think that you are he?

If you have trouble figuring out whether to use either *who* or *whom* or *whoever* or *whomever*, don't fret too much while you're writing. Instead, defer to writing *who* and *whoever* in all questionable instances and return to evaluate every *who* and *whoever* during the self-editing phase. Of note, it's best to defer to *who* and *whoever* because even if you end up using these pronouns incorrectly, their use is less conspicuous than *whom* and *whomever* and more closely follows transgressions made in informal speech. Moreover, by using *whom* or *whomever*, you risk hypercorrect usage.

Hypercorrect: Julian was surprised by the performance given by a man ~~whom~~ she believed was a magician.

Avoid using *whom* in order to sound fancy. You want your writing to sound clear, cohesive, comprehensible, concise, and correct (the 5 Cs) not jargonish, stilted, and hypercorrect.

During the self-editing phase ask yourself whether the relative pronoun that you plan to use is the subject of a verb, and is thus *who* or *whoever*, or whether the relative pronoun is acted on by a verb, and is therefore *whom* or *whomever*. As demonstrated in this section, when needed, you can transpose wording and substitute *he* (or *she*) to help determine proper usage.

Finally, with regard to corpus-based research, writing in *Change in Contemporary English*, Leech found that although uncommon, the frequency of *whom* in the English language is certainly not rare, with 129 instances per million words surveyed. He also found that *whom* is about 40 times more common in formal written texts than it is in spontaneous dialogue. In formal texts, people appear to overuse *whom* in hypercorrect usages. It's likely that many writers think that the inflection *whom* sounds more formal and use it to make their writing sound more formal.

Part II: Diction

11.
Attributive Nouns

Tip: Attributive nouns sound less technical and more relatable than adjective forms.

Key Points

- Meaning can differ based on whether an attributive noun or its corresponding adjective form is used.
- For clarity, consider recasting long noun strings which contain attributive nouns.

Is it *governmental office* or *government office*? How about *surgical suite* or *surgery suite*? In both these cases, either option is right.

The English language has a rich history of permitting words to change parts of speech. Nouns are commonly used as adjectives (for example, *Internet connection*, *telephone pole*, and *gas station*). When a noun is used as an adjective, it's called an *attributive noun*.

According to corpus-based research, attributive nouns were a new development in Middle English. They then became increasingly common after 1750, with a crescendo in use during the twentieth century.

Meaning can differ based on whether either an attributive noun or its corresponding adjective form is used. For instance, ambiguity would arise if *anemic management* were used instead of *anemia management* to describe the medical treatment and management of anemia by hematologists (physicians who specialize in treating blood disorders) and primary care physicians. Of note, anemia is a blood condition caused by a deficiency of red blood cells, which are needed for oxygenation.

In addition to being the adjective form of anemia, "anemic" has also taken on another meaning: lack of vigor or vitality. Thus, "anemic management" could be misconstrued to mean that the management itself was somehow dispirited ... perhaps the physicians responsible for management were listless or languid in their service.

Sometimes there's a clear preference as to whether either an attributive noun or an adjective form is used, and this preference depends on the noun being modified. For example, the term *chemical reaction* is common enough; however, the lab component of a chemistry course at university is called *chemistry lab*. After all, a *chemical lab* sounds like a place where they make chemicals like industrial solvents—not a place where students learn about chemistry.

Other times, the adjective form of a noun sounds too much like jargon to be used with a general audience. For instance, in the previous sentence, I write "adjective form" instead of "adjectival form" because "adjectival" sounds like a word that a linguist would use in an academic paper. Here's another example: The term "gynecology ward" is more inviting than "gynecological ward," which sounds too clinical.

For the sake of parallelism, it's best to avoid mixing attributive nouns and adjective forms in a series.

Faulty parallelism: The antiquities commission solicited input from government, business, and archaeological stakeholders.

Better: The antiquities commission solicited input from government, business, and archaeology stakeholders.

Most attributive nouns are singular. There's often no reason to make the attributive noun plural because it's common knowledge that the attributive noun refers to a group. For instance, *animal rights* refers to the rights of all animals, and *human rights* refer to the rights of all humans. However, two nouns in close apposition can sometimes cause a strain on cognitive processing and require undue inference. Thus, as suggested by corpus-based research, there's been a rise in frequency of plural attributive nouns used to modify nouns—especially when the plural form is irregular such as with the term *women* (for example, *women leaders*). These plural attributive nouns take some of the guesswork out of what's meant when two nouns directly appose each other.

In particular, there's been an increase in the number of plural attributive nouns taking the *-s* inflection—especially when the plural component takes a medial (middle) position in a longer sequence of nouns. For instance, the term *cluster munitions ban* is composed of the plural attributive noun *munitions* (more colloquially, "cluster bombs") in a medial position in the noun sequence. Because "cluster munitions" is plural, we know that there's a ban on not only one type of cluster bomb but all types, which is an important distinction because all types are destructive and notorious for the suffering that they spawn. Cluster bombs shoot out projectiles, or bomblets, mid-flight and raze whole areas, killing many civilians. Several countries (but not the United States) have signed the Convention on Cluster Munitions which bans the use of all cluster munitions under any circumstance.

Don't hesitate to use attributive nouns in your writing. Nevertheless, carefully consider the preceding guidance while writing and self-editing. Sometimes there's a better choice to make between an attributive noun and an adjective form, as in the case of parallelism.

Attributive Nouns in Noun Strings

By the fifteenth century a number of attributive nouns had faded into existence (for example, *cherry-stone* and *hall-door*). Over time, attributive nouns composed of two units became more common (for example, *coffee-house conversation* in 1752). By the twentieth century, we started seeing many longer noun strings that were confusing. (Corpus-based research has uncovered a whopping eight nouns in sequence!) Specifically, according to Leech in *Change in Contemporary English*, dated from 1961 and 1991/2, there's been a 33.8 percent increase in these "noun+common noun" constructions in British English and a 15.9 percent increase in American English, This practice follows a more general trend of *densification*, which is mainly attributable to journalists, government officials, and (technology) specialists who are looking to pack more concepts into smaller allotments of prose. However, such cumbersome noun phrases often benefit from being broken up.

NOUN STRING: Gymnast Simone Biles was the 2016 woman's all-around Olympic gold medalist.

BETTER: Gymnast Simone Biles won the gold medal in the woman's all-around at the 2016 Olympics.

While writing and self-editing your work, be on the lookout for long noun strings packed with attributive nouns. Remember that such constructions can be easily misconstrued and may benefit from being broken up.

12. Clear Antecedents

TIP: Make sure that the pronouns that you use have clear antecedents.

Key Points

- An antecedent gives meaning to a pronoun or relative pronoun.
- Be on the lookout for *this, that,* and *it.*

An *antecedent* is a word, phrase, clause, or sentence that gives meaning to another word such as a pronoun or relative pronoun. In your writing, you should keep a close eye on the pronoun *it* and the relative pronouns *this* and *that,* and when self-editing, make sure that these pronouns have clear antecedents.

Consider the following passage in which the relative pronoun *this* and the pronoun *it* lack clear antecedents.

> On January 14, 1963, at his inaugural address for the governorship of Alabama, George Wallace notoriously declared, "In the name of the greatest people that have ever trod this earth, I draw a line in the dust and toss the gauntlet before the feet of tyranny, and I say, segregation now, segregation tomorrow and segregation forever." This became a rallying cry against civil rights. It also stood in stark contrast to the message of hope and peace spread by Martin Luther King, Jr.

In the preceding example, the underlined relative pronoun, "this," and the underlined pronoun, "it," lack clear antecedents. It's unclear what "this" and "it" exactly refer to. This paragraph needs to be rewritten with clarity in mind.

> On January 14, 1963, at his inaugural address for the governorship of Alabama, George Wallace notoriously declared, "In the name of the greatest people that have ever trod this earth, I draw a line in the dust and toss the gauntlet before the feet of tyranny, and I say, segregation now, segregation tomorrow, and segregation forever." The phrase "segregation now, segregation tomorrow, and segregation forever" became a rallying cry against civil rights. This rhetoric also stood in stark contrast to the message of hope and peace spread by Martin Luther King, Jr.

Oftentimes, all that's required to clarify what a pronoun or relative pronoun is referring is to repeat a noun or phrase.

UNCLEAR: When Lucius visited New York City, he saw Times Square, the Empire State Building, and the Statue of Liberty. This was a gift from France, which was dedicated in 1886.

CLEAR: When Lucius visited New York City, he saw Times Square, the Empire State Building, and the Statue of Liberty. The Statue of Liberty was a gift from France, which was dedicated in 1886.

13. Comparisons

TIP: Be on the lookout for faulty comparisons.

Key Points

- When self-editing your own work, check to see if your comparisons could be miscomprehended and adjust them accordingly.
- In elliptical comparisons in which *than* is used, consider inserting elided words back into these comparisons to avoid any confusion.
- When considering differences in similar things of the same order, use *compare with* not *compare to*.

When writing for a general audience, you must assume that you're not only writing for native English speakers but all people—including those people for whom English is not a first language.

Faulty comparisons can confound readers—especially those who are less fluent in English. Thus, it's imperative that the comparisons that you use are clear, and the elements that you're comparing are clearly juxtaposed.

RIGHT: Warren is taller than Michael.

WORDY: Warren is taller than Michael ~~is~~.

This comparison is relatively simple, and there's no need to write "is" because this verb is implied.

EXAMPLE: The roof terrace of the new building is more spacious than the old building.

Here, the comparison is unclear, and more words are needed to clarify the comparison. Specifically, is the roof terrace of the new building bigger than the entirety of the old building, or is the roof terrace of the new building bigger than the roof terrace of the old building? Although a native English speaker may correctly assume the latter, the comparison is still faulty and could prove challenging to a non-native English speaker.

BETTER: The roof terrace of the new building is more spacious than that of the old building.

More generally, when self-editing your own work, check to see if your comparisons could be miscomprehended and adjust them accordingly.

Elliptical Constructions

Now, let's take a more detailed look at the concept of *ellipsis* as it relates to comparisons. Omission of words that complete or clarify a sentence is a form of ellipsis. Often, the native English speaker has no trouble interpreting the meaning of a sentence in which ellipsis is employed.

EXAMPLE: Despite scientific evidence to the contrary, global warming skeptics claim [that] concerns about climate change are unwarranted

In this zero-relative clause, *that* can be elided with little confusion as to intended meaning.

When used with comparisons, the word *than* can function as one of two parts of speech: a subordinating conjunction or a preposition. This difference can lead to confusion in sentence structures that employ ellipses.

CONFUSING: Noah walks with Ori more than Ariella.

When "than" functions as a subordinating conjunction, a clause follows.

Noah walks with Ori more than Ariella walks with Ori.

When "than" acts as a preposition, the meaning changes.

Noah walks with Ori more than with Ariella.

Remember that a preposition expresses a relationship between two things and takes an object.

During the self-editing phase, be on the lookout for elliptical comparisons in which *than* is used. Consider inserting elided words back into these comparisons to avoid any confusion.

Compare With vs. Compare To

With comparisons, most of the time, it's best to go with *compare with* instead of *compare to*. The term *compare with* is used to compare two entities that can be measured in similar terms. For example, two world-championship sprinters can be compared *with* each other in an athletic sense. However, if you were to compare one of these sprinters to a race car, then *compared to* would be used. The expression *compared to* is used to draw similarities between two things that are intrinsically nothing like each other: A human is nothing like a race car.

Depending on what words are elided in a comparison, you can simplify your prose by substituting *compare with* with *than*.

OKAY: The new goals are loftier compared with the old ones.

BETTER: The new goals are loftier than the old ones.

In this example, the meaning is the same if "than" is used as a preposition or subordinating conjunction. To help illustrate this point, let's reinsert the elided text using brackets.

The new goals are loftier than the old ones [are loftier].

14. Core Modals

TIP: Core modals can help qualify your meaning.

Key Points

- For nuanced writers, core modals like *can, could, will,* and *would,* are the most important auxiliary verbs to consider during the self-editing phase.
- Core modals can help hedge your language when writing about uncertainty (for example, in science).

Lots of information is presented in this chapter. For the nuanced writer, the goal here is to provide a comprehensive explanation of core modals so that you can better understand how to interpret and use them; pragmatics, genre, audience, and frequency all play a role in how core modals are used.

You can leverage the power of core modals to make your writing more refined and help you express meaning more precisely—especially when writing or reporting about science, where hedging is often necessary. Moreover, understanding gradations in the meanings of core modals will make you a better reader.

While writing and self-editing your work, it's a good idea to keep at least some of these concepts in mind. Whereas, you may never need to use the core modals *shall* and *ought,* there's a good chance you will want to use *can, could, will, would,* and so forth in certain contexts.

During the self-editing phase, it's not only helpful to recognize whether the core modals that you write are used properly but also to look for opportunities to effectively and prudently use them. Core modals can be a useful tool in a writer's toolbox.

To understand core modals in detail, we should first look at the more general categorization: auxiliary verbs. For good measure, we'll also look at quasimodals, a closely related construction.

Auxiliary verbs combine with other verbs to constitute a verb phrase. Auxiliary verbs complement *main verbs* (lexical verbs). They are separated into two categories: primary auxiliary verbs (primary auxiliaries) and modal auxiliary verbs.

Primary Auxiliary Verbs

The *primary auxiliary verbs* are conjugations of *be*, *have*, and *do.*

For instance, in the verb phrase *was debuted,* "was" is the auxiliary verb and "debuted" is the main verb (the past participle of *to debut*). Furthermore, in the verb phrase *had debuted,* "had" is the auxiliary verb and "debuted" is the main verb.

The primary auxiliary verbs *have* and *be* can combine with present participles and past participles to express a temporal perspective of an event (called *aspect*), and to express the passive voice.

Temporal view: In the past, Ibrahim <u>had competed</u> in marathons.

Passive voice: The marathon <u>was being run</u> by Henry.

Take note that a verb phrase can be made up of one or more auxiliaries. For example, in the verb phrase *was being debuted,* there are two auxiliaries, "was being," which precedes the main verb "debuted."

The auxiliary verb *do* is special for a few reasons.

First, unlike *have* and *be, do* can take a bare infinitive.

EXAMPLE: I do enjoy stand-up comedy.

Second, unless there's another auxiliary verb present, *do* is used to form interrogative or negative statements.

EXAMPLE: Do I like deadpan humor?

EXAMPLE: I don't like deadpan humor.

Third, *do* functions as a substitute verb.

EXAMPLE: I purchase more grapefruits than they do.

Here, "do" stands in for "purchase."

Modal Auxiliary Verbs

Modal auxiliary verbs convey modality. Modality is a category of linguistic meaning that expresses the attitude of the speaker or writer. There are two main types of modality: *epistemic* and *deontic*. These terms originated in philosophy.

Epistemic modality refers to the writer's or speaker's degree of confidence or belief in a proposition.

EXAMPLE: If hungry enough, Samir could eat a whole large pizza.

Deontic modality refers to the way the world should be according to the speaker or writer's desires, expectations, and so forth. Deontic can refer to duty or obligation.

EXAMPLE: Sven must attend the orientation.

Modal auxiliary verbs express shades of possibility, obligation, and certainty. Modal auxiliary verbs are fluid in meaning, and their meanings have shifted during the past several centuries. Nevertheless, however fluid they are in their meaning, they are just as unrelenting in their form. Specifically with modal verbs, one form serves all persons, there are no longer present or past contrasts, and there are no infinitive forms.

SINGULAR FIRST-PERSON: I will take the car.

SINGULAR SECOND-PERSON: You will take the car.

PLURAL THIRD-PERSON: They will take the car.

Unlike the primary auxiliaries *have* and *be*—but like the primary auxiliary *do*—modal auxiliary verbs take the bare infinitive.

Here's a list of core modals in order of decreasing frequency in language:

- would
- will

- can
- could
- may
- should
- must
- might
- shall
- ought
- need

Of note, the core modals *shall* and *will* can express future tense. (On an interesting, but somewhat unrelated point, *should* was once the past tense of the modal verb *shall*. Furthermore, *would* was once the past tense of the modal verb *will*.)

EXAMPLE: Dr. Bly shall go to the party.

EXAMPLE: Dr. Bly will bring his partner.

As a writer and self-editor, it's important to recognize the cline of meaning connoted in the usage of various core modals and leverage these shades of meaning. Consider the following table adapted from *The Cambridge Guide to English Usage* by Pam Peters.

	Ability	*Permission*	*Possibility*	*Necessity*	*Obligation*	*Inclination*	*Prediction*	*Habit*
Would						Weak	Medium	Weak
Will					Weak	Strong	Strong	
Can	Strong	Medium	Strong					
Could	Medium	Weak	Medium					
May		Weak	Medium			Weak		
Should				Medium	Medium	Weak	Weak	
Must				Strong	Strong		Weak	Weak
Might			Weak					
Shall					Weak	Medium	Medium	
Ought				Medium	Medium		Weak	
Need				Strong	Strong			

According to the table, both *can* and *could* connote root ability, with *can* having a stronger connotation. We can use this guidance when choosing when to use *can* or *could* in situations where ability is described.

EXAMPLE: Jerry can earn at least a C on the test.

EXAMPLE: If he studies hard enough, Jerry could earn an A on the test.

Earning at least a C on a test is a strong possibility for any student who shows up to class and does enough work. However, earning an A, although possible, is by no means guaranteed even if a student studies hard.

Please note that the table details grammatical meanings that are descriptive. The guidance in the table is historical, and more recently, we've seen changes in the corpora that blur the lines of connotation.

For instance, as a child you were probably taught to ask for permission to use the bathroom by using *may:* "May I use the bathroom, Mr. Azikiwe?" However, this advice is stylistic. In reality, *can* has been usurping the use of *may* with respect to root permission, and from a grammatical point of view, "Can I use the bathroom, Mr. Azikiwe?" has a stronger connotation of permission.

Furthermore, as suggested in the table, *can* indicates stronger root possibility than does *may.* In recent times, however, as evidenced by corpus-based research, *can* and *may* have become synonymous with respect to root possibility—probably because *may* sounds a bit stilted, and most speakers and writers tend to eschew stylistic heightening.

HISTORICAL USAGE: New World tapirs, which look like pigs with tusks, may be found in Central and South America.

RECENT USAGE: New World tapirs, which look like pigs with tusks, can be found in Central and South America.

According to the table, *may* has historically taken on a more definite connotation of root possibility than has *might*, which is a more tentative expression. However in spoken American English, *might* is gaining on *may* even in contexts in which things seem less possible. Much like *can* and *may,* these two modals have become somewhat synonymous.

HISTORICAL USAGE: Jack might hit a hole-in-one on a par-three hole.

RECENT USAGE: Jack may hit a hole-in-on on a par-three hole.

(In golf, it's pretty hard to hit a hole-in-one.)

As a general trend, the use of core modals is in decline. Nevertheless, core modals can add flair and subtlety to writing. Furthermore, they enable the writer to adjust language choice when describing scientific findings. In a world where so much is unknown and verification is paramount, core modals can be very useful when used judiciously. Watch out, however, because overuse of modals, especially when unnecessary, can appear evasive.

In his analysis of four corpora titled the Brown Family (two British and two English) dated from 1961 and 1991/2, Leech discovered the following patterns of usage:

- The decline for usage of all core modals is 10.6 percent on average.
- The decline in *could* is 2.2 percent.

- The decline in *shall* is 43.5 percent.
- The decline in *may* is 24.6 percent.
- The decline in *must* is 31.2 percent.
- The decline in *ought (to)* is 37.5 percent.
- The modal auxiliary *can* bucked the trend with a slight increase in usage of 1.3 percent.

According to Leech: "Compared to the subjunctive, the core modals are of course vastly more frequent and central to the grammar of the language." The decline in usage of core verbs has only been recently noticed. This decline is steeper in American English than it is in British English and is more pronounced in spoken American English than it is in written American English.

With respect to four written genre—fiction, learned, general prose, and press—core modals are most prevalent first in fiction and second in learned, or academic, contexts. With regard to fiction, this prevalence can be more generally explained by the fact that fiction most closely resembles speech, and usage of the modal auxiliary is more prevalent in speech.

Leech attributes the prevalence of core modals in academic contexts to the "habitual avoidance of categorical assertions of truth and falsehood. The qualification of such assertions, through modal concepts such as 'possibility,' 'necessity' and 'likelihood,' is deeply ingrained in academic habits of thought and expression, and might well be on the increase."

In other words, academics like to hedge their wording by using core modals, which makes sense because individual research findings accrete to knowledge and certainty, and when considered individually, often mean less.

On a related note, along with core modals, some writers also use additional hedge words in their writing to reinforce clarity, including *likely, probably,* and *possibly*.

EXAMPLE: Heidi will likely go to see the new Star Wars movie.

EXAMPLE: Depending on the size of my next paycheck, I could possibly loan you $1,000.

Corpus-based research suggests that certain less frequently used core modals have gravitated toward *monosemy,* or singular meanings, and have become more prevalent in these monosemic forms. For instance, *may* is becoming more epistemic than deotic.

EPISTEMIC (more common): I may go to the library.

DEONTIC (less common): You may use the car.

On the other hand, *should* has become more deontic than epistemic

DEONTIC (more common): You should use tissue when you blow your nose.

EPISTEMIC (less common): The mail should arrive by noon.

From a historical perspective, around the American Civil War, the modals *must, should,* and *shall* became less popular. These modals were associated with a social hierarchy that was slowly eroding. Nowadays, we rarely hear people tell others that they *must, should,* or *shall* do something. Doing so sounds bossy.

Finally, for good measure, let's look at quasimodals.

Quasimodals

Quasimodal verbs (also referred to a semimodals) are similar to core modals and paraphrase them. Like modal verbs, quasimodal verbs don't require *do* in negative constructions. However unlike modal auxiliary verbs, quasimodal verbs usually take the to-infinitive (and not the bare infinitive).

MODAL VERB: I will eat at In-N-Out Burger.

Quasimodal: I am going to eat at In-N-Out Burger.

Here are some modal verbs and their quasimodal equivalents.

Modal auxiliary	*Quasimodal*
will	be going to, be about to, be likely to
must	have to, need (to), be obliged to
should	ought to, be supposed to
would	used to, be willing to

Unlike core modals, which are shrinking in prevalence in both spoken and written English, certain quasimodals, such as *be going to* and *have to,* are becoming more popular in English—especially in spoken American English. Overall, however, core modals are still several times more frequent in the corpora. The increased prevalence of quasimodals in the corpora has led some experts to hypothesize that quasimodals, which are a relatively new construction, are on the path to taking on a new grammatical function, a process referred to as *grammaticalization.*

15. Figurative Language

TIP: Figurative language adds beauty, vigor, and meaning to your writing.

Key Points

- Metaphors use one image to explain another.
- Conventional metaphors are metaphors used in everyday language that provide a conceptual framework.
- With similes, the image is set alongside the statement using the words *like* or *as*.
- Metonymy is a trope in which the name of one thing is substituted for another term with which it is attributed or associated (for example, the "bar" for the legal profession).
- Avoid mixed metaphors.

Conventional metaphors are metaphors used in everyday language that provide a conceptual framework. The term *trope* refers to a word or expression that is used in a figurative sense and includes figures of speech like metaphors and similes. Figurative language leavens writing and speech. It would be an impossible challenge to communicate without using tropes because these literary devices touch on every aspect of thought. For instance, in the previous sentences, the verbs *leaven* and *touch* are tropes; figurative language doesn't literally *leaven* or *touch* anything.

"Primarily on the basis of linguistic evidence," write George Lakoff and Mark Johnson in *Metaphors We Live By*, "we have found that most of our ordinary conceptual system is metaphorical in nature. And we have found a way to begin to identify in detail just what the metaphors are that structure how we perceive, how we think, and what we do." The thought processes of humans are largely metaphorical.

More generally, tropes signify a relationship. According to the French philosopher Paul Ricœur in *The Rule of Metaphor*:

> The relationship through which tropes take place is one between ideas. More specifically, it is a relationship between two ideas; on the one hand, "the primary idea attached to the word," that is, the primitive signification of the borrowed word; and

on the other, "the new idea given to it," or the tropological meaning substituted for some other proper word that one did not wish to use in this particular situation.

With scientific writing, pundits recommend that linguistic devices, including figurative language, be limited in their use. According to the *Publication Manual of the American Psychological Association*: "Use metaphors sparingly; although they can help simplify complicated ideas, metaphors can be distracting.... Use figurative expressions with restraint and colorful expressions with care; these expressions can sound strained or forced."

Fortunately, not all writing is for scientific audiences. When writing for general audiences, the proper use of figurative language can fortify your prose, entertain your readers, and facilitate your message.

Metaphor

Metaphors allow us to experience and understand one thing in terms of another.

The great American mythologist, Joseph Campbell, defines metaphor as follows:

> A metaphor is an image that explains something else. For instance, if I say to a person, "You are a nut," I'm not suggesting that I think the person is literally a nut. "Nut" is a metaphor. The reference of the metaphor in religious traditions is to something transcendent that is literally not any thing. If you think that the metaphor is itself the reference, it would be like going to a restaurant, asking for the menu, seeing beefsteak written there, and starting to eat the menu.

Campbell then goes on to cite the metaphor that Jesus ascended into heaven, which if taken literally would mean that Jesus ascended into the sky and somehow thus entered heaven. If Jesus were literally to ascend into the sky, he would enter the galaxy and not heaven because there is no physical heaven in the galaxy. Instead, according to Campbell, Jesus went inward to "the kingdom of heaven within."

Ricœur defines metaphor as follows:

> Metaphor is the rhetorical process by which discourse unleashes the power that certain fictions have to redescribe reality.... The metaphorical "is" at once signifies both "is not" and "is like." If this is really so, we are allowed to speak of metaphorical truth, but in an equally "tensive" sense of the word "truth."

In this quotation, Ricœur describes metaphor as signifying what something not only *is* but what it *is not*.

For instance, if I were to write, "Flora's love for her children is an ocean," this expression has two meanings. First, Flora's love is vast, like an ocean. Second, Flora's love is not tiny, like a puddle.

In Aristotelian terms, the metaphor embodies three ideas:

- a deviation from ordinary usage
- a means of borrowing from an original domain
- a substitution for an absent but accessible ordinary word

Metaphors continue to define a term, and, with a metaphor, a transfer of meaning transpires. *Conventional metaphors* are metaphors used in everyday language that provide a conceptual framework. Different types of conventional metaphors exist. Let's look at three types of conventional metaphors: *orientational metaphors, ontological metaphors,* and *structural metaphors.*

Orientational metaphors organize an entire system of concepts with respect to a separate system of concepts. These metaphors use spatial terminology, such as *up-down, front-back, central-peripheral, in-out,* and *deep-shallow.*

EXAMPLE: Curtis is feeling down today.

EXAMPLE: Zach will need to wake up early today.

An *ontological metaphor* is one in which some abstract concept—such as an emotion, idea, or activity—is represented as an object (container), entity, substance or person.

EXAMPLE: Joan is going to get out of going to the meeting.

EXAMPLE: Ines's devotion is rock-solid.

In language, ontological metaphors serve several purposes. The most obvious ontological metaphors are ones in which an object or idea is specified as a person. These metaphors enable us to conceive of experiences with non-human entities in human terms, motivations, characteristics, and activities. The specific type of ontological metaphor also allows us to be more concise.

EXAMPLE: The research suggests that more money makes a person happier but not as happy as most people imagine.

Instead of: Based on the findings of numerous studies, researchers suggest that more money makes a person happier but not as happy as most people imagine.

EXAMPLE: The study finds that brain changes leading to autism are demonstrated using brain scans in infants aged between 6 and 12 months.

Instead of: Based on the data collected, the researchers found that brain changes leading to autism are demonstrated using brain scans in infants aged between 6 and 12 months.

Structural metaphors invite a wider breadth of meaning, and, unlike orientational and ontological metaphors, do more than orient, refer, and so forth. In structural metaphors, one—more nebulous—concept is structured in terms of another more detailed concept. For example, rational argument can be expressed in terms of war.

EXAMPLE: When Helga tried to defend her positions, her arguments were *shot down.*

Similes

Similes compare two unlike things using the words *like* or *as.* Unlike metaphors, similes are more explicit in their comparisons. In other words, with simile, the image is set alongside the statement; whereas, with metaphor the image is within the statement itself.

"[S]imile is a metaphor developed further," wrote Ricœur, "the simile says 'this is like that,' whereas, the metaphor says 'this is that.'"

EXAMPLE: Benicio's hair looks like the mane of a lion.

EXAMPLE: I will teach you as my father taught me.

Metonymy

Metonymy is a trope in which the name of one thing is substituted for another term with which it is attributed or associated. For example, "the bar" is a metonymy that refers to the legal profession as a whole. In reality, the bar is the railing that separates spectators from the lawyers, the judge, and the jury.

EXAMPLE: Iman was admitted to the bar in New York.

Another example of metonymy involves using "the Church" to represent the hierarchy of clergy in the Roman Catholic Church or the Church of England.

EXAMPLE: Under the leadership of Pope Francis, the Church seems more open to LGBTQ issues.

According to Lakoff and Johnson: "Metaphor is principally a way of conceiving of one thing in terms of another, and its primary function is understanding. Mentonymy, on the other hand, has primarily a referential function, that is, it allows us to use one entity to *stand for* another."

Synecdoche is a special form of metonymy in which the part is used to mean the whole. Or, with synecdoche, the whole can be used when referring to the parts.

EXAMPLE: Nathan needed an extra pair of hands to help build the tree house.

Here, "hands" is used to mean another worker and specifically stresses the importance of hands (as opposed to brain or voice) in helping with physical labor.

EXAMPLE: The orders came from Washington.

Here, Washington (as in D.C.), an entire physical area, is used to refer to the federal government that is located there.

Once again, according to Lakoff and Johnson:

> But metonymy is not merely a referential device. It also serves the function of providing understanding. For example, in the case of the mentonymy THE PART FOR THE WHOLE there are many parts that can stand for the whole. Which part we pick out determines which aspect of the whole we are focusing on.

When writing for international audiences, you should be careful when using metonymies that require a more nuanced or specific understanding of the English language. For example, although a native English speaker may understand that the term *suit* can be substituted for business executive or bureaucrat, this terminology may be lost on a non-native speaker.

EXAMPLE: The pop star has a meeting with the suits at her record label.

BETTER: The pop star has a meeting with the executives at her record label.

During the self-editing phase, it's useful to keep trope and metaphor in mind when writing for a general audience. With this guidance in mind, ask yourself whether the addition of figurative language can make your prose more engaging and help you better explain your meaning.

Also during the self-editing phase, you want to check your work for mixed metaphors. *Mixed metaphors* are overzealous extensions that conflate two separate metaphors to relate one idea. Mixed metaphors are universally derided and should be expunged from your writing.

WRONG: You shouldn't pass the buck but rather bite the bullet for your actions.

BETTER: You shouldn't blame someone else but rather be accountable for your actions.

For your entertainment, consider the following mixed metaphor written by columnist Frank Rich in the *New York Times:* "Top Bush hands are starting to get sweaty about where they left their fingerprints. Scapegoating the rotten apples at the bottom of the military's barrel may not be a slam-dunk escape route from accountability anymore."

Metaphor is a very useful tool in medical journalism and mirrors the communication of physicians with their patients. The circulatory system, with its numerable blood vessels, can be compared to plumbing; the brain, with a computer; and the kidney, with a filtration system or sieve.

Avoid false analogies. False analogies involve comparisons between two things that are too dissimilar to be compared. For example, comparing your boss to Kim Jong-un, supreme leader of North Korea, would (hopefully) be a false analogy.

Science of Analogy

A metaphor is a figure of speech in which a word or phrase referring to either an object or idea is used in place of another word or phrase to suggest a likeness or an analogy. An analogy, in turn, is an inference that if two or more things compare in some ways, they will compare in other ways, too.

In recent decades there has been increased interest in analogy among empirical researchers. One of the most prominent voices in analogical reasoning is Dedre Gentner, a psychologist who first suggested the *structure-mapping theory.*

In a 1983 article titled "Structure-Mapping: A Theoretical Framework for Analogy," Gentner states the following:

> The structure-mapping theory describes the implicit interpretation rules of analogy. The central claims of the theory are that analogy is characterized by the mapping of relations between objects, rather than attributes of objects, from base to target; and, further, that the particular relations mapped are those that are dominated by higher-order relations that belong to the mapping (the systematicity claim). These rules have the desirable property that they depend only on syntactic properties of the knowledge representation, and not on the specific content of the domain.

Gentner goes on to claim that this theoretical framework of analogy distinguishes analogy from literal similarity statements, abstractions, and other kinds of comparisons.

Essentially, an analogy is an assertion that the relationships that occur in one domain can be applied to another domain. The meaning of an analogy isn't derived from shared features but rather from shared relationships. For example, Gentner points to an analogy comparing a battery to a reservoir. In terms of physical characteristics, size, and so forth, these two things are nothing alike. However, they both store potential energy.

Finally, Gentner's theory has had broad implications in the fields of cognitive science, computer science, and artificial intelligence. Leveraging the power of the structure mapping theory, Kenneth Forbus and other computer scientists have been able to develop models that enable computers to think more like humans and engage in analogical problem solving. (This software algorithm is called the structure-mapping engine.)

16. Idioms

TIP: Avoid hackneyed idiomatic expressions.

Key Points

- Use idioms that are vivid and have flair.
- Define idioms that may be unfamiliar to the reader.
- Unless particularly apt, avoid hyperbolic idiomatic expressions like *groundbreaking* and *state-of-the-art.*

An *idiom* is a group of words that has a meaning that can't be deduced from its component words. When an idiom is trite or banal, it's best to use your own words. It's always a good idea to avoid clichéd language.

EXAMPLE: Track star Usain Bolt runs like the wind.

BETTER: Track star Usain Bolt runs very fast.

The key to using idioms is using them properly. Many non-native English speakers have trouble with idioms because they provide little context for meaning.

For instance, the expression *canary in a (the) coal mine* refers to a sign of impending danger. If you were to use this idiom, it's best to explain it.

UNCLEAR: The sea butterfly has been referred to as the ocean's canary in a coal mine because the shells of these creatures have begun dissolving in acidic waters secondary to carbon dioxide pollution.

BETTER: Carbon dioxide pollution has made the ocean's waters more acidic; consequently, the shells of sea butterflies have begun dissolving. Experts are concerned that these negative effects on sea butterflies portend future ecological disaster, which is why the sea butterfly has been referred to as the ocean's canary in a coal mine.

On a related note, the term "canary in a (the) coal mine" has a fascinating history. According to the United States Department of Labor, before electronic means of carbon monoxide detection, canaries were used to detect this lethal gas in mines. "Canaries—and sometimes mice—were used to alert miners to the presence of the poisonous gas. Following a mine fire or explosion, mine rescuers would descend into the mine carrying a canary in a small wooden or metal cage. Any sign of distress from the canary was a clear signal that the conditions underground were unsafe, prompting a hasty return to the surface. Miners who survive the initial effects of a mine fire or explosion may experience carbon monoxide asphyxia."

Semantic Bleaching

Certain hyperbolic idiomatic expressions have been overused to the point that they're now banal. Examples include *groundbreaking*, *earth-shattering*, and *state-of-the-art*. In linguistics, the reduction of a word's meaning is referred to as *semantic bleaching* and is due to broadened use.

You should reserve your use of words like groundbreaking and earth-shattering for truly extraordinary discoveries or ultramodern technologies, respectively. After all, the Internet is a disruptive technology that can deservedly be labeled groundbreaking. But the newest iteration of the iPhone is likely not a groundbreaking innovation but rather a direct extension of previous innovation. Moreover, the newest iPhone is never really state-of-the-art. Instead, a prototype sitting in Apple's lab is state-of-the-art; whereas, the newest iteration available to consumers is simply the newest model.

17.
Jargon

TIP: When writing for a general audience, use jargon sparingly.

Key Points

- Jargon is field-specific terminology and presents as shop talk or specialized lingo.
- If you must use jargon when writing for a nonspecialized audience, be sure to define it.

Merriam-Webster defines jargon as "the technical terminology or characteristic idiom of a special activity or group."

Jargon presents as shop talk or specialized lingo. It serves at least two purposes. First, it facilitates communication between professionals in the same field, such as physicians, engineers, architects, and psychologists. Second, it creates an in-group, or small group of people with shared interests in which a member feels solidarity and camaraderie.

When writing for a general audience, you want to do your best to avoid jargon and—whenever possible—find appropriate synonymous terms that everyone can understand. If you must use jargon, define it on first use.

Jargon should be reserved for specialized publications catering to like-minded professionals. If you confuse your readers with your writing, then you'll likely lose them. Using jargon doesn't make you look smart, it makes your readers feel dumb, and you don't want to make your readers feel dumb.

Let's consider some examples of jargon and how to revise this jargon so meaning isn't lost on the reader.

JARGON: In the United States, colorectal cancer is the second-leading cause of cancer death among men and women.

Okay, so what is "colorectal cancer"? Although you may already be familiar with this term, when writing for a general audience, you can take little for granted so err on the side of simplicity.

BETTER: In the United States, cancer that starts in the colon or rectum (colorectal cancer) is the second-leading cause of cancer death among men and women.

Importantly, I specified that this type of cancer "starts" in the colon or rectum. This point is important because colorectal cancer is particularly insidious and, if left untreated, spreads past the colon and rectum relatively quickly.

JARGON: Between 2004 and 2010, the five-year survival rate for stage 1 colon cancer is around 92 percent.

Stage 1 cancer is earliest stage cancer, or cancer that is local and hasn't yet spread to other organs. Five-year survival rate is a statistic referring to the percentage of people with the disease who live at least five years after diagnosis.

BETTER: Between 2004 and 2010, for earliest stage colon cancer, or cancer which has not yet spread to other organs, the percentage of people who were alive at least five years after diagnosis is 92 percent.

You will notice that I transposed this example for simplicity.

JARGON: In the United States, between 2003 and 2012, the incidence of cancer starting in the colon or rectum decreased.

"Incidence" indicates the number of people diagnosed during a certain time period, typically a year. When writing for a general audience, terms like *incidence* and *prevalence*—or total number of people with a disease—are best replaced with the more general term *frequency*.

BETTER: In the United States, between 2003 and 2012, the frequency of colon or rectal cancer decreased.

JARGON: For most people, colonoscopy is the best screening procedure for cancer starting in the colon or rectum.

What is a *colonoscopy*?

BETTER: For most people, colonoscopy, which is a method of visualizing the colon and rectum using a fiber-optic tube, is the best screening procedure for colon or rectal cancer.

Now, let's move on from examples of medical jargon to examples of technology and entertainment jargon.

JARGON: Cheaper hardware and more Wi-Fi has lead to an explosion in IoT.

Okay, so most people know that Wi-Fi refers to wireless Internet, and hardware refers to machines. But what does IoT refer to?

BETTER: Cheaper hardware and more Wi-Fi has lead to an explosion in the Internet of Things (IoT); IoT refers to devices that communicate using the Internet, such as a smart watch or smart car.

You'll notice that when clarifying jargon, you often need to use extra words, which makes things less concise. Using extra words or sentences to explain jargon is absolutely fine, just be judicious in your word choice.

JARGON: I used IFTT to connect my website to my blog's RSS feed.

The term IFTT is short for "If This Then That." It's a web-based service that allows you to automate tasks using recipes. An RSS (rich site summary) feed is a web feed that's automatically updated with new online content. If you have an RSS feed for your blog connected to your website using IFTT, then every time you publish a new post, your new post is automatically syndicated and displayed on your website.

BETTER: I used IFTT, a web-based service that automates tasks, to connect my personal website to my blog's RSS feed, which syndicates my newest blog postings.

JARGON: World of Warcraft is the most successful MMORPG.

BETTER: World of Warcraft is the most successful massively multiplayer online role-playing game (MMORPG), a type of online role-playing game where a large number of people simultaneously interact with each other in a virtual word.

JARGON: In filmmaker Wes Anderson's *The Grand Budapest Hotel,* the pink Mendl's pastry box is a hero prop.

BETTER: In filmmaker Wes Anderson's *The Grand Budapest Hotel*, the pink Mendl's pastry box is a hero prop. A hero prop is a special prop that gets more screen time and takes on a character its own.

If you're unfamiliar with a field and you're writing about, jargon won't come naturally, and it's likely that either you won't use jargon, or you'll automatically define it in your writing for not only the reader's sake but your own as well. However, if you're familiar with a field and the jargon associated with the field, then it may be hard to notice the jargon in your writing.

Instead of worrying about jargon when first writing, I suggest that you address jargon during the self-editing phase. Look for terms that others outside of the field may not understand. When writing for a general audience, imagine you are writing for a high school student who is learning about the topics that you discuss for the first time. How would you define complex and technical terms for this person? Alternatively, you can present your writing to a person unfamiliar with the topic that you're writing about—maybe your friend, partner, or grandmother—and ask for help identifying the jargon.

18. Left-Branching Sentences

TIP: Left-branching sentences work well on the web.

Key Points

- With a left-branching sentence, modifying elements come first followed by the subject and verb of the sentence.
- With right-branching sentences, the subject and verb of the sentence come first followed by modifying elements.

Left-branching sentences are weighted in the rear. With a left-branching sentence, the modifying clause or phrase ("branch") is placed before the subject and predicate of the sentence. Conversely, with a *right-branching sentence*, the subject and predicate come first. Right-branching sentences tend to work well with news, fiction, and narrative-driven prose.

Experts suggest that *left-branching sentences* work particularly well with online content and make it easier for readers, many of who are scanners, to hone in on the meaning. The practice of composing online content using left-branching sentences is likely influenced by broadcast journalism, where it has been effective and emphatic for listeners.

In all likelihood, the practice of using left-branching sentences dates even further back, and as advised in *The Elements of Style*: "The principle that the proper place for what is to be made most prominent is the end applies equally to the words of a sentence, to the sentences of a paragraph, and to the paragraphs of a composition."

When writing for an online audience, consider rearranging some of your sentences so that they're left branching. Not only does this construction promote clarity but it also sounds better when written aloud.

EXAMPLE (right-branching): Dmitry learned how to play both the guitar and piano while he was a child living in Tempe, Arizona.

BETTER (left-branching): While he was a child living in Tempe, Arizona, Dmitry learned how to play both the guitar and piano.

19. Misplaced Modifiers

TIP: Misplaced modifiers cause confusion for the reader.

Key Points

- A modifier can take the form of a word, phrase, or clause
- Limiting modifiers are single words, which cause confusion when misplaced.
- Dangling modifiers usually take the form of an introductory verb phrase.

Imagine a purse. If this purse were slung over the shoulder of a lady sitting at a café, you would presume that the purse belongs to the woman. If the purse were placed on the table immediately in front of this lady, you would likely presume that the purse belongs to her, too—especially if this woman were the only person sitting at the table. However, if the purse were sitting on a park bench across the street from the woman at the café, there's no way that you would know that this purse belongs to said woman.

To draw an analogy, a modifier, which can take the form of a word, phrase, or clause, is like the woman's purse. The farther away it is from what it's modifying, the less clear what the writer is referring to.

Let's first take a look at *limiting modifiers.* When misplaced, limiting modifiers cause absolute confusion. Examples of limiting modifiers include *only, merely, not, nearly, just, even,* and *almost.* For the sake of clarity, a limiting modifier needs to be placed before the noun, adjective, or verb it modifies.

EXAMPLE: The man had cried nearly the entire time.

EXAMPLE: The man had nearly cried the entire time.

In both of these examples, the placement of the limiting modifier "nearly" changes the meaning. Similarly, consider the placement of "only" in these sentences.

EXAMPLE: Hank is the only man with a plan.

EXAMPLE: Hank is the man with only a plan.

Next, consider the following sentence with the modifier, or restrictive clause, placed at two different points thus altering meaning.

EXAMPLE: There was a bumper sticker on the car that glowed in the dark.

EXAMPLE: There was a bumper sticker that glowed in the dark on the car.

Once again, the meaning of both sentences is different.

Now, let's look at two examples where the adverb phrase "only two days ago" is placed at different points.

Only two days ago, the man came into the shop with his daughter who applied for the cashier position.

The man came into the shop with his daughter who applied for the cashier position only two days ago.

Finally, let's consider the case of the *dangling modifier.* A dangling modifier usually begins a sentence and takes the form of a verb phrase. The reader would expect that the clause following this verb phrase to clearly identify the subject, or agent, first. With a dangling modifier, this clause doesn't clearly identify this subject first; thus, the sentence needs to be rewritten to avoid confusion.

UNCLEAR: While opening the Christmas presents, the snow began to fall.

In this example, it's unclear who is opening the presents, and the sentence seems to suggest that "the snow" opened the presents, which is nonsense.

BETTER: While opening the Christmas presents, we noticed that the snow began to fall.

Here, the independent clause following the dangling modifier is rewritten to name the agent first.

ALTERNATIVELY: While we opened the Christmas presents, the snow began to fall.

As shown in this example, for clarity, you can also name the agent in the modifying phrase.

When self-editing your own work, carefully consider whether the placement of your modifiers changes the meaning of your prose in unintended ways. If so, you should recast the sentence to ensure that your intended meaning is conveyed.

---

20. Negations

TIP: Rephrase not-negations in positive form.

Key Points

- Put not-negations in positive form to make your writing more assertive.
- Double-negative expressions are confusing and need to be reworded.
- Unlike not-negations, no-negations are used with purpose.

One of the most notable gems in Strunk and White's *Elements of Style* is the advice to "put statements in positive form."

"Make definite assertions. Avoid tame, colorless, hesitating, noncommittal language. Use the word *not* as a means of denial or in antithesis, never as a means of evasion.... Consciously or unconsciously, the reader is dissatisfied with being told only what is not; the reader wishes to be told what is."

EXAMPLE: Mariko did not acknowledge Yumiko.

BETTER: Mariko ignored Yumiko.

EXAMPLE: Finn did not speak softly to Amber.

BETTER: Finn yelled at Amber.

EXAMPLE: I wouldn't take the L Train today.

BETTER: I would avoid the L Train today.

As shown in the preceding examples, if you can find a positive alternative that's more specific than a not- (or *-n't*) negation go with it.

Not only does rephrasing a not-negation make for more specific writing but it also makes your writing more concise. Remember that when writing for publication, word counts are important and being concise pays.

Legitimate Uses of Not-Negations

Importantly, not-negations do have their uses. As explained by Strunk and White, not-negations are useful in statements of denial or antithesis.

EXAMPLE: Arif told the police that he did not steal the motorcycle.

Furthermore, Strunk and White also point out that contrasting a negative with a positive can reinforce a message.

EXAMPLE: I want to buy this car, not that car.

Double-Negative Expressions

In double-negative expressions, two (or more) negative expressions are used in apposition.

DOUBLE-NEGATIVE: Elizabeth would not rarely go to the zoo.

BETTER: Elizabeth would go to the zoo.

If you find double-negative expressions confusing, simply strike through the opposing negative expressions, which cancel each other out.

EXAMPLE: Elizabeth would ~~not rarely~~ go to the zoo.

DOUBLE-NEGATIVE: Kim's boss didn't dissuade her from seeking new employment.

BETTER: Kim's boss encouraged her to seek new employment.

No-Negations

Please keep in mind that negative words other than *not* are usually strong and used to make a point. Linguists call these other negative words *no-negations,* which include the following assertive words:

- no
- no one
- nobody
- none
- nothing
- nowhere

EXAMPLE: No amount of money is worth breaking the law.

EXAMPLE: The sequel was nowhere near as good as the original movie.

In the *Longman Student Grammar of Spoken and Written English,* Biber reports that no-negations are much less common in written language and downright rare in spoken language. This finding seems to make sense because in impromptu speech it's easier to reach for a not-negation than think about a no-negation. Of note, not-negations are about twice as common in spoken English than written English.

---

21. Nominalizations

TIP: Try to convert nominalizations back to active verbs.

Key Points

- Converting a verb to an abstract noun is known as a *nominalization.*
- Although the connotations of nominalizations are sometimes useful, prefer the active verb when prudent.

Nouns and verbs—as opposed to adverbs and adjectives—are the most common types of lexical word classes in the English language. Conversation has more verbs, and informative writing, such as academic writing and journalism, has more nouns. Because adverbs are attached to verbs, you'll find more adverbs in spoken language, as well as in fiction, which is heavily influenced by spoken language (think dialogue). Whereas, in informative writing, there are more adjectives, which are linked to nouns.

In linguistics, there's a hypothesis that nouns and verbs are diametric. A nominal style of writing, or one which uses plenty of (mostly abstract) nouns as well as adjectives, is wordy and the opposite of a verbal style. Certain corpus studies done by Douglas Biber and others tend to support this hypothesis and demonstrate that a higher proportion of nouns to verbs does correspond to longer clauses and longer phrases located within these clauses.

This hypothesis is debatable, and other linguists have demonstrated that an increase in nouns doesn't necessarily come at the expense of verbs but rather of other parts of speech (function word classes), such as determiners, articles, and prepositions that make up noun phrases.

When a base verb is changed into an abstract noun it's called a *nominalization*. Nominalizations convert verbs to nouns, or one extreme to the other. Nominalizations do have their uses in official and theoretical prose, where abstraction is sometimes needed. However, institutional language is also full of nominalizations, which makes the language harder to read. Nominalizations are stereotyped language, which make writing easier to reproduce. Style guides suggest to revert nominalizations back to their original verb forms.

EXAMPLE: The teacher made a suggestion about how to prepare for the spelling bee.

Here, "made a suggestion" is a nominalization with the base verb being "suggest." In an attempt to be concise, the prudent writer would rephrase this sentence with limited periphrasis. In other words, use fewer words by converting nominalizations back into their base forms.

BETTER: The teacher suggested how to prepare for the spelling bee.

Let's take a look at another example of nominalization.

EXAMPLE: After seeing a spider, Chandan uttered a loud shriek.

Here, "uttered a loud shriek" is a nominalization and could be replaced by the base verb "shriek."

BETTER: After seeing a spider, Chandan shrieked.

From a linguistics perspective, like noun strings and s-genitive constructions, nominalizations are another example of a trend toward *densification* of the noun phrase. Densification refers to condensation of information and is evident in the use of noun strings, s-genitive constructions, and nominalizations. Densification is the countervailing force to *colloquialization,* and the practice of densification seems to have spread from academic writing. Today, densification is most prevalent in journalism and least prevalent in spoken English.

In a bid to attain information density, there's been a trend for modern writers to use longer noun phrases. Additionally, in the continuous push-pull between densification and colloquialization, modern writers have riddled speech-like language with more complex noun phrases. Consequently, the writing of today often takes the form of nominal blather rather than verbal eloquence.

While self-editing, be on the lookout for nominalizations that can be replaced with active verbs. Often, nominalizations end in the following suffixes:

- -ance
- -ancy
- -ence
- -ency
- -ent
- -ity
- -ment
- -ness
- -tion

EXAMPLE OF NOMINALIZATION: The anatomists performed a dissection of the elephant lung.

BETTER: The anatomists dissected the elephant lung.

Please note that not all words that end in these suffixes are nominalizations. Furthermore, it's sometimes okay to use nominalizations. However, it's usually a good idea to prefer a base verb when meaning is retained.

EXAMPLE: The judge determined a punishment for the defendant.

INSTEAD OF: The judge punished the defendant.

Here, converting the nominalization "punishment" to the base verb "punish" can invite undue implications and connotations. After all, a judge is supposed to be an impartial arbiter of justice; thus, a periphrastic approach may sound better.

EXAMPLE: Cheryl turned in her application for graduate school at noon.

INSTEAD OF:: Cheryl applied for graduate school at noon.

The process of applying for graduate school involves more than just turning in an application. Thus, the nominalization "turned in an application" is probably preferable to "applied."

22.
Noun Choice

TIP: Choose nouns that best express your meaning.

Key Points

- You can normally do away with many adjectives and adverbs.
- Identify nouns, nominalizations, and noun phrases that have better alternatives.

When writing for a general audience, it's best to steer clear of vocabulary that most people won't understand. For the most part, you want to use big or complicated words only when simpler words fail to suffice, and even then, you want to place a big word in a context from which the reader can infer the meaning.

For example, according to *Merriam-Webster,* the word *auteur* means "a film director whose practice accords with the auteur theory." In turn, *auteur theory* means "a view of filmmaking in which the director is considered the primary creative force in a motion picture."

No better word for auteur exists, and alternatives to this single word are wordy phrases. Therefore, although most people may not know the word auteur, if you needed to express this idea, then this "big" word is best.

Consider the following:

John Hughes changed filmmaking forever with 1980s touchstones, such as *The Breakfast Club, Pretty in Pink,* and *Ferris Bueller's Day Off.* The unique vision and voice of these films established Hughes as a true *auteur.*

The reader may not know what "auteur" means. But the reader can likely infer that John Hughes was a screenwriter and director famous for examining teenage angst and indignities. Based on the surrounding context, a reader would be able to infer that auteur means visionary filmmaker.

In June 2017, Preet Bharara, the former U.S. Attorney for the Southern District of New York, did his first television interview ever since being fired from office by President Donald Trump in March 2017. In this interview with ABC News, Bharara was asked whether he thought that former FBI director James Comey—who, like Bharara, was also fired by Trump—lied under oath.

Bharara, who was a colleague of Comey's, said he doesn't think that Comey lied and that Trump has a history of making untrue accusations. He described

Comey as having a "reputation for probity" and "a reputation for telling the truth."

The word "probity" is well chosen by Bharara and in tune with his intended meaning. Probity not only means truthful but also possessing a devotion to telling the truth. It connotes high moral character.

You can normally do away with many adjectives and adverbs. But with nouns, like verbs, you can often choose the best one. Ideally, you want to use words that your audience will understand in context—which is why in the ABC interview, Bharara immediately qualifies his use of probity with a more familiar "reputation to tell the truth." Ultimately, there is wonderful latitude in noun choice. Just keep in mind that you don't want to pick a noun that is so obscure that it makes your writing sound contrived. In other words, don't succumb to stylistic heightening.

During the self-editing phase, identify nouns, nominalizations, and noun phrases that have better alternatives. Doing so will more clearly express your meaning and help you be more concise. When looking for good nouns to use, have a good thesaurus on hand.

EXAMPLE: During the Cuban Missile Crisis, the specter of nuclear war loomed large.

"Specter'" means something that is widely feared as a source of terror. In the preceding sentence, using the word "specter" is more concise and meaningful than several other words used to represent this term. Furthermore, in the context of nuclear war and the Cuban Missile Crises, the meaning of scepter can be inferred.

EXAMPLE: The poisoning of the city of Flint's water supply in 2014 became a cause célèbre among politicians, celebrities, and activists.

The compound word "cause célèbre" refers to a controversial issue that generates a lot of public interest. In the preceding example, cause célèbre captures this complex meaning in a term.

23. Noun Strings

TIP: Avoid complex noun strings.

Key Points

- Corpus-based research demonstrates that noun phrases are becoming denser.
- A noun string is a type of noun phrase in which the final noun is modified by a series of nouns or adjectives.
- While self-editing, think about how you can break up long noun strings for clarity.

A noun phrase is a group of words formed by a head noun and all its modifiers and determiners. A noun phrase functions as either a subject, an object, or an object of a preposition.

EXAMPLE: These German luxury cars cost a lot of money.

In this example, the noun phrase "these German luxury cars" is the noun phrase and "cost" is the verb. The word "cars" is the head noun.

EXAMPLE: Ziggy bought a pink luxury sedan.

In this example, "a pink luxury sedan" is a noun phrase and serves as an object of the verb "bought."

EXAMPLE: Ziggy bought the certified pre-owned car with his year-end bonus.

In this example, "his year-end bonus" is a noun phrase that serves as an object in the prepositional phrase "with his year-end bonus."

Corpus-based research suggests that the usage of nouns and adjectives in the form of noun phrases is increasing. More generally, in English, we're observing an increase in *open-class categories* (also called lexical word classes or "content words"), such as nouns and adjectives, and a decrease in *closed-class categories* (also called function word classes or "function words"), which are defined in terms of their use, such as determiners, articles, auxiliary verbs, and prepositions. Closed-class categories have grammatical function, and open-class categories carry information and can accept new members. Of note, *determiners* are articles, possessives, quantifiers, or demonstratives that make noun phrases specific. For instance, *the, which, each, his, all, some, its,* and *that* are all determiners.

Corpus-based research also suggests that noun phrases are becoming more densely packed with information, a phenomenon referred to as *lexical density* (or *densification*).

Writing in *Change in Contemporary English*, Leech states that this increase in lexical density suggests "an increase in the proportion of content words to function words, which in turn indicates a tendency to condense more information about the world into a smaller number of words." This trend has been going on for some time and is evidenced in medical, legal, and scientific writing.

Interestingly, this pattern of densification likely started in the American press and spread to spoken language. Typically, evolution of the English language happens in the opposite direction, with innovation in speech effecting changes in written language.

On a related note, the use of nouns and pronouns varies inversely. In general, written language is more information-packed and uses specific nouns; whereas, spoken language is, of course, more colloquial, with nonspecific pronouns predominating.

Examples of increased lexical density include constructions in which two nouns are juxtaposed, such as the noun phrases composed of the s-genitive (e.g., "Miss Thistlebottom's Hobgoblins") and noun-plus-noun sequences, or noun strings.

A *noun string* (also called a *noun chain*) is a type of noun phrase in which the final noun is modified by a series of nouns or adjectives. According to Bryan A. Garner in *A Dictionary of Modern American Usage*, "English has long been noted for its ability to allow words to change parts of speech. The transmutation of nouns into adjectives is one of the most frequently seen shifts of this kind."

Contempt for noun strings among style experts dates way back. In Follett's *Modern American Usage*, Follett called the practice of stringing nouns together "noun plague." According to Follett: "Modern style is sorely afflicted with misplaced emulation of the abstractness of the scientific and technical report."

Some noun strings are quite familiar and completely acceptable, including *randomized controlled trial*, *search engine optimization*, and *below-knee amputation*. If a noun string has established itself, and its meaning is apparent to many, then using it is fine.

However, be wary of noun strings that are difficult to discern or inscrutable. In *On Writing Well*, William Zinsser calls noun strings "creeping nouns" and explains, "This is a new American disease that strings two or three nouns together where one noun—or, better yet, one verb—will do."

"In general," writes Theodore M. Bernstein in *The Careful Writer*, "two or more polysyllable nouns used as adjectives are undesirable."

You'll often find noun strings in bureaucratic, government, and legal circles. For instance, the U.S. Department of Health and Human Services (HHS) offers an early commissioning program titled the following: Senior Commissioned Officer Student Training and Extern Program (SRCOSTEP). This noun string is unbearable.

Understanding what this program does may help us untangle this noun string in an attempt to better explain it. According to the HHS website: "This highly competitive program is available to full-time students about to begin their final year of academic study or professional training. Those selected for the program will become Commissioned officers in the U.S. Public Health Service (USPHS) and receive full pay and benefits of an active duty officer for up to 12 months just for finishing their education and training."

With this explanation in mind, let's restructure this noun string in plain terms: "training program for senior students becoming commissioned officers." Typically, when breaking up longer noun strings, you identify the head noun and chop off any modifiers. You then tack this information back on using determiners, prepositions, and so forth.

Here's another gem from the Federal Bureau of Prisons: "Inmate DNA Sample Collection Procedures."

According to the Bureau's website, these are "procedures for identifying persons in Bureau of Prisons (Bureau) custody from whom DNA (deoxyribonucleic acid) samples will be collected, as well as the DNA sample collection procedures, as authorized by current statutes and Federal regulations."

No doubt the following would be clearer: "procedures for the collection of DNA samples from inmates."

Finally, here's a noun string which might be found in scientific writing: *well-funded multicenter randomized controlled trials.* This noun phrase could be restructured as follows: multicenter randomized controlled trials that are well funded.

Because people are more inclined now than ever before to use noun strings, you may find noun strings in your own writing. If these noun strings are short and their meanings are widely recognized by the audience that you're writing for, you can keep them. However, if these noun strings sound jargonistic or contrived, consider restructuring them in plain terms during the self-editing phase.

---

24. Parallelism

TIP: Always keep parallelism in mind.

Key Points

- Correlative conjunctions link elements in parallel form.
- Lists should contain items in parallel form.

When you write any document, the goal is to have your reader understand your message. If your reader doesn't understand what you've written, then you've failed in a fundamental way. You've committed a fatal error. To this end, a writer has tools that help keep the flow of information, or continuity, going.

One tool is transitions, or the words that glue sentences together. Paragraphs also provide structure and render prose digestible and comprehensible. (Identifying concepts, limiting the use of jargon, and providing examples are other ways to boost readability.) Importantly, parallelism can make the words that you write easier to understand for the reader.

The law of correlative conjunctions applies to conjunctions that are paired, including *either ... or, neither ... nor, not only ... but (also)*, or *whether ... or.* In *The Careful Writer*, Theodore M. Bernstein writes, "The law, which like most laws is occasionally broken for a noble purpose, simply states that such conjunctions should connect two of the same thing—that is, elements of the same grammatical value and in parallel forms." Of interest, Theodore Bernstein was a journalism professor at Columbia University and a longtime editor at the *New York Times*. He also wrote many guides on English language usage.

NONPARALLEL STRUCTURE: Someday, presidential historians will take great interest in the fact that Donald Trump was not only voted president of the United States but also his starring role in *The Apprentice.*

PARALLEL STRUCTURE: Someday, presidential historians will likely take great interest in the fact that Donald Trump was not only voted president of the United States but also starred in *The Apprentice.*

Another place in your writing where parallelism is important is in list items—whether they constitute run-on lists or displayed lists.

For example, consider the following displayed list.

Here are some interesting facts about Michigan:

- The Detroit Zoo was the first zoo to feature open, cageless exhibits.
- Lots of craft breweries
- Battle Creek, Michigan, is the home of Kellogg's and has been nicknamed the Cereal City.
- Birthplace of Madonna, Sonny Bono, and Anthony Kiedis
- Produces more tart cherries than any other U.S. state.

In this list, the parallelism of the items is off. Some of the items are independent clauses, and some are phrases. Preferably, all items should either be phrases or independent clauses but not a mix of both.

Let's consider the displayed list written as a series of phrases.

Here are some interesting facts about Michigan:

- Home of the first zoo with cageless exhibits (the Detroit Zoo);
- Lots of breweries;
- Home of Kellogg's cereal;
- Birthplace of Madonna, Sonny Bono, and Anthony Kiedis;
- Biggest producer of tart cherries of any U.S. state.

Now, let's consider the displayed list written as a series of independent clauses.

Here are some interesting facts about Michigan:

- It was the first state to have a zoo with cageless exhibits (the Detroit Zoo).
- It has lots of breweries.
- It is the home of Kellogg's cereal.
- It is the birthplace of Madonna, Sonny Bono, and Anthony Kiedis.
- It produces the most tart cherries of any state in the United States.

25. Passive Voice

TIP: Prefer the active voice to the passive voice.

Key Points

- Use the passive voice when the process or action described is more important than the agent.
- Use the passive voice when the agent is unremarkable, unimportant, or uninteresting.
- Use the passive voice when the agent can be guessed from the context.
- Use the passive voice to conceal the agent.

You've likely heard that it's best to avoid the passive voice and prefer the active voice. This advice is especially prevalent in American style guides.

According to *The Chicago Manual of Style*, "As a matter of style, passive voice is typically, though not always, inferior to active voice."

With the passive voice, the object becomes the subject, and is followed by a conjugation of the verb *to be* and a past participle. The subject is thus acted on. In other words, the subject experiences the action or process that is expressed by the verb. The passive voice emphasizes the process. On a related note, only transitive verbs have voice.

EXAMPLE: The movie was watched.

In passive constructions, the importance of the agent is minimized, and the agent often goes unnamed. In the preceding example, for instance, it's unclear who watched the movie. The agent, however, can be specified with the addition of a phrase beginning with *by*.

EXAMPLE: The movie was watched by the children.

In more lively narrative, you typically want to know who is performing an action. Thus, many would prefer the following construction, which is active.

ACTIVE: The children watched the movie.

Passive Voice Usages

The passive voice does have some legitimate uses.

First, the passive voice is useful when the agent is unremarkable—as in scientific writing.

EXAMPLE: The participants were asked to fill out the questionnaire.

Here, it's implied that *the researchers* asked the participants to fill out the questionnaire, which is a common practice. There's little need to repeatedly mention "the researchers" (or "we" as it refers to the researchers) and doing so can sound redundant.

"The *passive* also allows scientists to avoid implying any particular cause and effect to their statements," writes Pam Peters in *The Cambridge Guide to English Usage*, "and to concentrate on what happened until they are ready to look for explanations in physical laws and principles."

In other words, the passive voice helps the researchers objectively detach from study participants who they are observing and helps the reader focus on the scientific process.

Nevertheless, using the active voice is gaining traction in the sciences, especially in biology, medicine, and engineering. Thus, specifying "we" (a generalized subject pronoun) instead of writing in the passive voice is acceptable in peer-reviewed journal articles.

EXAMPLE: We asked the participants to fill out the questionnaire.

Linguistics scholar Robert Dixon writes in *A Semantic Approach to English Grammar* that passive constructions are written "to give an illusion of total objectivity, whereas in fact the particular personal skills and ideas of a scientist do play a role in his work, which would be honestly acknowledged by using active constructions with first person subject."

Second, in journalism when the agent can be readily inferred or is inconsequential, the passive can be used to cut down on word count. When reporting on crime, for example, there's little need to mention *the police*, which is implied and could read redundant if used too many times.

EXAMPLE: The perpetrator was apprehended shortly after midnight.

Third, the passive voice is useful in situations where diplomacy or sensitivity is important. In other words, the passive voice can be used to avoid specifying the agent to save the agent from criticism, censure, embarrassment, or so forth.

EXAMPLE: The employees will be laid off.

EXAMPLE: The guest was accidently vomited on.

Fourth, the passive voice is used in judicial, legal, and corporate documents.

EXAMPLE: The defendant was ordered to be held without bond.

Technically, this construction is known as the *double passive*, with the second verb being a passive infinitive, and historically many experts have censured double passives. Thus, some American publications have developed the following workaround.

WORKAROUND: The defendant was ordered held without bond.

Passive and Passive-Like Constructions

So far, we've examined the passive voice no more deeply than it's been detailed in numerous style guides. But the story of the passive voice is more complex.

In addition to the passive voice as it's commonly observed—the *be-passive*—there are also passive-like constructions like the *get-passive* and the *middle voice*, or *mediopassive* construction. Both passive and passive-like constructions are similar in that they lack an agent. Furthermore, the verbs in passive and passive-like constructions are *stative verbs*, which means they describe a state of being. (Dynamic verbs are the opposite of stative verbs and indicate an action.)

The Be-Passive

EXAMPLE OF THE BE-PASSIVE: The expensive vase was cracked.

In the corpora, examples of the be-passive are decreasing. In other words, linguistic studies of the be-passive suggest that there's a trend toward disuse of the be-passive. (Textbooks are an exception, with use of the be-passive on the rise.) Instead, according to Robert Dixon, "Everything else being equal, a speaker of English will prefer to use a verb with two or more core roles (a transitive verb) in an active construction, with subject and object stated." This move away from the passive is likely rooted in the strong prescriptive tendencies of American style guides, which instead extol the active voice as a more direct and striking means of presenting a situation.

The Get-Passive

EXAMPLE OF THE GET-PASSIVE: The traitor got hanged.

The get-passive is considered an informal and colloquial, or slang, variant, which is sometimes heard in speech. From a semantic perspective, the get-passive is adversative, or oppositional, and usually used during face-to-face conversations. Even in spoken English, however, the get-passive is rare and only accounts for 0.1 percent of all verbs used. The get-passive is used even less frequently in conversation than the be-passive, probably because of its adversative connotation.

The get-passive was first documented at the end of the seventeenth century and became more frequent at the end of the eighteenth century. More recently, there's been a slight increase in the usage of the get-passive. Currently, the get-passive is about 400 times more common than the be-passive in written texts.

The get-passive could be considered a *grammaticalization;* grammaticalization denotes the process by which words change to take on a grammatical function.

The Mediopassive

The *mediopassive* is a term borrowed from Greek that refers to a third voice: the middle voice. With the mediopassive, the subject is most important. It's almost as if the subject were doing the action. The mediopassive straddles a meaning between the active and passive voices.

MEDIOPASSIVE: The boat steers easily.

MEDIOPASSIVE: The album sold well.

The be-passive, get-passive, and mediopassive exist on a cline of meaning. The subject in the be-passive takes little responsibility, and the process is the focus. With the get-passive, the subject takes more responsibility. Finally, the subject in the mediopassive takes the most responsibility as compared with the be-passive and get-passive. Moreover, the subject in the mediopassive either facilitates or hampers the process. In fact, mediopassive constructions have modal meanings with possibility, certainty, necessity, willingness, and ability expressed by the writer.

Studies of the corpora indicate that there's been only a slight increase in the use of the get-passive. Furthermore, the mediopassive has mostly experienced an increase in prevalence in advertising publications, thus reflecting a niche use.

EXAMPLE: Levi's jeans wear well.

EXAMPLE: The new Lexus drives smoothly.

Should You Use the Passive Voice?

While self-editing, be on the lookout for passive constructions in your writing. In many contexts—even scientific ones in which the passive voice is permitted—it's better to use the active voice instead of the passive voice. However, exceptions do exist.

Before using a passive construction ask yourself the following:

- Is the process detailed more important than the agent?
- Is the agent unremarkable, unimportant, or uninteresting?
- Is the agent easy or hard to infer from the context?
- Is it more tactful or less hurtful to conceal the agent?

---

26. Powerhouse Verbs

TIP: Choose the best verb for the job.

Key Points

- Look for variety in the verbs that you use.
- Use a thesaurus to discover powerhouse verbs.

An exception to the rule of thumb that simple words are usually best is a class of verbs that I call *powerhouse verbs.* The synonyms of these verbs are so particular and often descriptively befitting that it's wise to use a thesaurus to seek out these synonyms. In other words, with powerhouse verbs, it's often a good idea to use the thesaurus and find the perfect synonym even if this synonym is a big word.

While self-editing, it's a good idea to check whether the verbs that you use have better powerhouse alternatives.

Let's consider the following example.

OKAY: With her sartorial flair and false promises of new and disruptive technology, Elizabeth Holmes tricked investors out of many millions.

POWERHOUSE VERB: With her sartorial flair and false promises of new and disruptive technology, Elizabeth Holmes inveigled investors out of many millions.

Lots of powerhouse verbs exist in English. Here are some more examples.

Powerhouse Verb	***Synonyms***
run	dash, scamper, scoot, scurry, sprint, bolt, flee, fly, make off
hit	strike, slap, punch, swat, beat, thrash, wallop, whack, bash, clip, slug, clobber
talk	speak, chat, prattle, babble, blather, yak, chatter, articulat, maunder
cry	weep, sob, wail, howl, bawl, whimper, bleat, grieve, mourn, blubber

Although the word *say* is a powerhouse verb, when writing out quotations, it's usually best to write *say* or *state* instead of using another synonym. Furthermore, the expression *according to* should be used only with written or authored text. In other words, you don't write "according to Bill Gates" if you're quoting a speech given by Gates.

In conclusion, you can use big words when they're powerhouse verbs. You can also use big words with certain nouns that perfectly express ideas. You should largely steer clear of complicated words with all other parts of speech. Moreover, you should endeavor to use as few adverbs and adjectives as possible.

27. Preposition Stranding

TIP: It's fine to place a preposition at the end of a sentence.

Key Points

- Ending a sentence with a preposition is called *preposition stranding* and is preferred in most contexts.
- Placing a preposition at the head of a relative clause is referred to as *pied-piping* and is more formal.

In nearly all contexts, it's perfectly fine to place a preposition at the end of a sentence. In linguistics, this practice is called *preposition stranding.*

STRANDING: Oregon is the state that Mrs. Witucki lives in.

Alternatively, you can place the preposition at the head of the relative clause. This practice is referred to as *pied-piping.* In technical terms, the relative clause gap functions as a prepositional complement.

PIED-PIPING: Oregon is the state in which Mrs. Witucki lives.

You'll notice that in the pied-piping construction, "in which" is restrictive, which makes sense because "in that" sounds wrong. Pied-piping constructions always introduce restrictive clauses and thus require no preceding comma.

Corpus-based research published in *Change in Contemporary English* by Leech shows that pied-piping is seen in more expository and formal registers—academic writing and general prose—and stranding in more colloquial, or less academic, registers such as fiction as well as the press. Stranding is rare in formal registers. (The term "register" refers to a style or variety of language.) Although stranding has become increasingly common in less academic registers, it is still less common than pied-piping.

We must take in account, however, that these research results were calculated using corpora (the Brown Family) that were dated from 1961 and 1991/2. By nature, corpus-based research is retrospective, and as with any retrospective study, a time lag exists. More recently, the advice of style mavens is to stick with stranding.

When writing and self-editing your work, for most audiences, stranding is usually fine. Keep in mind that pied-piping can sometimes sound pretentious.

28.
Progressive Tense
A Linguistics Perspective

TIP: Stative uses of the progressive tense are usually wordy.

Key Points

- Use the progressive tense with actions that are durative or dynamic.
- For conciseness and clarity, take "non-durative" or stative situations out of the progressive tense.

We have already looked at the progressive tense from the vantage point of style. Now, let's look at the progressive tense in parallax: from the vantage point of linguistics.

Style teaches us only so much about language and does so in a prescriptive fashion. Corpus linguistics, or the study of language in the real world, gives us a greater appreciation and understanding of the progressive tense. Put another way, corpus linguistics proffers a descriptive appreciation for the different uses of the progressive tense. To truly understand the progressive tense and how to use it in your writing, it's a good idea to appreciate how it's actually used in the real world.

Linguistic Definition of the Progressive Tense

In the analytic text *Change in Contemporary English*—a work that has been formative in this and several other chapters of the book—Leech writes that the progressive tense is typically associated with notion of aspect or "the manner in which the internal temporal constituency of a situation is represented."

Remember that the progressive tense consists of a conjugation of *to be* followed by a participle ending in *-ing*.

EXAMPLE: President Trump will be relaxing at Mar-a-Lago.

EXAMPLE: President Obama has been vacationing in his birth state of Hawaii.

In both these examples, the progressive aspects are clear. In other words, it's clearly understood that the situations described are *durative* and continue for a certain duration of time. Furthermore, these situations also indicate change and are thus *dynamic*.

However in a minority of contexts, the progressive tense can also be used to describe situations that are apparently unlinked to a duration of time ("non-durative") and are instead *stative*, or refer to a state of being. According to some linguists, in these contexts, it's questionable whether the term "progressive" actually applies.

EXAMPLE: Despite having emphysema, Sherry is always smoking cigarettes.

EXAMPLE: Adam will be graduating from architecture school next year.

EXAMPLE: This year's total number of donations is appearing to surpass that of last year.

In these non-durative and stative constructions, the progressive tense appears to be taking on an expanded meaning in the English language. Unlike the subjunctive, which has for the most part dwindled in real-world usage, the progressive has become increasingly popular and widespread.

History of the Progressive Tense

Although its exact origins are unclear, the progressive tense took on its durative meaning between the sixteenth and eighteenth centuries. By the late eighteenth century, the progressive passive emerged followed by more complex forms of the progressive tense, including the past perfect, present perfect, future, and modal paradigms. Unlike today, when the passive progressive is mostly used in British reportage, in the early days of the tense, it was used in even more informal contexts.

PROGRESSIVE PASSIVE: Hotels and venues are being constructed mere days before the start of the Olympics.

MODAL PASSIVE: Due to his symptoms, the man could be having a heart attack.

In English, the progressive tense has taken on more paradigmatic complexity. Furthermore, the progressive tense has become increasingly popular—especially in spoken language. In linguistics, the word *paradigm* is jargon for the different forms (inflections) that a verb, noun, or adjective can take.

Progressive Tense Trends

In both American English and British English, the rapid rise in the use of the progressive tense is mostly attributable to increased use of the present progressive. Otherwise, trends with respect to the progressive tense somewhat differ between American and British English.

First, unlike in American English, in British English, the passive progressive is becoming more popular. This trend is especially apparent in semi-formal contexts dependent on fact, such as newspaper reporting or opinion pieces. In American English, flagging use of the passive progressive follows a more general decline in use of the passive voice, which has been proscribed in many style guides.

In many instances in American English, use of the passive progressive has been supplanted by use of the present progressive in which the subject is a generic pronoun, such as *you* or *we*.

PASSIVE PROGRESSIVE: The pendulum has swung the other way toward the descriptive, and instead of being quick to label certain examples of unconventional speech or writing "bad grammar," more prescriptive practices are being eschewed.

PRESENT PROGRESSIVE WITH GENERIC PRONOUN: The pendulum has swung the other way toward the descriptive, and instead of being quick to label certain examples of unconventional speech or writing "bad grammar," we are eschewing more prescriptive practices.

Second, in British English, there's been increased popularity in the use of the progressive tense in combination with modal auxiliary verbs, or the modal progressive—especially in expressions that begin with *will be*. In these specific constructions, the predicted event is devoid of volition or intent and considered normal or expected. We usually observe these constructions in the first- or second-person.

EXAMPLE: I will be going to the play tomorrow night.

In American English, much like the passive progressive, the modal progressive is also losing ground. And again, just as decreased prevalence of the passive progressive can be traced back to the passive voice falling into disfavor, so too can the decline in the use of the modal progressive be linked to a more general erosion of modal auxiliary verb usage in modern American English.

While self-editing your own work, you want to keep an eye out for any uses of the progressive tense. As indicated by the corpora, we're seeing more people use the present progressive, which is commonly misunderstood.

Finally, while self-editing, keep in mind that stative uses of the progressive can often be replaced with more concise alternatives. Let's look at some previous examples to prove this point.

WORDY: Despite having emphysema, Sherry is always smoking cigarettes.

BETTER: Despite having emphysema, Sherry smokes cigarettes.

WORDY: Ezra will be graduating from the hotel school next year

BETTER: Ezra will graduate from the hotel school next year.

Now, let's take a look at some additional examples.

WORDY: This year's total number of donations is appearing to surpass that of last year.

BETTER: This year's total number of donations appears to surpass that of last year.

WORDY: I will be going to the play tomorrow night.

BETTER: I will go to the play tomorrow night.

29. Relative Pronouns

TIP: American style guides prescribe the use of *that*—not *which*—to introduce restrictive clauses.

Key Points

- American style guides prescribe using *that* to introduce restrictive clauses.
- A case can be made—especially in written British English—for the use of *which* to introduce restrictive clauses.
- The relative pronoun *who*—not *that*—is used to describe people.
- A *zero-relative clause* is a relative clause in which the *that* or *which* relativizer has been elided, or removed, without affecting meaning.

The distinction between *that* and *which* is particularly important when writing for American audiences. The relative pronoun *that* begins a restrictive modifying clause (essential clause) and introduces information that is necessary to the meaning of the sentence.

Example: Flying birds that colonize islands with no predators evolve toward flightlessness.

If the restrictive clause "that colonize islands with no predators" were removed, the resulting sentence would make no sense—obviously, all birds don't evolve toward flightlessness.

Unclear: Birds ~~that colonize islands with no predators~~ evolve toward flightlessness.

The relative pronoun *which* begins a nonrestrictive modifying clause (nonessential clause) and introduces information that is not integral to the meaning of the sentence. A nonrestrictive clause can be set off with commas.

Example: The bananaquit, which is a bird found in the Caribbean, has evolved toward flightlessness.

Many writers have difficulty deciding whether to use *that* or *which*. When in doubt, eliminate all restrictive and nonrestrictive modifying clauses from a selection and evaluate the resulting sentences for comprehension. Clauses that are integral to the meaning of the text need to begin with *that*.

Consider the following selection with restrictive and nonrestrictive clauses intact.

> Predictable evolutionary trends help us better understand the diversity of plant and animal species which populate every habitat on earth. For example, birds that colonize islands with few natural predators evolve toward flightlessness in predictable patterns. Over time, populations of small-island birds develop smaller flight muscles and longer legs. Without predators, these birds no longer need to fly as much and lose the ability. However, invasive predators introduced on these islands endanger such small bird species which have evolved toward flightlessness.

Now, let's strike all restrictive and nonrestrictive clauses, which begin with *that* and *which*, respectively, from this paragraph and evaluate the resulting sentences for comprehension.

> Predictable evolutionary trends help us better understand the diversity of plant and animal species ~~which populate every habitat on earth~~. For example, birds ~~that colonize islands with few natural predators~~ evolve toward flightlessness in predictable patterns. Over time, populations of small-island birds develop smaller flight muscles and longer legs. Without predators, these birds no longer need to fly as much and lose the ability. However, invasive predators introduced on these islands endanger such small bird species ~~which have evolved toward flightlessness~~.

For the most part, this selection still makes sense, which means that most of these clauses are, in fact, nonrestrictive. The only clause that is necessary to the meaning of this paragraph is "that colonize islands with few natural predators." With its removal, the resulting sentence doesn't make sense. Thus, "that colonize islands with few natural predators" is restrictive. All other clauses in this selection are nonrestrictive.

Some people have a tendency to prefer *that* to *which* when constructing modifying clauses. If you exhibit this tendency, when self-editing, by default, consider all the restrictive clauses that you've written as nonrestrictive clauses and evaluate for meaning. In other words, if you tend to overuse *that,* substitute all instances of "that" with "which" and evaluate for meaning.

Use "Who" for People

All professional writers recognize that relative pronoun *who*—not *that*—is used to describe people, and professional editors, who historically have served as gatekeepers to publication, can easily recognize whether a writer understands this crucial distinction.

> Wrong: To the surprise of many, the candidate ~~that~~ garnered the Republican presidential nomination in 2016 was Donald Trump.
>
> Right: To the surprise of many, the candidate who garnered the Republication presidential nomination in 2016 was Donald Trump.

However, *that* can sometimes be used to refer to groups of people or teams—things related to people. In these cases, the group or team is more important than the individuals on it and thus can be viewed as a non-human entity.

> Right: During the 2016 election, it was often Trump's team that was left explaining the candidate's musings.

Linguistics

In terms of grammar, the prescriptive value of distinguishing between *that* or *which* is less important. Linguists are much more concerned with how *that* and *which* are actually used in various contexts. Remember that grammar is descriptive and describes language as it is—not as it "should be."

A *zero-relative clause* is a relative clause in which the *that* or *which* relativizer has been elided, or removed, without affecting meaning. According to Leech, in American English, between the year 1961 and 1991/2, there's been a 6.1 percent rise in the number of zero-relative clauses compared with that of 8.2 percent in British English.

Although zero-relative clauses are usually understood in spoken English, when writing, it's probably best to avoid them. The use of *that* and *which* makes your writing clear and helps readers—especially international readers—better grasp your meaning.

ZERO-RELATIVE CLAUSE: The orange car we rented had GPS and an incredible sound system.

BETTER: The orange car that we rented had GPS and an incredible sound system.

In the *Longman Student Grammar of Spoken and Written English,* Biber found that in speech, *that* is the most frequent relativizer, followed by the zero- (or no) relativizer. However, in writing, *wh-* (*which, who,* and *whom*) relativizers are most common.

Apparently, *wh-* relativizers can carry a heavier load in formal writing and signal not only the beginning of nearly all nonrestrictive clauses but also some restrictive clauses. (In the corpora, the *wh-* relativizer *who* is strongly preferred to *that* when referring to human antecedents.)

In *Change in Contemporary English*, Leech argues:

> The informational registers have by far the greatest complexity of noun phrase structure, and the *wh-* pronouns are useful here because they can bear a heavier functional load than *that* and zero, and can give a stronger, more unambiguous signal of the beginning of a relative clause, thus mitigating the structural ambiguities and processing difficulties associated with syntactically more complex NPs [noun phrases].... Overall, moreover, *wh-* relativizers are the most versatile in that they can be used with the greatest variety of syntactic functions.

Leech found that in American English, when introducing restrictive clauses, *wh-* relativizers are much less common than *that* relativizers. In fact, Americans tend to view *wh-* relativizers as more formal and best suited for formal written texts. Importantly, American style guides specify that only *that* relativizers be used to introduce restrictive clauses.

In British English, however, *wh-* relativizers are more commonly used to introduce restrictive clauses. Nevertheless, there has been attrition in British written registers due to *colloquialization*, or preference of *that* for *which* in speech. Moreover, many spell checkers and grammar checkers, which are created in the United States, are programmed with prescriptive guidance from American stylebooks and dispatched across the world.

30. Subjunctive Mood

TIP: Proper use of the subjunctive
can make your writing more graceful.

Key Points

- Use of the subjunctive is optional, but when used properly, the subjunctive can energize your writing.
- Core modals (for example, *would, could,* and *should*) are usually used in lieu of the subjunctive.
- The subjunctive is used in *if* expressions to express an idea that will never happen, or represent unreal or impossible situations.
- When something may or might happen, don't use the subjunctive.
- Think of the subjunctive mood as the *other* way to say something using a verb or verb phrase.
- The mandative subjunctive is on the rise in English and refers to the following: use of the subjunctive in contexts when a specific action is called for.

Once upon a time, when English existed as Old English, there was a fully functional subjunctive. This subjunctive existed in person-number-tense combinations. Nowadays, we see much less of the subjunctive because core modals (for example, *should* and *would*) can serve as semantic alternatives to the grammatical subjunctive and also express obligation, necessity, hope, demand, and expectation.

In light of a long march toward a more analytic language rooted in logic and free of irregularity, some experts have even gone so far as declaring the subjunctive dead. Pam Peters, author of *The Cambridge Guide to English Usage* (2004), writes that "the subjunctive is a pale shadow of what it used to be." Nevertheless, the subjunctive still exists in pockets of the English language and is of interest to writers, style mavens, and linguists alike.

Adherents hope that the revival of certain forms of the subjunctive, particularly in American English, may indicate a more pervasive resurgence. Linguists doubt a complete resurrection of the subjunctive but acknowledge that certain uses, such as the *mandative subjunctive* and *were-subjunctive,* both iterations that we will examine at length, will endure into the foreseeable future.

Let's take a look at the subjunctive in parallax: first, from the vantage point of linguistics and grammar, and second, from lexical (dictionary) and stylistic perspectives. Remember that style is *prescriptive* and defines writing as it "should be." Grammar, however, is *descriptive*, or more permissive, and describes language and writing as *it is* or *could be*.

I'll be drawing from different sources when describing each vantage point. In the first section titled "Subjunctive: Lexicon and Style," I'll be looking at dictionaries (lexicons) and style guides. The first section is probably most important to writers interested in using the subjunctive. In the second section titled "Subjunctive: A Linguistics Perspective." I'll examine linguistics texts, which base findings on corpus-based research. For good measure, I'll present how these different disciplines explain concepts like the mandative subjunctive. We'll round out our examination with a case for the continued use of the subjunctive.

Subjunctive: Lexicon and Style

According to *Fowler's Dictionary of Modern English Usage:* "The subjunctive mood is one of the great shifting sands of the English grammar. Its complexity over the centuries is such that the standard reference work on historical English syntax by F. Th. Visser (4 vols., 1963–1973) devoted 156 pages to the subject (Visser called it the "modally marked form") and listed more than 300 items in its bibliography."

Here is what the *New Oxford American Dictionary* has to say about usage of the subjunctive:

> In English, the subjunctive mood is fairly uncommon (esp. in comparison with other languages such as French and Spanish), mainly because most of the functions of the subjunctive are covered by modal verbs such as might, could and should. In fact, in English the subjunctive is often indistinguishable from the ordinary indicative mood since its form in most contexts is identical. It is distinctive only in the third person singular where the normal indicative –s ending is absent … and in the verb "to be".… In modern English, the subjunctive mood still exists but is regarded in many contexts as optional. Use of the subjunctive tends to convey a more formal tone, but there are few people who would recognize its absence as actually wrong. Today it survives mostly in fixed expressions.

Among Latin languages, such as French and Spanish, the subjunctive mood is a highly distinct form. (English is a Germanic language.) The subjunctive was commonly used in the English language before the year 1600. By the late eighteenth century, writers of English had already started writing obituaries for the subjunctive, and it is hard to find too many examples of usage between 1600 and 1900. After 1900, usage of the subjunctive became prevalent once again, especially in American English. More recently, however, use of the subjunctive has been discouraged by many. Style guides and writing instructors alike point to the mood's undue complexity and unintended connotations as reasons to discourage its use.

Nevertheless, although subtle, the subjunctive does have its uses, and the mood endures. Specifically, the subjunctive is useful when expressing what is wished, demanded, exhorted, proposed, and so forth.

In Latin and Greek, *mood* is used to distinguish fact and hypothesis. In English, mood signals modality, or the intent or commitment of the speaker. There are three main ways for a writer to express *mood:* the indicative, the imperative, and the subjunctive. Notably, mood and tense are different things. Tense is expressed in past, present, and future.

The *indicative* is most commonly used to express mood. The indicative is used to make factual statements.

INDICATIVE: The leaves are green.

The imperative is used with orders, advice, or commands.

IMPERATIVE: Call your mother!

The subjunctive mood is used to describe something hypothetical, contrary to fact, or imagined like a wish, desire, doubt, or hope. Conditional statements that begin with *if* are common examples of the subjunctive mood.

Fluent English speakers will recognize the subjunctive as the *other* way to say something using a verb or verb phrase. For instance, you'll often encounter the subjunctive in *if* expressions that are used to express an idea that will never happen, or to represent unreal or impossible situations. Even with a singular subject, these *if* expressions take *were* (the were-subjunctive) and not *was* in the dependent clause. Furthermore, the independent clause takes a core modal, such as *would, should,* or *could.*

SUBJUNCTIVE: If Clark <u>were</u> to travel to Mars, he would miss his cat.

INDICATIVE: If Clark <u>was</u> to travel to Mars, he would miss his cat.

MODAL AUXILIARY: If Clark <u>would</u> travel to Mars, he would miss his cat.

Here, although still okay, the usage of the indicative is less preferable than the usage of the subjunctive because travel to Mars is not yet possible. Moreover, as with many cases where the subjunctive can be used, many people would reach for the modal auxiliary.

With verbs other than conjugations of *to be,* the subjunctive is formed using the past tense of the verb.

SUBJUNCTIVE: If I held my breath for 25 minutes, I will break the world record

INDICATIVE: If I hold my breath for 25 minutes, I will break the world record.

Again, the subjunctive is preferred, because there is no way I'm holding my breath for that long nor would I even try.

Don't use the subjunctive when something may or might happen.

WRONG (SUBJUNCTIVE): If Charlie finished the marathon, he will have completed 11 marathons.

RIGHT (INDICATIVE): If Charlie finishes the marathon, he will have completed 11 marathons.

One final use of the subjunctive involves *that* expressions following verbs like *advise, recommend, ask, insist, order, command, propose,* and *urge,* as well as with words such as *essential* and *important*. In these mandative constructions, a specific action is called for.

SUBJUNCTIVE: Dr. Norton urges that Terrance watch his weight.

INDICATIVE: Dr. Norton urges that Terrance watches his weight.

SUBJUNCTIVE: I wish that Jerry volunteered at the soup kitchen, but he will never do that.

INDICATIVE: I wish that Jerry volunteers at the soup kitchen, but he will never do that

Once again, the subjunctive is preferred in both sets of examples.

Subjunctive: A Linguistics Perspective

There are idiosyncratic and ancient uses of the subjunctive that exist in the English language. For example, consider the following Bible verse from Proverbs 26:5: "Answer a fool according to his folly, lest he be wise in his own eyes."

In this verse, we observe the subjunctive mood used in a subordinate clause beginning with "lest." Lest means "to avoid the risk of."

We also find the subjunctive used in more isolated instances, such as "if need be" and "God save the Queen."

However, linguists tend to concern themselves with the subjunctive as used in three instances.

First, linguists focus on the mandative subjunctive as used in third-person singular present tense forms. In these forms, the ending or inflection is changed. For instance, in the next example, "takes" is changed to "take."

EXAMPLE: Requesting that she take her raincoat, Donna's mother always watched out for her daughter's best interest.

Second, linguists pay attention to the past subjunctive as used with the first- and third-person singular (the *were-subjunctive*).

EXAMPLE: If I were more impulsive, I can only imagine my reaction.

EXAMPLE: Bernie routinely urinated in the pool, as if this were completely acceptable.

Third, linguists are interested in the subjunctive as used with the verb *be* in the bare form.

EXAMPLE: If the truth be told, then Zaid is in love with Ivanna.

Let's first take a closer look at the mandative subjunctive, which is experiencing a renaissance in American grammar. We'll then take a look at the were-subjunctive.

Use of the Mandative Subjunctive

The mandative subjunctive (also called either the mandatory subjunctive or "suasive" expressions) occurs in subordinate clauses that are usually introduced with the following expressions:

- consider
- demand
- essential
- important
- insist
- move
- necessary
- require
- suggest

EXAMPLE: It is important that Zander take the blue car.

Although you'll mostly see the mandative subjunctive tense used in restrictive clauses that begin with "that," sometimes these clauses don't begin with "that" and are thus zero-relative clauses.

EXAMPLE: Stacey insisted Kamran remove his hat.

However, in the preceding zero-relative clause, "that" is understood and could be stuck back in as a relativizer. (Remember that relativizers help facilitate meaning for non-native readers of English.)

RELATIVIZER USED: Stacey insisted that Kamran remove his hat.

American writers have revived the use of the mandative subjunctive with more vigor than have writers of British English. (The mandative subjunctive is more frequently found in written discourse because its use is more salient in writing.) The fact that Americans have more fervently embraced this grammatical atavism is somewhat surprising and bucks a common pattern: American English typically leads British English in change that embraces novel usage.

"The post-colonial revival of the mandative subjunctive," writes Leech in *Change in Contemporary English: A Grammatical Study*, "has been attributed to language contact in the Mid-West of the United States (immigrants transferring the subjunctive from their native languages in the acquisition of English)."

On a related note, although use of the mandative subjunctive is on the rise in American English (and to a lesser degree in British English), it's most frequently found in more formal texts, such as administrative prose, which jibes with the perception that some have that the subjunctive is stuffy and erudite. The rise of the mandative subjunctive in administrative texts is also somewhat counterintuitive because formal texts are usually more resistant to change.

In American English, use of the mandative subjunctive has actually become less prevalent in the press and in general prose. Use of the mandative subjunctive in American English has become much more frequent in fiction; however, because fiction is more permissive with respect to diversity of style and grammar, less can be inferred from this phenomenon. Furthermore, with respect to academic and administrative texts, there's been a slight bump in the use of the mandative subjunctive.

Notably, these distinctions don't apply to British English, where use of the mandative subjunctive has risen across all text types.

According to *Comparative Studies in Australian and New Zealand English*: "Regional variation of the mandative subjunctive has come to light during the twentieth century, with corpus-based research showing it to be standard usage in American English whereas its currency in British English was limited."

The subjunctive is semantically related to core modals, such as *might*, *could*, *would*, and *should*. In fact, sentences written in the subjunctive that convey sentiments like obligation and necessity can be rewritten using the core modals (typically *should*) without changing meaning. Such core modal alternatives, however, are a bit wordier and indirect. In linguistics, these alternatives are referred to as *periphrastic constructions* or *modal periphrasis*.

SUBJUNCTIVE: The college counselor suggests that Olivia <u>visit</u> the university.

MODAL PERIPHRASIS: The college counselor suggests that Olivia should visit the university.

EXAMPLE: Dr. Trunsky insisted that his student attend the meeting.

MODAL PERIPHRASIS: Dr. Trunsky insisted that his student should attend the meeting.

Interestingly, modal periphrasis is less frequent in American English than it is in British English. In American English, the mandative subjunctive is preferred. Moreover, use of the indicative instead of the mandative subjunctive, although prevalent in British speech and informal British English, is discouraged in American English. In other words, using the indicative instead of the mandative subjunctive is a Briticism.

AMERICAN ENGLISH (subjunctive): Dr. Trunsky insisted that his student attend the meeting.

BRITISH ENGLISH (indicative): Dr. Trunsky insisted that his student attends the meeting.

Use of the Were-Subjunctive

Use of the past subjunctive *were* compared with indicative forms in adverbial subordinate, or dependent clauses, has been studied much less in corpus linguistics than has the mandative subjunctive. Use of the *were-subjunctive* in such hypothetical or conditional contexts is only now being elucidated. Let's take a look at a couple of examples of the were-subjunctive.

EXAMPLE: If the infection were to spread to the blood, shock could ensue.

EXAMPLE: The bodybuilder lifted the burlap bag filled with rice as if it were a small book.

Now, consider these examples as written in the indicative.

INDICATIVE: If the infection was to spread to the blood, shock could ensue.

INDICATIVE: The bodybuilder lifted the burlap bag filled with rice as if it was a small book.

Although use of the were-subjunctive in counterfactual-if clauses is decreasing in both British and American English, its attenuation in favor of the indicative *was* is more prevalent in spoken British English. Notably, in British English, the were-subjunctive is not being replaced by modal periphrasis (would + be).

Moreover, Americans are more hesitant to use the indicative in lieu of the were-subjunctive. This phenomenon is likely rooted in more prescriptive style practices in the United States. In fact, such prescriptive guidance may have pushed some American writers over the edge with use of the were-subjunctive in contexts that aren't hypothetical or counterfactual at all, so-called hypercorrect constructions.

HYPERCORRECT: If I *were* typing at the computer, I would listen to music.

RIGHT: If I *was* typing at the computer, I would listen to music.

A Case for the Subjunctive

Frankly, use of the subjunctive is optional and a minor self-editing point. While self-editing your work you can likely get away with using the indicative or core modals and few readers will ever notice. Nevertheless, for those of you wish to use the English language in its fullest, when used correctly, the subjunctive adds nuance to your voice.

Our collective use of the subjunctive guarantees that in some iteration this mood will survive in the English language. And if history is any guide, English can contract. For instance, when the Vikings, who were Scandinavian pirates, invaded the British Isles starting in the late eighth century, they simplified the English language. They had to because the Vikings weren't kids, they were adults who had trouble learning new languages as most adults do. Furthermore, they occupied the lands that they conquered and needed to communicate with the indigenous people.

Unlike French, which is prescriptive by nature, English is both *prescriptive* and *descriptive.* More specifically, France has a council called the Académie française, which regulates (prescribes) French grammar, usage, and vocabulary. English speakers are open to change, as evidenced by the fact that the *Oxford English Dictionary* is descriptive and describes how language *is used* instead of how it *should be used.*

The reality that the English language transmutes is wonderful. This change makes the language nimble, current, and receptive. Nevertheless, English speakers still like to hold on to certain aspects of the language.

For instance, in an online poll conducted by the Oxford Dictionaries, 70.27 percent of respondents expressed preference for dictionaries that are both prescriptive and descriptive instead of either descriptive (16.22 percent) or prescriptive (13.51 percent). People long for both change and familiarity. Perhaps continued use of the subjunctive could extend a sense of nostalgia for a mood that was once more eminent than it is now.

If we, as writers, don't make an effort to use the subjunctive, it could someday just as easily phase out, and another embellishment of the language will be lost, which is just kind of sad.

In "The Sad Decline of the Subjunctive," a 1984 article published in the *Contemporary Review,* John Elsom writes: "To ignore the subjunctive … means that we no longer consider it important in our speech to separate fact from possibility, that which has happened from that which could occur … the language which has lost its subjunctive has lost its soul."

Now, consider the following passage concerning the subjunctive from the modern children's classic *The Dangerous Book for Boys* by Conn and Hal Iggulden, a wonderfully illustrated and typeset book, which aims to teach skills and life lessons to all boys aged between "eight and eighty."

"Mind you, don't expect to 'get it' immediately—this is one of the really tricky forms of English. The answer, however, is not to stop teaching it and watch it wither away as generations come through school with little knowledge of their own language. The answer to difficulty is always to get your hands around its throat and hold on until you have reached an understanding."

31. Transition Words and Phrases

TIP: Transitions glue sentences together.

Key Points

- Transitions are words or phrases that create narrative flow.
- The transition *moreover* is different from *furthermore* or *additionally.*

When writing, transitions are important. Transitions link sentences and create narrative flow.

Here are some transitional words or phrases.

- additionally
- but
- despite
- finally
- first, second, third …
- for example

- furthermore
- however
- in other words
- in the meantime
- moreover
- more recently
- next
- of note
- so
- this

A subject that is either repeated or implied can also serve as a transition. Furthermore, a quotation can serve as a transition.

The use of transitions in your writing may seem formulaic, but their proper usage is necessary. Although it's best to be judicious in your use of transitions and use them only when flow is improved, the good writer ends up using plenty of transitions.

Consider the following passage from which most of the transitions are removed.

> Placing a tattoo in a visible area has both economic and social consequences. Research suggests that a visible tattoo can affect employment opportunities.
>
> Tattoos have been associated with society's out-groups and fringe elements, including bikers, prisoners, circus performers, gang members, and punk rockers. They historically used tattoos to symbolize various things, such as rejection of mainstream society, physical strength, aggression, group affiliation, and religious beliefs. Research suggests that people with tattoos are not more aggressive, rebellious, and so forth.
>
> Lots of people from all walks of life have been getting tattoos, and in a general sense, body modifications, including tattoos, have gained more acceptance among members of the public. Nearly 36 percent of Americans between 18 and 25 have at least one tattoo, with many Americans wearing more than one tattoo. Discrimination against tattoos—in particular, those that are situated in visible areas like the face, neck, and wrist—is alive and well.

Now, let's put these transitions back in.

> Apparently, placing a tattoo in a visible area has both economic and social consequences. In particular, research suggests that a visible tattoo can affect employment opportunities.
>
> Tattoos have been associated with society's out-groups and fringe elements, including bikers, prisoners, circus performers, gang members, and punk rockers. These individuals (or groups) have historically used tattoos to symbolize various things, such as rejection of mainstream society, physical strength, aggression, group affiliation, and religious beliefs. Despite such personal intentions, however, research suggests that people with tattoos are not more aggressive, rebellious, and so forth.
>
> In recent years, lots of people from all walks of life have been getting tattoos, and

> in a general sense, body modifications, including tattoos, have gained more acceptance among members of the public. Nearly 36 percent of Americans between 18 and 25 have at least one tattoo, with many Americans wearing more than one tattoo. Despite more and more people getting inked, however, discrimination against tattoos—in particular, those that are situated in visible areas like the face, neck and wrist—is alive and well.

You'll notice that although both passages make sense, the passage with more transitions flows better. Furthermore, the meaning is clearer when transitions are used and the language sounds less stilted.

On a final note, although *furthermore* and *additionally* are synonymous, and these transitions can be used alternately for the sake of variety, the transition *moreover* has a slightly different meaning more akin to *besides*.

OKAY: I'm happy to take the kids to McDonald's; furthermore, I'm hungry myself.

BETTER: I'm happy to take the kids to McDonald's; moreover, I'm hungry myself.

---

32. Using "As Well As"

TIP: When used properly, the phrase "as well as" can add variety to your writing.

Key Points

- The conjunction *as well as* can be used to insert nonessential information into a sentence.
- Remember that when acting as a "tucked in addition" *as well as* doesn't affect subject-verb agreement.

According to *Fowler's Dictionary of Modern English Usage,* one undisputed use of *as well as* is as a synonym of "in as satisfactory a manner as."

EXAMPLE: Frits climbs as well as Angie does.

Furthermore, *as well as* can mean the following:

- and also
- and in addition

- and not only
- besides
- both ... and
- in addition to
- not only ... but also
- together with

According to Follett's *Modern American Usage:* "Various locutions, of which this [as well as] is probably the most useful and popular, allow the writer to tuck in additional subjects before a verb in such a way that the grammatical number of the subject, and hence of the verb, remains unchanged."

As a "tucked-in addition," the conjunction *as well as* introduces information that is subordinate or parenthetical, which can be removed without compromising the meaning of the resulting sentence. In other words, *as well as* can introduce nonessential information into a sentence. To drive this point home, feel free to enclose this parenthetical clause or phrase in commas. Remember that *as well as* has no bearing on subject-verb agreement.

EXAMPLE: The gruesome nature of the crimes, as well as the defendant's lack of contrition, is why the judge handed down a stiff sentence.

If the crimes were truly gruesome, it's likely that no amount of contrition will substantially influence a judge's decision to sentence a criminal. In fact, in a 2013 study published in the *Cornell Law Review*, Rachlinski and co-authors write that "in some criminal settings, apologies can induce judges to be more lenient, but overall, apologizing to a judge is often unhelpful and can even be harmful." Thus, "as well as the defendant's lack of contrition" is parenthetical and doesn't affect subject-verb agreement.

EXAMPLE: The Detroit Pistons' defensive-style play and head-coaching by Chuck Daly, as well as Vinnie Johnson's buzzer-beating shot in Game 5 of the NBA finals, garnered the team a repeat championship in 1990.

Although dramatic, Vinnie Johnson's buzzer-beating shot was less important than the physicality of Detroit's players or the leadership skills of future Hall of Fame coach Chuck Daly; thus, Johnson's shot is parenthetical to the meaning of the sentence.

EXAMPLE: The artist Prince was a musician and innovator, as well as avid ping-pong player, who won eight Grammy Awards during his lifetime.

Prince will be remembered as many things but not as a ping-pong player.

33. Verbals

TIP: When the substitution makes sense, use a verbal instead of a preposition.

Key Points

- A verbal is a word that combines the characteristics of a verb with the characteristics of either a noun or an adjective.
- Verbals include gerunds, participles, or infinitives.

A *verbal* is a word that combines the characteristics of a verb with characteristics of either a noun or an adjective. Many writers commonly deploy prepositions in phrases where substitution with a verbal—such as a gerund, participle, or infinitive—would read better.

EXAMPLE: The radiologist helped diagnose the fracture by X-ray.

BETTER: The radiologist helped diagnose the fracture using X-ray.

EXAMPLE: We arrived at the park via the metro.

BETTER: We arrived at the park using the metro.

ALTERNATIVELY: We arrived at the park by taking the metro.

EXAMPLE: Joon's academic improvement was evident after her recent report card.

BETTER: Joon's academic improvement was evident after reading her recent report card.

EXAMPLE: An examination to figure out whether a piece of jewelry is made of real gold involves visualization with a magnifying glass and tests for density.

BETTER: An examination to figure out whether a piece of jewelry is made of real gold involves inspection using a magnifying glass and tests to determine density.

34.
Word Usage

TIP: Some word usage distinctions are trivial or baseless, but some are important.

Key Points

- Whenever you hear that certain words "need to" or "have to" be used in a certain way, ponder these claims.
- The jargon of certain fields mandates particular word usage.
- Use a dictionary or style guide when unsure about word usage.

Purists are often sticklers for word usage. Furthermore, many writers and editors become enamored with the idea that certain words should be used only in certain ways.

In reality, the world is moving away from the more prescriptive dictates of style and toward a more encompassing embrace of grammar, which is descriptive. After all, there are many ways to use words to express ideas, and as long as the message is clear, the specifics of delivery are less important. Much of the prescriptive guidance concerning word usage that was embraced in the twentieth century is making way for more permissive word usage in the twenty-first century.

As a writer, every time you hear that certain words "need to" or "have to" be used in a certain way, think about these claims. Do they sound arbitrary? Or, is there good reason for these recommendations? For instance, if scientific experts within a field have good reason to suggest certain words be used in specific ways for scientific reasons, then this advice is very well valid. Moreover, if the style preferences of the publication that you're writing for prescribe certain word usage preferences, then follow them. Finally, use a dictionary or style guide when unsure about word usage.

Outmoded Solecisims

Different From, Different Than, and Different To

For all intents and purposes, *different from*, *different than*, and even *different to* can be used interchangeably most of the time. Prescriptivists have long argued that *different from* is correct, For instance, in *The Elements of Style,* Strunk and White writes that "one thing differs *from* another, hence, *different from.*" However, this advice is contentious and *different than* has a long history of usage.

CORRECT: Leasing a car is different from buying a car.

CORRECT: Leasing a car is different than buying a car.

CORRECT: Leasing a car is different to buying a car.

Although all three choices of the following alternatives are correct, corpus-based research shows that there's some preference for *different than* when written before *what.*

CORRECT: The vacation package was different from what we expected.

CORRECT: The vacation package was different than what we expected.

CORRECT: The vacation package was different to what we expected.

Corpus-based research done by Pam Peters suggests that British writers favor *different from* compared with *different to* at a rate of 6:1; whereas, American writers prefer *different from* to *different than* at about 4:1. American writers rarely write *different to.*

Hopefully

In English, there is no synonym for the word *hopefully* as it is most commonly defined: *it is hoped.* Nevertheless, prescriptivists have long had a bone to pick with the use of *hopefully* in this capacity. Specifically, purists take issue with any use of *hopefully* other than "with hope." Strunk and White decry any superfluous uses as ambiguous, offensive, and silly.

Consider the following sentence:

Hopefully, Elias will finish studying for the exam by midnight.

The prescriptivist would argue that it's unclear whether either Elias will be in a hopeful frame of mind when he's studying, or it is hoped that he will finish studying by midnight. However for most of us, the latter meaning is what immediately comes to mind; thus, there's no ambiguity.

The ire that the word *hopefully* draws when used to mean *I hope* or *it is hoped* is irrational. The sentiment expressed by the word *hopefully* is universal and should have a word to describe it. Notably, other languages have a single word for *hopefully.* For instance, in German the word *hoffentlich* means *hopefully.* The Arabic equivalent of *hopefully* is *inshallah,* or God willing, and this expression is widely used for nearly any future event that bodes well for the speaker from passing a test to buying a car.

Pulitzer Prize–winning author Jean Stafford, who was famous for writing short stories and novels that examined gender roles, posted the following message on her door: "The word HOPEFULLY must not be misused on these premises. Violators will be humiliated." Sadly, Stafford, who died in 1979, led a life devoid of hope: She suffered through three bad marriages, alcoholism, and illness.

Warranted Guidance Concerning Word Usage

Exercise, Physical Activity and Physical Fitness

Kinesiologists, sports physiologists, epidemiologists, and more have very different definitions for these terms and don't use them synonymously in their own specialist literature.

Exercise refers to physical activity that is planned, purposeful, repeated, and structured, such as jogging or weight lifting. The objective of exercise is to attain or maintain physical fitness.

Physical activity is any activity that results in body movement that uses energy. For instance, walking to the refrigerator to grab a Gatorade is physical activity.

Physical fitness is a set of attributes which are related to health or skill, such as balance, endurance, flexibility, and agility.

Adverse Effect and Side Effect

According to the *AMA Manual of Style,* which serves as principle style guidance for medical clinicians and researchers intent on publication, the terms *side effect* and *adverse effect* have different meanings.

Specifically, a side effect is any consequence of a drug—whether good or bad. For instance, for many, one desirable side effect of caffeine is wakefulness. On the other hand, adverse effects are always bad.

EXAMPLE: One side effect of beta blockers, which are medications sometimes used to treat high blood pressure, is fatigue.

BETTER: One adverse effect of beta blockers, which are medications sometimes used to treat high blood pressure, is fatigue.

OR: One negative side effect of beta blockers, which are medications sometimes used to treat high blood pressure, is fatigue.

For ease, let's take a look at additional guidance concerning word usage in tabular format.

Word Usage	*Rationale*	*Examples*
affect vs. effect	*Effect* is typically used as a noun. *Affect* is typically used as a verb. Less frequently, effect can be used as a verb to mean "to cause." In psychiatry and psychology, affect is used as a noun to refer to an emotion or emotional response.	*Affect* as verb: This change will affect Sally's test score. *Effect* as a noun: We expect positive effects from the change. *Effect* as a verb: I hope these improvements will effect substantial change. *Affect* as a noun: The patient had a depressed affect.
among vs. between	Although some uses of *among* and *between* can be more nuanced, generally *among* is used to express a relationship that involves three or more things, and *between* is used to express a relationship that involves two things.	Example: The child could choose among 31 flavors of ice cream. Example: The child could choose between chocolate and vanilla ice cream.
attain vs. obtain	*Obtain* usually means to acquire. *Attain* means to achieve.	Example: Sandy obtained 10 dollars. Example: Sandy attained a college degree. Example: After waiting a few days, Nadau obtained a hard copy in the mail. Example: Most people hope to attain career success.
show vs. demonstrate	The verb *show* is typically used when something is visualized. Often, people write *demonstrate* because they think that it sounds fancier than show (stylistic heightening). However *demonstrate* is best used to describe a procedure, result, or step that is illustrated.	Example: The clock shows the time. Not: The clock demonstrates the time. Example: Loretta demonstrated to the crowd how to use the synthesizer.

Word Usage	*Rationale*	*Examples*
fewer vs. less	*Fewer* is used for countable quantities. *Less* is used for uncountable qualities. On a related note, *many* and *number* are used with countable nouns; whereas, *much* and *amount* are used with uncountable nouns.	Example: There were fewer Tasmanian devils in 2006 than in 1996 due to a contagious cancer known as devil facial-tumor disease.
comprise vs. compose	When all the parts of the whole are specified, use *comprise*. Importantly, *comprise of* is wrong. The word *compose* is used with parts of the whole.	Example: The continental United States comprises 48 states. Example: A car is composed of many parts
farther vs. further	*Farther* is used with physical distances. Hint: Think of the a in f*a*rther as *a*way. *Further* is used with degree. Hint: Think about the meaning of *further* in furthermore.	Example: Hong Kong is farther away from New York than it is from Tokyo. Example: There will be no further discussion.
assure, ensure, and insure	The word *assure* means to comfort, assuage, or reiterate. The word *ensure* primarily means to make a guarantee. The word *insure* is used to describe insurance (a financial guarantee).	Example: The mother assured her son that everything would be okay. Example: Regular training ensured that Scott would be ready for the marathon. Example: All cars must be insured.
sex vs. gender	The word *sex* is a biological distinction, and the word *gender* is a sociocultural construct.	Example: Caitlyn Jenner is of the female gender. Example: Bruce Jenner was assigned the male sex at birth.
male vs. men female vs. women	Many scientific publications recommend using *male* and *female* only as adjectives when describing humans.	Example: There were four men in the room. Not: There were four males in the room.

Word Usage	*Rationale*	*Examples*
since vs. because	To avoid confusion, use *since* in a temporal sense, and *because* in a causal sense. Hint: When used in a temporal sense, write *ever since.*	Ambiguous: Since Joanne took the car, her cousins have been at home. Better: Because Joanne took the car, her cousins have been at home. Or: Ever since Joanne took the car, her cousins have been at home.
participants vs. subjects	When referring to people who are part of a research study, the word *subject* sounds impersonal and possibly derogatory. Use *participant* instead.	Example: Ten research participants experienced headaches
patient vs. person	Outside of a clinical setting (like an office or hospital) refer to *patients* as *people.*	Not: Many patients with glaucoma lived in the trailer park. Not: Many glaucoma patients lived in the trailer park. Better: Many people with glaucoma lived in the trailer park.
unique	Use *unique* only when something is one-of-a-kind.	Not: Diamonds that are more than 10 carats are unique. Better: Diamonds that are more than 10 carats are rare.
dose vs. dosage	A *dose* is a one-time administration. The word *dosage* is used to describe a regimen (i.e., amount and frequency).	Example: Mali took a small dose of pain medication. Example: The prescribed dosage is 81 mg of aspirin every day.
if vs. whether	Use *if* with a conditional statement and *whether* when illustrating two alternatives.	Example: If you take the bus, don't forget your bus pass. Example: I am unsure whether I will take the bus. Not: I am unsure if I will take the bus.

Word Usage	*Rationale*	*Examples*
Age groups	Specific terminology for age is tricky. Here are definitions provided by the *AMA Manual of Style.* *Neonates* or *newborns* are aged between 0 and 1 month. *Infants* are children between 1 month and 1 year. *Children* are aged between 1 and 12 years. Sometimes the term *children* more inclusively refers to *boys* and *girls* aged between birth (0 months) and 12 years. *Adolescents, adolescent boys, adolescent girls,* and *teenagers* are aged between 13 and 17 years. *Young adults* are aged between 18 and 24 years. *Adults, men,* and *women* are aged older than 18.	Wrong: The newborn is 6 months old. Better: The infant is 6 months old.
into vs. in to	The word *into* is used with a verb of motion to indicate inclusion, insertion, or entry, and this single word has a single meaning. The term *in to* is an adverb followed by a preposition; both "in" and "to" retain their individual meanings.	Example: The demonstrators blocked entry into the building. Example: The caterpillar turns into the butterfly. Example: Zufi turned the books back in to the library.
onto vs. on to	The word *onto* indicates that X is to be moved atop Y. Alternatively, *onto* can be used to indicate attachment or awareness. The term *on to* is an adverb plus a preposition with each word retaining its meaning.	Example: The ball was thrown onto the court. Example: Jacqueline pinned the broach onto her lapel. Example: The detectives were on to the suspect. Example: The small boy held on to the kite string.

35. Wordiness

TIP: Tightening up wordy expressions will make your writing more concise.

Key Points

- Use as few words as possible to convey meaning.
- A word processor's search functionality can be used to find wordy expressions.

When writing any document—especially one for publication—it's a good idea to use as few words as possible to express meaning. Oftentimes, more concise expressions can be substituted for wordier ones.

EXAMPLE: In spite of the fact that Vladimir Putin denied such allegations, it's widely believed that the Russian government interfered with the 2016 U.S. presidential election.

BETTER: Although Vladimir Putin denied such allegations, it's widely believed that the Russian government interfered with the 2016 U.S. presidential election.

In many instances, you can omit the word *fact* from your writing.

WORDY: The fact that the United Kingdom will leave the European Union came as a surprise to many.

BETTER: The United Kingdom's departure from the European Union came as a surprise to many.

WORDY: Due to the fact that the electronics giant RadioShack went bankrupt twice in two years, many stores were closed.

BETTER: Because the electronics giant RadioShack went bankrupt twice in two years, many stores were closed.

Certain phrases such as *there is*, *there are*, *it is*, and *it was* are expletive constructions and can often be omitted.

WORDY: There are three main languages spoken in Luxembourg: French, German, and the national language Luxembourgish.

BETTER: Three main languages are spoken in Luxembourg: French, German, and the national language Luxembourgish.

Here are some more examples of wordy expressions and some concise alternatives.

Wordy	*Concise*
a majority of	most
a number of	several, many
as of yet	yet
as to whether	whether
at this point	currently
by means of	by, using
commented to the effect that	said, stated
draws to a close	ends
during the course of	during
exerts a lethal/deadly effect	kills
file a lawsuit against	sue
for the reason that	because
hold a meeting	meet
in a quick manner	quickly
in a sufficient manner	sufficiently
in all instances/cases	always
in attendance at	attend
in case	if
in close proximity to	near
in connection with	about, concerning
in regard to	regarding, about
in the event that	if
in the initial instance	initially
in those areas where	where
is equipped with	has
on account of	because
prior to	before
regarded as being	regarded
she is the woman who	she
still remains	remains
subsequent to	after
take into consideration	consider
the present study/article	this study/article
the question as to whether	whether
there is no doubt that	doubtless, no doubt
through the use of	by, with, using
was of the opinion that	thought
with limited effort	easily
with reference to	about, concerning
with regard to	about, concerning

Certain words or expressions can usually be removed from your writing without affecting meaning. Consider the following list of needless phrases:

- as already stated
- in other words
- it is interesting to note
- it stands to reason that
- needless to say
- take steps to
- to be sure

The words *quite, rather,* and *very* can often be omitted from writing.

Example: Darla was ~~very~~ ecstatic with her new iPad.

Better: Darla was ecstatic with her new iPad.

Example: Denise was ~~rather~~ disappointed with her new iPhone.

Better: Denise was disappointed with her new iPhone.

Certain words and phrases are redundant. Consider the following examples with the excess words stricken through:

- 1 ~~out~~ of 4
- ~~12~~ noon
- ~~advance~~ planning
- ~~completely~~ over
- consensus ~~opinion~~
- count ~~up~~
- covered ~~over~~
- ~~end~~ result
- ~~fellow~~ colleagues
- fewer ~~in number~~
- filled ~~to capacity~~
- fuse ~~together~~
- ~~future~~ plans
- ~~in order~~ to
- interval ~~of time~~
- lift ~~up~~
- ~~major~~ breakthrough
- ~~past~~ history
- period ~~of time~~
- ~~personal~~ friend
- pink ~~in color~~
- raise ~~up~~

- split ~~up~~
- ~~still~~ continues
- sum ~~total~~
- ~~time~~ period
- ~~true~~ fact
- ~~up~~on (except "once upon a time")

You can usually omit the *of* after *all*. The exception being when *all of* precedes a nonpossessive pronoun.

EXAMPLE: All thc toys were piled in a corner of the room.

INSTEAD OF: All of the toys were piled in a corner of the room.

BUT: All of those statements are lies.

Typically, the expression *whether or not* is redundant and using *whether* alone is preferred. Occasionally, when both alternatives are equally important, *whether or not* can be used in full.

EXAMPLE: I am unsure whether it will rain.

NOT: I am unsure whether or not it will rain.

EXAMPLE: Whether or not Freya chooses to pursue a career as a veterinarian, she will always help stray dogs and cats.

Sometimes writers double up on transitions, such as *furthermore* and *also*. In these cases, one of the redundant transitions can usually be omitted.

EXTRA TRANSITION: According to the advertisement, the caterer works weekends. Additionally, the caterer is also a bartender.

BETTER: According to the advertisement, the caterer works weekends. The caterer is *also* a bartender.

OR: According to the advertisement, the caterer works weekends. Additionally, the caterer is a bartender.

When first writing an article or other type of document, it may be difficult to identify areas where wordy expressions can be cut down and made more concise. Instead of fretting about where you can cut down on wordiness with the initial draft, it's a good idea to use the preceding list and guidance to identify wordy phrasing that you're prone to using, and then searching the article or document for this phrasing. For example, if you tend to overuse *fact*, while self-editing, you can use search functionality to identify all uses of this word and make changes accordingly.

Part III: Mechanics

36. Abbreviations

Tip: Spell out abbreviations on first use.

Key Points

- An abbreviation is a shortened form of a longer word or phrase.
- Abbreviations that are formed using the initial or principal letters of a phrase are called acronyms.
- Typically, acronyms are written without periods.
- Try to avoid introducing abbreviations into short documents.
- When spelling out an abbreviation, use capital letters only when what's being spelled is a proper noun.

There are no formal rules in English concerning abbreviations; instead, there exist some general observations and guidance that can help you as a writer.

Terminology

An *abbreviation* is a shortened form of a longer word or phrase. Abbreviations are formed by omitting certain letters from a word. Here are some examples of abbreviations:

- appt. = appointment
- NV = Nevada
- capt. = captain
- prof. = professor
- Dec. = December
- i.e. = *id est,* which in Latin means "that is"
- e.g. = *exempli gratia,* which in Latin means "for example"

Abbreviations that are formed using the initial or principal letters of a phrase are called *acronyms.*

- CIA=Central Intelligence Agency
- NRA=National Rifle Association
- FYI=for your information
- EEG=electroencephalogram
- OSHA= Occupational Safety and Health Administration
- FEMA=Federal Emergency Management Agency
- ZIP code=Zone Improvement Plan code
- AWOL=absent without official leave
- LMAO=laughing my ass off (slang)
- YOLO=you only live once (slang)

Some acronyms are pronounced as words, such as OSHA, FEMA, and AWOL. Others are pronounced as letters. Some people make the distinction that when acronyms are pronounced using letters, then they should be called *initialisms.* This distinction is minor.

Typically, acronyms are written without periods. When an abbreviation contains more than one letter of the original word, however, a period is used. For example, "govt." is the abbreviation for government and "cont." is the abbreviation for continued.

Using Abbreviations

In any document, it's always best to define abbreviations on first use. Typically, in short documents, where a term that could be abbreviated is used only once or twice, it's best to spell out terms and avoid abbreviations. Abbreviations can be confusing for a reader, so it's best to use them judiciously. For instance, the *Publication Manual of the American Psychological Association* suggests that it may be a good idea to use an abbreviation for a term used more than four times in a document.

In longer documents, it is best that an abbreviation be defined shortly before it's used. For instance, if a term that could be abbreviated shows up once on page 5 and then several times after page 25, then you have two options. First, you can introduce the abbreviation on both pages 5 and 25. Second, you can introduce the abbreviation on page 25.

In scientific papers, abbreviations are spelled out in the abstract *and* the body of the paper itself.

If you're using a lot of abbreviations, it's a good idea to use a key to define them. This practice is common in scientific papers.

In fiction, abbreviations are rarely used. After all, it would look weird to see a bunch of abbreviations in a novel or short story.

When spelling out an abbreviation, only use capital letters when what's being spelled out is a proper noun. For instance, you would write *EU leader* as *European Union* leader—with capital letters—because the *European Union* is a proper noun, but *UV light* as *ultraviolet light*—without capital letters—because *ultraviolet light* is a common noun. Similarly, write *human immunodeficiency virus* for *HIV*.

Try to avoid beginning a sentence with an abbreviation.

INADVISABLE: WHO officials spend more money on travel than on fighting AIDS, hepatitis, tuberculosis, and malaria.

BETTER: More money is spent by WHO officials on travel than on fighting AIDS, hepatitis, tuberculosis, and malaria.

Certain abbreviations are well recognized and understood by a general audience without being spelled out, such as *NFL*, *FBI*, *HIV*, and *ATM*. Furthermore, certain abbreviations are well recognized among specialized audiences and don't need to be spelled out when writing for these specialized audiences. For instance, basic medical science and biology researchers readily recognize certain lab tests, such as *PCR (polymerase chain reaction)* and *ELISA (enzyme-linked immunosorbent assay)*.

Plural abbreviations without periods take an *-s*, for example, *CPUs (central processing units)* and *PPOs (preferred-provider organizations)*. On a related note, avoid redundancy when using abbreviations, such as *CPU processor* and *PPO organization*.

Remember that when choosing whether to use the indefinite article *a* or *an* before an abbreviation, the right choice depends on how the abbreviation sounds when pronounced. If an abbreviation sounds like it starts with a consonant sound, for instance, *a POW (prisoner of war)* or *a U.S. soldier*, then use the definite article *a*. If the abbreviation sounds like it begins with a vowel sound, use *an*, for example, *an HBO movie*, *an ER visit*, or *an FBI agent*.

Corpus-Based Research: Proper Nouns and Abbreviations

According to corpus-based research dated from 1961 and 1991/2, Leech found that the number of proper nouns in the form of acronyms (for example, *UNICEF* and *IMF*) has nearly tripled. (Leech suggests that the number of common-noun abbreviations such as GPS and COPD, has increased, too.) This increase follows a more general trend of increased usage of proper nouns in the English language. Both proper nouns and abbreviations derived from them can pack a lot of information into a tightly budgeted space, which explains why they're popular—especially in the press.

Densification is a more general trend in grammar and language usage; it refers to the condensation of information into nouns or noun phrases. For instance, the single-word proper nouns *Drake*, *Prince*, and *Disney* take very few letters to bring vivid images to mind. Similarly, acronyms like *GOP (Grand Old Party)* and *ICE (Immigration and Customs Enforcement)* bring vivid—yet more polarizing—images to mind. Ultimately, proper nouns and abbreviations are popular in written documents because they're efficient at carrying a heavy load.

37. Capitalization

Tip: Up style works well for the Internet.

Key Points

- Adherents to down style capitalize more parsimoniously.
- Adherents to up style capitalize more liberally.
- Be consistent in your use of either up style or down style

We're taught about capitalization from a young age. Most of the time, it's apparent what things need to be capitalized. For example, we all know to capitalize the proper name George Washington or the city name London; both George Washington and London are proper nouns. However, it may be less apparent that common nouns like *pharmacist, doctor,* or *internist* are not capitalized.

Classically, book editors have preferred *down style* as opposed to *up style*. With down style, capitalization is minimized. Importantly, *The Chicago Manual of Style*, which guides much book publication, prefers down style. (The *New York Times* switched from up style to down style in 1999.)

On the other hand, newspapers, magazines, and online publications typically follow up style, and prefer capitalization. More recently, the pendulum has swung toward up style because capital letters work better onscreen and draw in reader attention.

Down Style vs. Up Style

Let's look at three examples of down style in practice.

First, adherents to down style will minimize capitalization with respect to the common noun element of a proper noun (for example, Obama administration, Fields medal committee).

Second, down-style adherents may choose not to capitalize the first word that begins a new sentence and follows a colon.

The through line of this book is as follows: authors can successfully self-edit their own work before publication.

Third, when following down style, bulleted or numbered list items may not be capitalized.

In the preceding examples, adherents to up style would capitalize the common noun element of a proper noun, such as Obama Administration or Fields Medal Committee. Furthermore, they would also capitalize the first word that begins a sentence following a colon and capitalize the first letter in list items.

When preparing documents for publication, try to be consistent in your use of either up style or down style.

Specific Guidance

Now, let's take a look at some more specific guidance concerning capitalization.

Capitalize a title when attached to a proper name, but don't capitalize a title when used alone.

EXAMPLE: Many criticized Secretary of the Interior James Watt, who served under Ronald Reagan, for being an "anti-environmentalist."

EXAMPLE: The secretary of the interior manages and sustains American lands.

Avoid capitalizing parts of disease names that are common nouns, for example, Alzheimer's disease. Similarly, in Munchausen syndrome the word "syndrome" isn't capitalized. Finally, you wouldn't capitalize diabetes mellitus because this term doesn't contain a proper name.

Do capitalize brand names like Tylenol, but don't capitalize generic names like acetaminophen.

Sometimes terms may appear to be common nouns, which aren't capitalized, when in fact, they're actually proper nouns. Whereas, a common noun generically refers to a whole bunch of things, such as televisions, printers, and refrigerators, a proper noun refers to one very specific thing, or something that's one-of-a-kind.

Example: The lawyer discussed Exhibit A.

Here, "Exhibit A" refers to a very specific exhibit and is therefore capitalized.

Example: Please examine Figure 1 in Chapter 3 of the text.

Again, we're talking about a specific figure and chapter found in a specific text.

Finally, remember to capitalize proper nouns in their entirety. For instance, it's necessary to capitalize "small" in Small Satellite Conference. The Small Satellite Conference is actually a large event dedicated to satellites that are small in size.

38. Contractions

Tip: Use contractions sensibly.

Key Points

- Contractions are fine in informal contexts and can be used with many publications appealing to a general audience.
- With formal writing for a specialist audience—like a peer-reviewed scientific journal—don't use contractions.

Punctuation can be used to indicate omission. In a contraction, an apostrophe indicates the omission of a letter or letters, such as *it's* (it is), *aren't* (are not), *let's* (let us), *we've* (we have), *I'm* (I am), and *we'll* (we will).

When writing research papers, journal articles, and other formal documents, contractions are rarely used; they're considered too colloquial. For example, in both the *AMA Manual of Style* and the *MLA Handbook for Writers of Research Papers,* the use of contractions is discouraged. However, in general prose, fiction, and the press, you'll find contractions used—especially in dialogue or quoted speech. Of note, *The Associated Press Stylebook* recommends avoiding excessive use of contractions but, in informal contexts, permits those found in the *Webster's New World College Dictionary* (the preferred dictionary of the Associated Press) and other recommended dictionaries.

Contractions as Colloquialization

The use of contractions in writing is probably the best example of colloquialization. The term *colloquialization* refers to the process by which features of speech are incorporated into written language. In the book *Longman Student Grammar of Spoken and Written English*, Biber distinguishes between spoken language and written language in a number of ways, including the following:

- avoidance of elaboration or specifics regarding what's discussed;
- shared context between the speakers;
- interactive nature;
- concern about feelings, attitudes, and assessments of likelihoods.

When writers use contractions, they assume the reader understands the omission thus saving time and keeping things relatable.

Based on corpus studies, Leech found that there's been a substantial increase in the frequency of contractions used in writing. For instance, the contraction *let's* was used instead of *let us* 51.3 percent of the time in 1961. By 1991/2, *let's* was used 71.1 percent of the time. Furthermore, *let us* was almost never found in written samples of fiction.

Using *let's* instead of *let us* makes perfect sense. For instance, "let us go to the park this afternoon" sounds much more grandiloquent than "let's go the park this afternoon." On a related note, the contraction "aren't I" is universally preferred to the more pretentious alternative: "am I not."

Who's vs. Whose

The contraction *who's* can mean either *who is* or *who has.*

Example: Who's the winner of the contest?

Example: Who's been to London?

Although *whose* sounds the same as *who's,* its meaning is different. Just like *its* (not *it's*) is the possessive form of *it, whose* is the possessive form of *who.* Remember that unlike possessive nouns, possessive pronouns never take apostrophes.

Example: Whose keys are these?

When self-editing your work, keep an eye out for contractions. If you're writing for a publication, consider the preferred or house style. Typically, with formal (peer-reviewed scientific) publications, you should avoid contractions. Many newspapers, magazines, book publishers, and website are okay with the sensible use of contractions.

If you're writing and publishing on your own and for a general audience, prudent use of contractions is also good idea. A certain number of contractions will make your writing more fluid and relatable. However, too many contractions may sound too informal. When in doubt, check with a dictionary to make sure that the contraction that you're using is formally defined.

39. Interjections

Tip: When used sparingly, interjections add texture to your writing.

Key Points

- Interjections make writing more interactive and colloquial.
- Interjections usually begin a clause.

In writing, interjections make things more colloquial and interactive. They signal relationships between the listener and the speaker and exist on the periphery of grammar. Interjections can stand alone or be loosely connected to a clause or non-clausal grammatical construction. When used with a clause or non-clausal construction, interjections are usually placed at the beginning

Example: *Hey*, can you believe how much money Apple has stockpiled!

Until recently, grammar and style texts have paid little heed to interjections—considering their use outside the domain of formal writing. In fact in 1989, the Oxford Dictionary labeled the interjection a "natural ejaculation expressive of some feeling or emotion." Moreover, the Chicago Manual calls certain interjections "meaningless utterances."

The ancient Greeks, however, categorized interjections as their own class of word with emotive meaning. Interjections are a lot more important than many people realize. They've even found their way into the records of the British Parliament. According to linguist Pam Peters, interjections serve as sort of mini-sentences that communicate attitudes, social orientations, and "reaction signals." They can function either independently, often taking an exclamation point, or as part of a sentence.

In the text *Longman Student Grammar of Spoken and Written English,* Biber categorizes *inserts* as outlined in the following table. Of note, the term insert is preferred by some grammarians as a more general grouping for interjections.

Insert type	***Key points***	***Examples***
Interjection	• exclamatory function • emotive reaction to something that has been uttered or something that has occurred	Oh, did you try this cake! Ah, I did try the cake! Wow, I did try the cake! Ugh, I hate chocolate cake. (*Ugh, ow,* and *ouch* express negative emotions.)
Discourse markers	• indicate how the speaker plans to lead the dialogue	Well, I don't like cake.
Response getters	• added to the end of a question, statement, or directive	You don't like the cake, right? You don't like cake, huh? British variant of *huh:* You don't like cake, eh?
Response forms	• brief responses to a previous remark or question	Yes, I tried the cake. Yeah, I tried the cake. Yep, I tried the cake. Uh huh, I tried the cake. No, I didn't try the cake. Nope, I didn't try the cake. Okay, I will have some cake. (The response form *okay* is much more common in American English than in British English.)
Hesitators	• also called pause fillers • can co-occur with other dysfluencies	Um, there's no more cake left. There's, um, no more cake left. Uh, there's no more er cake left.
Attention grabbers		Hey, don't hog the cake! Yo, you ate all the cake!
Polite formulae		Excuse me, is there any more cake left? Do you want more cake? Please.
Greetings and farewells		Hi, did you try the cake? Hello, did you try the cake? Farewell, I hope that you liked the cake.
Expletives	• taboo or semi-taboo expressions	God, why did somebody eat all the cake! Jeez, why did somebody eat

Insert type	*Key points*	*Examples*
		all the cake! *(Jeez is short for Jesus)* Fuck, why did somebody eat all the cake! Somebody ate all the cake! For shit's sake!

Data from corpus-based research done by Biber suggest that inserts are increasingly common in both American English and British English, and overall probably even more common in American English. Furthermore, certain inserts are preferred by certain social groups.

Writers of fiction and poetry find plenty of use for inserts when writing dialogue. However, writers of nonfiction can occasionally make good use of inserts.

First, when journalists are transcribing quotations for use in articles, it's a common temptation to eliminate dysfluencies, or speech irregularities. However, inserts, like *uh*, *er*, and *um*, do have meaning and should be retained in contexts when hesitation is expressed.

For instance, the statement "Uh, I would go out on a date with Sam" sounds a lot different from "I would go out on a date with Sam."

Second, good writers can sometimes use interjections as a way to convey tone and make writing more personal. Interjections can be more than one word, and one function of interjections is to provide support to another person.

EXAMPLE: Of course, cocaine can be snorted or sniffed. But it can also be injected intravenously.

EXAMPLE: As you probably know, cocaine can be snorted or sniffed. But it can also be injected intravenously.

Finally, in the first line of an email, people often write "Hello John Smith" or "Greetings John Smith:." However, "hello" and "greetings" are interjections after which commas are placed: "Hello, John Smith:" or "Greetings, John Smith:." A similar argument could be made for "Hi, John Smith." Keep in mind that publication often begins with an email sent to an editor, who may or may not notice that you were cognizant to place a comma after "hello" or "greetings" (cue soft skills). Furthermore, there is no comma in the salutation "Dear John Smith" because *dear* acts as an adjective that modifies the name John Smith; *dear* is not an interjection.

40. Italics

TIP: Use italics sparingly and in specific instances.

Key Points

- Italics are used when the genus and species names are specified.
- Italics are used with court cases.
- Italics are used with unfamiliar foreign words.
- Italics are used to distinguish single letters from surrounding words
- Italics are used for titles of complete works.
- Italics are used when introducing key terms.
- Italics are used for words used as words.

Once upon a time, all words were printed in italics. Nowadays, italics are used only for contrast. The plural noun *italics* is preferred in the United States, Canada, and Australia; whereas, the singular noun *italic* is used in the United Kingdom.

Uses of Italics

When writing, there are several contexts in which to use italics.

First, italics are used when the genus and species names are specified, for example, *Streptococcus pneumonia* and *Felis catus* (the feral house cat).

Second, italics are used with court cases, for example, *Korematsu v. United States,* which in 1944, upheld the internment of Japanese citizens during World War II, and *Obergefell v. Hodges,* which legalized same-sex marriage in all 50 states in 2015.

Third, italics are used with certain unfamiliar foreign terms, such as *pas devant les enfants*, which means "not in front of the children" or "not in present company." However, more common foreign words and Latin abbreviations aren't italicized, including the following:

- ad hominem
- et al.

- ibid.
- in situ
- prima facie
- via
- viz.

Deciding whether or not to italicize can be tricky. Some sources suggest that if a foreign term is listed in a dictionary it's familiar; however, which dictionary are they referring to? Descriptive dictionaries like the *Oxford English Dictionary* contain many more entries than do prescriptive dictionaries like *Webster's New World College Dictionary.* Furthermore at any given time, the number of entries in any given dictionary is in flux. Thus, the decision to italicize foreign terms is often arbitrary and based on the best judgment of a writer or editor.

Foreign proper nouns should not be italicized such as Académie des Arts et Techniques du Cinéma, which presents the César Awards. (The César Awards are national French awards for film akin to the Oscars, BAFTA Film Awards, or the Goya Awards.)

Fourth, italics can be used to distinguish single letters from surrounding words, such as "this word aardvark has three *a*'s."

Fifth, the names or titles of the following things should be italicized:

- books
- journals
- musical compositions
- paintings
- periodicals
- planes
- plays
- podcasts
- radio programs
- sculptures
- ships
- space vehicles
- submarines
- television series
- trains

Notably, all these things are essentially entities onto themselves. Something that is part of a larger entity, such as an episode of a television show, specific journal article (which belongs to a periodical), or a book chapter, isn't italicized and is instead placed in quotation marks. On a related note, when no preference by a publisher is explicitly specified, it's a good idea to use title case with titles.

Please note that the titles of sacred texts such as the Quran and the Bible, as well as the various books of the Bible, are neither italicized nor placed in quotation marks.

Sixth, italics are used for emphasis. For instance, key terms or particularly salient sentences can be italicized. However, this effect should be used sparingly.

Finally, italics are used for words used as words. EXAMPLE: Abbreviations like *CIA* and *IRS* are readily understood by most American readers.

More About Italics

According to *The Chicago Manual of Style*: "Good writers use italics for emphasis only as an occasional adjunct to efficient sentence structure. Overused, italics quickly lose their force. Seldom should as much as a sentence be italicized for emphasis and never a whole passage."

Key terms need only to be italicized on first use and are not italicized on subsequent uses. For instance, if the key term *cardiomyopathy* (a type of chronic heart disease) is italicized (and defined) on first usage, there's no need to italicize cardiomyopathy with subsequent usage. Moreover, you can define an italicized word using parentheses.

Importantly, use of italics is different from use of *scare quotes*. Scare quotes refer to quotation marks used to highlight text that's nonstandard or ironic. It's best to limit your use of scare quotes. Remember that it's important to embrace the words that you write, and scare quotes place distance between you and your words.

EXAMPLE: Gavin makes "bullshit" arguments.

MUCH BETTER: Gavin makes bullshit arguments.

Some writers like to use underlining, capitalization, or all-caps to emphasize. These practices are ill-advised. If you have this habit, keep an eye out for this transgression during the self-editing phase and rectify it. Moreover, during the self-editing phase, you must also ask yourself whether emphasis is truly needed.

Web designers and publishers sometimes use boldface for emphasis. Some older research indicated that using boldface or color helps the reader distinguish emphasis better than does the use of italics because there's less resolution on the screen compared with the written page. This research is somewhat dated, however, and screen resolution has greatly improved during the past several years. Nevertheless, this thinking is entrenched among certain designers and publishers who are wary of using italics for emphasis.

Online publishers recommend against hyperlinking italicized text. On a related note, underlining anything in an electronic document is a bad idea because underlining is most closely associated with hyperlinking.

Finally, let's take a look at inflections of italicized terms and what to do with punctuation following italicized words.

With respect to plural forms of proper nouns that are italicized, such as newspaper or magazine titles, the *-s* or *-es* is not italicized, for instance, two *Cosmopolitan*s when referring to two issues of the magazine *Cosmopolitan.* Similarly, the s-genitive isn't italicized, for example, *Cosmopolitan*'s audience. Nevertheless, it's probably best to recast two *Cosmopolitan*s and *Cosmopolitan*'s audience a "two copies of *Cosmopolitan*" and "the audience of *Cosmopolitan,*" respectively.

Periods, commas, semicolons, and colons—but not exclamation points and question marks—are usually italicized when they follow an italicized word. It may look weird to italicize a semicolon or colon but apparently this convention is preferred by certain publishers.

41. Numbers

TIP: Be consistent in how you present numbers.

Key Points

- Reword a sentence to avoid beginning with a numeral.
- Use commas to separate numbers that have four or more digits.

One of the biggest questions any writer has is whether to spell out numbers or use Arabic numerals instead. This decision is based on style. The key is to be consistent when writing out numbers within a document.

The Chicago Manual of Style, which is often the style guide of choice when writing books, suggests that in nontechnical contexts, numbers between zero and one hundred be spelled out. Additionally, numbers followed by the words *hundred, thousand,* or *million* should be spelled out (for example, *fifty-eight pennies, fourteen thousand readers,* and *114 dimes*).

The American Psychological Association recommends that numbers that are only one or two words be spelled out (for example, *eight dogs, five thousand ants,* and *584 grasshoppers*).

The American Medical Association recommends that numerals be used unless a number begins a title, sentence, or heading. The Council of Science Editors makes similar recommendations.

The Associated Press recommends that numbers one through nine be spelled out, and numerals be used for numbers 10 and greater. Numbers used at the beginning of a sentence should be spelled out.

When writing, don't start a sentence with a numeral. In these cases, it's often best to recast the sentences.

WRONG: 185 people attended the ceremony.

BEST: In total, 185 people attended the ceremony.

Finally, use commas (or spaces) to separate numbers that have four or more digits (for example, *5,983 tables* and *129,345 chairs*).

42. Orthography

TIP: When writing for a British audience, use British spelling and word usage consistently.

Key Points

- Some spelling and word usage differs between the United States and the United Kingdom.
- If you're unsure about British spellings and you intend to write for a British audience, you can always check with the *Oxford English Dictionary.*

According to *Merriam Webster,* the word *orthography* has three meanings:

- the art of writing words with the proper letters according to standard usage (as in, *the rules of English orthography*);
- the representation of the sounds of a language by written or printed symbols;
- a part of language study that deals with letters and spelling.

The word *orthography* is derived from the Greek words *orthos,* which means "right or true," and *graphein,* which means "to write." This field of study is younger than you may think. People paid little heed to orthography until after the introduction of the printing press in the 15th century, when the printed word became more widely disseminated.

The 1755 publication of Samuel Johnson's *Dictionary of the English Language* standardized much written English. However, there were spelling reforms—most notably, that launched by Noah Webster who, in 1806, published *A Compendious Dictionary of the English Language,* and then in 1828, his greatest work, *An American Dictionary of the English Language.* This second dictionary is arguably the most influential dictionary ever—even more influential than Johnson's original invention.

The success of Webster's *An American Dictionary of the English Language* is rooted in Webster's clear vision, sense of aesthetics, and American sensibility. He wanted the United States to have its own distinct cultural identity, which would be reflected in American idiom, style, and pronunciation. To research the origins of the English language, Webster learned 26 languages, including Sanskrit and Old English. Webster's second dictionary had 70,000 entries—up from 37,000 entries in his first dictionary—and served as a gold standard for future reference works.

Webster was tired of the status quo: Inconsistencies in English spelling and British textbooks dominating American classrooms. Webster's approach was distinctly American, and he employed a common sense and logical strategy with language, doing away with spelling conventions that were complicated and artificial. Changes that he made included dropping the second *-l* from words like *cancel* and *travel,* and dropping the *-k* from words like *publick* and *musick.* Webster also introduced American words into the vocabulary of the English language, such as *hickory, skunk,* and *chowder.* (Some of Webster's suggestions didn't take, such as modifying *tongue* to *tung* or changing *women* to *wimmen,* a spelling that he saw as truer and older.)

To this day, orthographic debates still fume, albeit a far cry from the conflagrations fueled by Webster and other lexicographers. For example, probably the most spirited orthographic debates in recent times focus on the use of apostrophes to indicate the possessive, or genitive, case.

Webster's work was foundational in the evolution of American and British spelling variants. The following table details some important distinctions between American and British spelling.

American spelling	***British spelling***	***Considerations***
offense (-ense ending)	offence (-ence ending)	
theater (-er ending)	theatre (-re ending)	
aging	ageing	
analyze (-yze ending)	analyse (-yse ending)	

American spelling	*British spelling*	*Considerations*
anesthesia	anæsthesia	British digraph –æ (a digraph represents a combination of two letters that have a single sound)
etiology	œtiology	British digraph –œ
plagiarize (-ize ending)	plagiarise (-ise ending)	The –ize ending is also used in British spelling.
program	programme	However, *computer program* is the same in both American and British spelling.
while	whilst or while	
among	amongst or among	
artifact	artefact	
color (-or ending)	colour (-our ending)	
traveled	travelled	
learned	learned or learnt	Similarly in British usage, the past tense of *dream* and *burn* can be written *dreamt* and *burnt*.

When writing and editing your own work, you should adopt American or British spelling conventions based on your audience and remain consistent—don't switch between American and British spellings willy-nilly, or with the intention of appearing "smart." If you're writing for an American or most international audiences, American spelling is often preferred. British conventions work for British audiences. If you're working with a publication, heed the publisher's preference, which is outlined in its preferred style guide or editorial style sheet.

If you're unsure about British spellings and you intend to write for a British audience, you can always check with the *Oxford English Dictionary.*

On a related note, word usage also varies between American and British speakers, and when writing for either audience, you should keep such conventions in mind and remain consistent. In other words, don't refer to "my apartment" in one sentence and "my flat" in another. Here are some examples of differing word usage.

American usage	*British usage*
cookie	biscuit
vacation	holiday
drugstore	chemist's
elevator	lift
soccer	football
subway	tube
preschool	crèche

Part IV: Punctuation

43. Colons

Tip: Colons are used to direct attention to a matter.

Key Points

- Use colons to introduce lists.
- Use colons to join two independent clauses when the second clause explains the first.

A colon means "that is to say" or "here is my meaning."

The following table explains when to use a colon.

Colon usage rules	***Examples***
To introduce a series of items in either a run-on or displayed list	Ted requested the following: a note book, a pencil, a pen, and a folder.
To join two independent clauses when the second independent clause modifies the first independent clause. In other words, the second independent clause explains, illustrates, or paraphrases the first clause.	After losing the popular vote to Hillary Clinton in the 2016 presidential election, Donald Trump appeared irate: He intended to launch an investigation.
To introduce a noun or phrase that illustrates a preceding independent clause.	Everyone in the room garnered a scholarship: a good day for all! Winston Churchill had an endearing nickname: Winnie.
To introduce a long quotation	During a 1940 radio broadcast, Sir Winston Churchill stated: "We shall defend every village, every town and every city. The vast mass of London itself, fought street by street, could easily devour an entire hostile army;

Colon usage rules	*Examples*
	and we would rather see London laid in ruins and ashes than that it should be tamely and abjectly enslaved."
After the salutation in a business letter or other formal missive.	Dear Colonel Sharpe: Greetings, Ms. Rita:

When a colon is used to transition between two independent clauses, the first word in the second clause can be either capitalized or not, depending on either your personal preference or the style of your intended publication. Specifically, capitalizing the first word is *up style* and not capitalizing it is *down style.*

After losing the popular vote to Hillary Clinton in the 2016 presidential election, Donald Trump appeared irate: *H*e intended to launch an investigation.

After losing the popular vote to Hillary Clinton in the 2016 presidential election, Donald Trump appeared irate: *h*e intended to launch an investigation.

Finally, with informal communications, like email, the salutation doesn't need to be followed by a colon and instead can be followed by a comma. For instance, when starting an email you could write either "Dear John," or "Greetings, John,."

44. Commas

Tip: Use commas with purpose.

Key Points

- Read sentences aloud and pay close attention to pauses indicated by commas to check whether the comma placement adds clarity and helps organize your writing.
- Visually inspect your work for *dependent clause markers* and other indicators of comma usage.
- Avoid disruptive markers like the plague.

In his first remarks as a public citizen on January 20, 2017, Barack Obama told his closest friends and supporters to not lose faith in progress. "This is not a period," Obama said. "This is a comma in the continuing story of building America." For some, this metaphor may seem curious. With respect to Obama, however, it reminds us that he is a writer who thinks in terms of writing.

A comma is a pause in thought. It's a pause in the flow of words in a sentence. A comma helps to clarify meaning by not only separating words but also by grouping words together. Commas can also introduce related thoughts. A period, however, is a full stop and an end to an idea. Obama was encouraging his supporters to still believe in their cause even if their party had lost and their ideology seemed in jeopardy because democracy is an ongoing process that won't be stopped by any one election.

When a comma is encountered while reading a sentence, oftentimes the short pause in message makes sense and helps clarify meaning. Sometimes the pause makes less sense, and comma placement is directed by convention.

When editing your own work, you can read sentences aloud and pay close attention to pauses indicated by commas to check whether the comma placement adds clarity and helps organize your writing. This auditory check should follow a more complete visual inspection that looks at words both individually and as components of phrases and clauses to figure out where commas go.

There are several comma tips that guide visual inspection (some are debatable). For ease, I've outlined them in tabular format.

Comma tips	*Examples*
To separate two independent clauses in a compound sentence joined by a coordinating conjunction (e.g., but, and, for, or, nor, so, yet)	Example: Xylem carries water and minerals from a plant's roots to its leaves, and phloem carries glucose from the leaves to the rest of the plant. Example: Oliver was saddened by the loss of his gold watch, for the watch was a gift from his late grandfather. Example: Harry made a lot of money, yet he wanted more. Example: Amir wanted more money, so his boss gave him a raise.
To set off an introductory dependent clause from the rest of a sentence	Example: Although Alvin is self-absorbed, he still cares deeply for his brothers.
To set off an introductory dependent phrase from the rest of a sentence	Example: Running toward the gate, Erica nearly tripped on another passenger's suitcase.

Comma tips	*Examples*
	Example: Wanted for grand theft auto, the perpetrator turned himself in.
To set off introductory words such as transitions (i.e., sentence adverbs)	Example: Initially, Danny refused the tickets to the opera. Example: Well, it's really up to you to buy earthquake insurance. Example: Moreover, I disagree with your assessment.
To set off dependent clauses that begin a sentence	Example: While Edna traveled by boat, Blake took the train.
To set off parenthetical expressions that interrupt the flow of the sentence (e.g., nevertheless, thus, however, moreover, of course, conversely, on the other hand, by the way, after all)	Example: Although Lance wanted to go alone, he, nevertheless, invited his wife to come along. Example: The mail, of course, is in the mailbox. But: The buyer didn't agree to the deal thus no deal. (no comma)
To set off nonrestrictive, dependent clauses	Example: Danny, who is Justin's sister, finished college in three years. Example: The car, which is only three years old, requires extensive repairs. Example: Bobak wants a new car, even though his car is only three years old.
To set off a nonrestrictive adjective phrase (prepositional phrase or verb phrase)	Prepositional phrase: The school, with its rustic field, hosted the alumni game. Verb phrase: Changing course quickly, the hummingbird darted off into the distance.
To separate items in a series	Example: Lawrence ate steak, mashed potatoes, pasta, and stewed carrots. Example: Lawrence's favorite sandwiches, in order of preference, are tuna, corned beef, peanut butter and jelly, and pastrami. (Because "peanut butter and jelly" acts as a unit, no comma is needed between "peanut butter" and "jelly.") Wrong: Lawrence's favorite sandwiches, in order of preference, are tuna, corned beef, peanut butter, and jelly, and pastrami.
To separate a compound predicate for emphasis or clarity	The leader's order closed the nation's borders, and blocked many refugees from entering the country.

Comma tips	*Examples*
To set off contrasting parts of a sentence	Example: The dog belongs to Sloane, not Bertrand.
To introduce a direct quotation	Example: Archibald said, "I will come back to visit you next year after I finish my exams." But: Archibald said "Wait!" (no comma)
To break up a direct quotation	"I will come back to visit you next year," Archibald said, "after I finish my exams."
Before attribution of a direct quotation	"I won't do it," said Vasilios. "I won't do it," he said.
To separate a statement from a question	Example: Edward didn't take the cake, did he?
To separate a city from a state	Example: Peter remembers visiting Centerville, Ohio, with his friends.
To separate the day and month from the year	Example: On July 4, 1976, Americans celebrated the nation's bicentennial. But: The U.S. bicentennial was celebrated in July 1976. (No comma separates month from year.)
To set off nonrestrictive, parenthetical elements following *for example, including, such as, that is, namely, or,* and equivalents	Example: Billy brought several of Ethan's favorite desserts, including sugar cookies, chocolate cake, and strawberry cheesecake, to the surprise birthday party. But: Factors including genetics and environment shape human development. (restrictive)
To separate interchangeable (coordinate) adjectives	Example: Alice adopted a young, energetic puppy. But: It was an expensive three-day pass. (Here, there is no comma because the adjectives can't be interchanged. In other words, "three-day, expensive pass" doesn't sound right.)
In elliptical constructions that are interdependent	Example: In soccer, a yellow card signifies caution, and a red, dismissal.
To set off a nonrestrictive appositive	The first president of the United States, George Washington, was 6 feet 2 inches tall.
To separate parts of a salutation that introduces a letter, email, and so forth. Note that when the	Greetings, Mr. Jones: or Greetings, Mr. Jones, (informal)

Comma tips	*Examples*
first word is *dear* no comma is needed because "dear" is an adjective. Instead, commas in salutations separate two nouns.	Hello, Mr. Jones: or Hello, Mr. Jones, (informal) But: Dear Mr. Jones: or Dear Mr. Jones, (informal)

Here is a list of *dependent clause markers.* If you find any one of these words at the beginning of a sentence, you've identified a dependent clause that should be followed by a comma.

- after
- although
- as
- as if
- as long as
- because
- before
- if
- unless
- until
- when
- whenever
- while

Here are some things to look for in the first two or three words of a sentence that indicate a dependent phrase is present which should be followed by a comma.

- expressions beginning with *–ing*
- expressions beginning with *–ed*
- expressions beginning with *to*
- expressions beginning with a preposition

Optional Uses of Commas

Sometimes, comma use is optional and depends on the style of your intended publication. When not specified in a style guide or editorial style sheet, it's up to you to decide whether to use a comma or not. The serial (Oxford) comma is the highest profile optional use of a comma. The serial comma refers to a comma placed before the *and* or *or* following the penultimate item in a list. Notably, *The Chicago Manual of Style* promotes use of the Oxford comma; whereas, *The Associated Press Stylebook* discourages use of the Oxford comma in simple series. (The rock band Vampire Weekend isn't a fan of the Oxford comma either.) Scientific style guides like the *AMA Manual of Style* and the *Publication Manual of the American Psychological Association* recommend use of the serial comma.

OXFORD COMMA: The stars Alkaid, Mizar, and Alioth comprise the Big Dipper's handle.

When two very short introductory elements begin a sentence, using only one comma is fine. (Some editors argue that using two commas is more "illustrative.")

EXAMPLE: Incredibly in 2017, the four finalists in the Australian Open—Rafael Nadal, Roger Federer, Serena Williams, and Venus Williams—were all more than 30 years old.

ALSO FINE: Incredibly, in 2017, all four finalists in the Australian Open—Rafael Nadal, Roger Federer, Serena Williams, and Venus Williams—were all more than 30 years old.

Please note that when you use commas with a personal title, you must use two, not one.

WRONG: Lawrence Altman, MD wrote a book titled *Who Goes First? The Story of Self-Experimentation in Medicine.*

RIGHT: Lawrence Altman, MD, wrote a book titled *Who Goes First? The Story of Self-Experimentation in Medicine.*

EXAMPLE: Neil Plank, MD, PhD, teaches pathophysiology at the medical school.

Similarly, depending on the specified style of a publication, it's also optional to enclose titles like Jr., or Sr., in commas.

EXAMPLE: Martin Luther King, Jr., matriculated at Morehouse College when he was 15 years old.

ALSO FINE: Martin Luther King Jr. matriculated at Morehouse College when he was 15 years old.

When Not to Use a Comma

Knowing when to avoid using commas is just as important as knowing when to use commas. When commas are inappropriately placed, they can become *disruptive commas.* Disruptive commas can break up the following:

- subject and verb
- compound objects
- certain compound verbs

Disruptive comma: An estimated 5 million refugees from Syria, had fled the country by 2017.

Here, the disruptive comma breaks up the subject "5 million refugees" and verb "had fled the country."

Right: An estimated 5 million refugees from Syria had fled the country by early 2017.

Disruptive comma: Globally by mid–2015, the number of refugees fleeing from persecution, and violence totaled 60 million.

Here, the disruptive comma improperly breaks up two objects of a prepositional phrase: "from persecution and violence."

Right: Globally by mid–2015, the number of refugees fleeing from persecution and violence totaled 60 million.

Of note, in the preceding example, the introductory elements, "globally" and "by mid–2015," are short therefore only one comma need be used, not two.

Wrong: The politician sat, and listened.

Here the compound predicate, consisting of "sat" and "listened," is disrupted by a comma.

Don't use a comma to separate two independent clauses. Doing so yields a dreaded *comma splice.*

Wrong: I went with friends to the cafeteria for lunch, you ate lunch in your office alone.

Better: I went with friends to the cafeteria for lunch; you ate lunch in your office alone.

Finally, don't use a comma to split up correlative conjunctions (for example, *not only ... but also, either ... or,* or *neither ... nor*).

Wrong: Rostam not only took his laptop, but also his tablet.

Right: Rostam not only took his laptop but also his tablet.

45. Ellipsis Points

TIP: Ellipsis points can add narrative flair to your writing.

Key Points

- Ellipsis points are used to indicate the omission of words, phrases, paragraphs, and so forth.
- In quoted material, if one or more sentences are omitted, then you can use four points (....).

Whereas, em dashes are used to signify abrupt changes in thought, ellipsis points (ellipses) are more subtle. In writing, ellipsis points can indicate speech that is trailing off. Furthermore, ellipsis points can convey emotion, confusion, hesitation, anxiety, insecurity, suspense, or so forth. Finally, ellipsis points can impart importance.

Ellipsis points are used to indicate the omission of words, phrases, paragraphs, and so forth.

One way to type out ellipsis points is to place a single space both before and after three equally spaced periods (...). (If interested, there's a keyboard shortcut for writing out ellipsis points.)

EXAMPLE: In an unspeakable tragedy, Malaysia Airlines flight MH370 crashed in March 2014 ... killing 239 people on board.

EXAMPLE: After the diner burned her entire arm on the hibachi grill, the hostess didn't know what to do ...

In quoted material, if one or more sentences are omitted, then you can choose to use four points (....).

Consider the following quotation from *Life on the Mississippi* by Mark Twain. "I'm the man they call Sudden Death and General Desolation! Sired by a hurricane, dam'd by an earthquake.... When I'm playful I use the meridians of longitude and parallels of latitude for a seine, and drag the Atlantic Ocean for whales! I scratch my head with the lightning and purr myself to sleep with the thunder."

In the preceding quotation, the omitted sentences are unnecessary when getting the point across. Specifically, the speaker continues with his braggadocios claims, in part: "I take nineteen alligators and a bar'l of whiskey for breakfast when I'm in robust health, and a bushel of rattlesnakes and a dead body when I'm ailing!" Ultimately, words and sentences from quoted text can be omitted when the resulting text is comprehensible, and when meaning isn't misrepresented or distorted.

Now, let's consider two more points about ellipses. First, with quoted materials, don't use ellipsis points either before the quotation begins or after it ends. This practice is antiquated, and it's understood that the quotation is merely a snippet. Second, the first letter following the three ellipsis points is capitalized if it begins a new sentence.

EXAMPLE: Hmm … You know I'm scared to go skydiving.

Proper use of ellipsis points can infuse your writing with narrative flair. During the self-editing phase, while more generally assessing the transitions that you use, consider whether ellipsis points could be employed for good effect. Remember that as a writer, your reader can't hear you utter the words you write out loud.… Ellipsis points can help you convey meaning that would otherwise be lacking.

46.
Exclamation Points

TIP: In rare instances, use exclamation points to convey genuine surprise.

Key Points

- Exclamation points are overused.
- Infrequently do you use one exclamation point. Use of three exclamation points is exceedingly rare. Never use only two exclamation points.

Nowadays, we see exclamation points everywhere: in text messages, social media points, emails, and so forth. Exclamation points have lost their impact.

To be fair, the overuse of exclamation points has a history. For some time, exclamation points have been overused in comic books and ad copy. But never before has the usage of exclamation points been so prolific.

Consider the following excerpt from linguist John McWhorter's book titled *Words on the Move:* "The potency of the single exclamation point has faded over time. Originally intended to indicate surprise or emphasis, the exclamation point has seen its connotation diluted in the same way, and for the same reason, that a joke fades, a fashion ceases to distract, or shock value diminishes. A marker once used to summon attention can now be used merely to show that you're *paying* attention, in places where an old-fashioned Strunk and White sensibility would use just a period."

McWhorter also points that "today three exclamation points means what just one exclamation point did originally."

You should never write just two exclamation points. The vast majority of the time, one exclamation point is sufficient. Very rarely, should you use three exclamation points; using three exclamation points is reserved for something truly spectacular—like a paradigm shift.

EXAMPLE: I just won 10 grand in Vegas!

EXAMPLE: The research team just discovered extraterrestrial life!!!

The exclamation point has become hackneyed among Scandinavian speakers, too. For instance, a Swede or Finnish writer will often place an exclamation point after a person's name when beginning a cover letter, email, or so forth.

Now that we've established that the exclamation point has lost its vigor, the question becomes how can the exclamation point reclaim its meaning. One solution is to use exclamation points judiciously.

First, an exclamation point can be used to indicate strong emotion.

EXAMPLE: I am so angry that you stole my gold watch!

Second, an exclamation point can be used to call attention to something.

EXAMPLE: Halt! Don't step on the broken glass in your bare feet!

Third, an exclamation point can be used to capture someone's attention and focus the reader on some specific point.

EXAMPLE: Albert crashed six cars in three months!

Fourth, an exclamation point can be used with a question that is essentially an exclamation.

EXAMPLE: Isn't it great to be free to vote for whomever you please!

Don't use an exclamation point to feign surprise.

WRONG: Jared was so hungry that he ate three tacos!

RIGHT: Jared was so hungry that he ate three tacos.

Some writers will end a rhetorical question with both a question mark and an exclamation point (?! or !?). This usage is clumsy. If you feel a real need to double punctuate the end of a rhetorical question or exclamation, you may consider the interrobang (‽), which is a combination of a question mark (?) and an exclamation point (!).

The interrobang is a new punctuation mark and was first introduced in 1962 by an adman named Martin K. Spreckter. It is accessible using a keyboard shortcut.

According to *Merriam-Webster*: "Most punctuation marks have been around for centuries, but not the interrobang: it's a product of the 1960s. The mark gets its name from the punctuation that it is intended to combine. *Interro* is from 'interrogation point,' the technical name for the question mark, and *bang* is printers' slang for the exclamation point. The interrobang is not commonly used—its absence from standard keyboards can explain its paucity in print perhaps just as well as its paucity in print can explain its absence from standard keyboards. Most writers who want to communicate what the interrobang communicates continue to do as they did before the advent of the mark, throwing in !? or ?! as they feel so moved."

INADVISABLE: Who would turn down a Pulitzer Prize?!

OKAY: Who would turn down a Pulitzer Prize‽

Style Considerations

Let's consider some conventions governing the use of not only exclamation points but also question marks.

Unlike commas and periods, which are placed within quotation marks in American English, exclamation points and question marks are placed outside of quotation marks unless these punctuation marks apply to, or are part of, the quoted text.

EXAMPLE: I will not "go gentle into that good night"!

EXAMPLE: Did you see the sign that read "enter at your own risk"?

EXAMPLE: Liam screamed, "I just burned down the house!"

EXAMPLE: The authorities asked Liam, "Why did you burn down the house?"

When an exclamation point or question mark follows an italicized title, then you should avoid italicizing these terminal punctuation marks if not part of a title..

EXAMPLE: Don't let the kids watch *The Exorcist*!

NOT: Don't let the kids watch *The Exorcist!*

EXAMPLE: I remember watching *Mars Attacks!*

NOT: I remember watching *Mars Attacks*!

Don't follow an exclamation point or question mark with a period.

WRONG: The disgraced mayor sobbed, "I'm being indicted!."

RIGHT: The disgraced mayor sobbed, "I'm being indicted!"

WRONG: The perpetrator demanded, "Why am I being indicted?."

RIGHT: The perpetrator demanded, "Why am I being indicted?"

Neither periods nor commas accompany exclamation points or question marks because the force of an exclamation point or question mark is stronger than that of a period or comma. In other words, exclamation points and question marks supersede periods and commas.

An exclamation point or a question mark will occasionally serve as internal punctuation. In these uncommon instances, don't change the surrounding text and don't follow the exclamation point by a comma.

EXAMPLE: When Ernie screamed "D'oh!" we laughed because he sounded like Homer Simpson. (Note: no comma after "D'oh!")

EXAMPLE: Luna was dumfounded and could only mutter "Why?" after being left at the altar.

During the self-editing phase, you should carefully consider every use of an exclamation point. Don't use an exclamation point unless you have a darn good reason to use one!

Please don't take your reader for granted. Remember that your reader is more observant than you may assume. If you've written well, your reader will realize when something is somewhat more substantial without you calling extra attention to it. In fact, the professional writer rarely uses exclamation points and can rely on the limpidity of the prose to convey meaning.

Finally when possible, prefer italics to exclamation points to stress something specific.

INADVISABLE: I was happy that she chose me!

BETTER: I was happy that she chose *me.*

47. Interrupters

TIP: Carefully consider whether to use parentheses, commas, or em dashes to set off interrupters.

Key Points

- Parentheses are used to set off de-emphasized interrupters and examples.
- Commas are used to set off neutral content and examples.
- Em dashes (long dashes) are used to set off emphasized interrupters or interrupters that contain internal punctuation.

Oftentimes, it's necessary to break the flow of a sentence with an interrupter. An interrupter nests one idea into another more substantial idea. An interrupter can serve several purposes including the following:

- to digress
- to provide commentary
- to provide detail
- to provide emphasis
- to provide examples

Three different types of punctuation are used to set off an interrupter that occurs mid-sentence: parentheses, commas, and em dashes (also referred to as long dashes). Each of these punctuation choices exists on a cline of meaning.

Typically, parentheses are used to enclose an idea that is de-emphasized ... a throwaway remark or observation, which doesn't add much to the sentence and is truly tangential.

EXAMPLE: The iPhone 7 (much to the chagrin of many Apple aficionados) has no headphone jack and instead supports wireless headphones.

Here, parentheses are used because the comment is extraneous, and—like with all interrupters—elimination of the interrupter results in a sentence that still makes sense.

Commas enclose interrupters that are more neutral in meaning.

EXAMPLE: Apple CEO Tim Cook announced, in an exclusive May 2017 interview with CNBC, that Apple plans to invest $1 billion in a fund to promote advanced manufacturing jobs in the United States.

Here, commas are a good idea because the interrupter is more of a neutral idea. Providing specific attribution for the information is probably of limited relevance to most but could be useful to some who would like to look up the source for either verification or reference.

Em dashes are used to emphasize the interrupter.

EXAMPLE: Apple's cash reserves swelled to $256.8 billion—more than the entire market value of General Electric—in May 2017.

Here, the information enclosed by the em dash, that Apple has more cash on hand than General Electric is worth, is truly staggering and warrants emphasis using em dashes.

Parentheses are used to enclose other types of information including the following:

- abbreviations; for example, *National Endowment for the Arts (NEA)*;
- cross-references; for example, *(see Figure 3)*;
- numerical equivalence; for example, *1 stone (14 pounds)*;
- technical synonyms; for example, *surgical incision into the abdomen (laparotomy).*

Of note, cross references such as Figure 1 or Table 1 are capitalized because they are proper nouns and refer to a specific figure or table.

When an interrupter contains internal punctuation, such as commas or parentheses, em dashes can be used to enclose it.

EXAMPLE: Human beings and the great apes of Africa—chimpanzees (including bonobos) and gorillas—share a common ancestor, which lived more than 6 million years ago.

Em dashes are also used to enclose longer grammatical constructions.

EXAMPLE: Many people ignore their chronic health problems—resulting in conditions that are incredibly difficult for a physician to treat such as advanced heart disease—and avoid routine health care.

The following expressions provide further detail or specification and can be enclosed in parentheses, commas, or em dashes:

- for example (e.g.)
- for instance
- including
- like
- more specifically
- or

- such as
- that is (i.e.)

Example: Certain drugs, including cocaine, methamphetamine, and heroin, are illegal in all states.

Example: Certain drugs (including cocaine, methamphetamine, and heroin) are illegal in all states.

Example: Certain drugs—including cocaine, methamphetamine, and heroin—are illegal in all states.

Example: Certain states, such as Massachusetts, Michigan, and Arizona, have legalized the use of medical marijuana.

Example: Certain states (such as Massachusetts, Michigan, and Arizona) have legalized the use of medical marijuana.

Example: Certain states—such as Massachusetts, Michigan, and Arizona—have legalized the use of medical marijuana.

However: Certain states such as Michigan have legalized the use of medical marijuana. (Commas or parentheses are unneeded when *such as* or *like* are used to introduce one element.)

Example: Certain states, for instance, Mississippi, Ohio, and Illinois, have decriminalized the possession of small amounts of marijuana.

Example: Certain states (for instance, Mississippi, Ohio, and Illinois) have decriminalized the possession of small amounts of marijuana.

Example: Certain states—for instance, Mississippi, Ohio, and Illinois—have decriminalized the possession of small amounts of marijuana.

Example: A variety of medical conditions, for example, anxiety, irritable bowel disease, and cancer, can be treated with medical marijuana.

Example: A variety of medical conditions (for example, anxiety, irritable bowel disease, and cancer) can be treated with medical marijuana.

Example: A variety of medical conditions—for example, anxiety, irritable bowel disease, and cancer—can be treated with medical marijuana.

Example: According to the DEA, marijuana is a Schedule 1 drug; in other words, it has a high potential for abuse.

Example: According to the DEA, marijuana is a Schedule 1 drug (in other words, it has a high potential for abuse).

Example: According to the DEA, marijuana is a Schedule 1 drug—in other words, it has a high potential for abuse.

Sometimes expressions like *including* and *such as* are used to introduce restrictive elements. In these situations, the expression is not an interrupter and doesn't need to be enclosed in commas or parentheses. For instance, in a restrictive sense, the word *including* means "that included"; whereas, in a nonrestrictive sense, it means "which included."

Restrictive: The group including tenth and eleventh graders needs to be retested.

Finally, some experts recommend against using the abbreviations *i.e.* and *e.g.* in body text and instead argue that such abbreviations should be used only in tables, figures, and so forth. Nevertheless, the practice of using *i.e.* and *e.g.* in body texts is common among many online and print publishers.

---

48. Possessive Forms

TIP: Be consistent when using apostrophes to indicate possessive forms.

Key Points

- With singular common nouns that don't end in *–s,* add an *'s.*
- With plural common nouns that end in *–s* or *–es,* add an apostrophe only.
- With plural common nouns that don't end in *–s,* add an *'s.*
- Attributive nouns aren't possessive and don't take apostrophes.

In English, possessive forms of nouns can be expressed in two ways: the *of-genitive* (for example, the house of Mr. Payne) and the *s-genitive* (for example, Mr. Payne's house). As explained by Leech in *Change in Contemporary English,* corpus-based research suggests that in both American English and British English, there's been about a 24 percent decline in the use of the of-genitive in favor of the s-genitive, and toward the end of the twentieth century, the s-genitive had overtaken the of-genitive in usage. Furthermore, both the of-genitive and s-genitive are more frequent in American English than they are in British English; however, the decline of the of-genitive is more pronounced in British English.

The rise of the s-genitive is likely multifactorial and has been attributed to pragmatic, semantic, syntactic, and phonological factors.

From a historical perspective, in Old English, the of-genitive was rarely used and, instead, became more popular in Middle English. In Modern English, the of-genitive has seen a decline in favor of the s-genitive. In particular, the s-genitive has seen increased use in the press, where denser noun phrases decrease word counts.

Here are three general rules regarding the possessive case which cover a lot of scenarios:

- With singular common nouns that don't end in *-s,* add an *'s* (for example, *cat's purr, dog's bark, my father-in-law's suit,* and *lion's roar*).
- With plural common nouns that end in *-s* or *-es,* add an apostrophe only (for example, *the soldiers' weapons, the students' exams, the enemies' retreat,* and *the buildings' shadows*).
- With plural common nouns that don't end in *-s,* add an *'s* (for example, *men's game, children's party,* and *teeth's enamel*).

The term *common noun* refers to nonspecific things, people, or places. Whereas, a proper noun refers to specific people, things, and places. Although with proper nouns all you usually need to do is add an *'s* (for example, *Mr. Suarez's motorcycle* and *Juan's calculator*), things can get more complicated.

Imagine that Mr. Jones had a dog named Skippy. Skippy is *Mr. Jones's dog.* But what happens if the dog not only belonged to Mr. Jones, but also to his wife, Alice, and their kids, Ricardo and Betty. Skippy would be the *Joneses' dog.* In both cases, pronunciation is the same; however, spelling is different.

Oftentimes, your ear can guide you on how to write out possessive forms of nouns. You will hear the added sibilant *s* sound that accompanies a possessive form. For instance, you can hear the *s* sound in *candidate's tax returns. Paris's arrondissement system,* or *ABC News's anchor.* In the case of *Mr. Jones's dog* or the *Joneses' dog,* however, the derivations (inflections) of *Jones* sound the same, and your ear won't guide you as to where to place the apostrophe. Instead, you must think that the plural of *Jones* is *Joneses,* which like plural forms of common nouns ending in *-s* or *-es,* takes only an apostrophe. Similarly, consider the following examples:

- Mr. Williams's car
- The Williamses' Winnebago
- Mrs. Cummings's desk
- The Cummingses' in-ground pool

One major change in the 16th edition of *The Chicago Manual of Style* involves the addition of an *'s* to proper nouns that end in a silent *s* or the *-eez* sound.

- Euripides's writings
- Xerxes's conquests
- Albert Camus's oeuvre
- Descartes's Rule of Signs

The Chicago Manual of Style holds an esteemed position in the realm of writing and editing and guides much book publishing. When writing and publishing on your own, nobody is going to fault you for following either *The Chicago Manual of Style* or *The Associated Press Stylebook,* another formidable style treatise, which specifically guides news and magazine writing. However, the guidance found in the AP Stylebook on possessive forms is confusing for many people. In this section, much of the advice provided can be found in *The Chicago Manual of Style.*

When writing for a publication, you should follow the style—more specifically, the style guide or editorial style sheet—of the publication. When writing for your own blog, website, or platform, however, you can choose an approach that best suits you. As always, the key is to be consistent in your approach and refrain from switching strategies. For example, don't write *Mr. Wells's desk* in one sentence and *Mr. Wells' lamp* in another.

Some publications and style guides, as well as writers themselves, have their own idiosyncratic approaches to forming possessive nouns. For instance, many magazines and newspapers add an *'s* to common nouns ending in *s* and an apostrophe alone to proper nouns ending in *s,* for example, the *grass's color* and *Mr. Charles' son,* respectively.

Conversely, some writers add an apostrophe to all common nouns ending in *s* and an *'s* to every proper noun ending in *s,* for example, the *dress' color* and *the Gaines's daughter*, respectively.

An alternative system, explained in *The Chicago Manual of Style,* and once much more popular, is to simply add only an apostrophe to all words ending in *s,* for example, *Mr. Christmas' plan* or the *actress' script.* The problem with this strategy, however, is that it's blunt and discounts pronunciation, with no indication of the extra *s* sound on reading. A more sophisticated writer would likely eschew this approach.

Some pundits (adherents to Follett's *Modern American Usage*) argue that inanimate objects shouldn't take a possessive form because an inanimate object can't *own* anything. This view is a fringe one and bucked by many publications; it's fine to write *California's wildfires* or the *office's cubicles.* Nevertheless, it's sometimes a good idea to reword the possessive form of an inanimate object when it sounds weird or wordy.

For example, the *business's security system* grates on the ears with its sibilant *s* sounds. Instead, many copywriters will write the *firm's security system* or the *company's security system.* Alternatively, you can write the *security system of the business,* and replace the apostrophe with the of-genitive. The AP Stylebook deals with sibilant possessives individually and recommends that the writer look at the word that follows a possessive form and punctuate accordingly. According to the AP Stylebook, you would write *the heiress's fortune* but *the heiress' sapphires.*

When forming the possessive with compound words, or nouns that act as a unit, you want to make sure that you are making the proper elements possessive. If an entire phrase functions as a unit, use only one apostrophe. Consider the following:

- my daughter-in-law's birthday
- *Bill & Ted's Excellent Adventure*
- Billy Bob Thornton and Angelina Jolie's marriage

In the last example, we consider the marriage shared by Thornton and Jolie. However, if we were to refer to the several marriages between Jolie and Pitt, we would write *Billy Bob Thornton's and Angelina Jolie's marriages.*

Another underappreciated use of the apostrophe to indicate possessive forms involves proper nouns that end in *–s* and appear plural but, in fact, represent single entities. For example, the United States is plural in presentation but singular in meaning.

RIGHT: The students learned about the United States' stance on landmines.

RIGHT: Falgun read about Bloomfield Hills' cultural history.

Attributive Nouns

So far, we've looked at the possessive form as it relates to common and proper nouns. Another important principle that guides the use of apostrophes is whether the noun that you're thinking about punctuating is truly possessive, or instead is an adjective. Nouns that serve as adjectives and modify other nouns are called *attributive nouns, noun premodifiers, noun adjuncts,* or *converted adjectives.* Keep in mind that adjectives don't take apostrophes.

Figuring out whether a noun is attributive or is in the genitive case can be tricky. In the genitive case, the apostrophe can be substituted with *of.* Thus, you could drop the *'s* and substitute *of* instead. However, in the attributive case, the relationship is better expressed by *for* or *by.* Often, an argument could be made for either, which is why this subject is nebulous and certain style guides make specific recommendations.

To illustrate this point, let's look at some more examples.

Correct: Boys aren't offered membership to the girls' club.

Here, "girls'" club means "club of the girls."

ALSO CORRECT: Boys aren't offered membership to the girls club.

Here, "girls club" means "club for the girls" or "club (organized) by the girls."

Although the first example, "girl's club," is more widely accepted and makes sense (the club *of* the girls), a case can be made for the second usage, or the nonpossessive case. The word "girls" could describe the club itself and not indicate any possession thus functioning as a modifier.

To keep things more standard, *The Chicago Manual of Style* recommends that it's best to go with the apostrophe when punctuating most common nouns, as in "girl's club," but recommends that plural head nouns in proper names of companies, corporations, and institutions be written without an apostrophe and instead treated as attributive nouns. For example, *The Chicago Manual of Style* recommends that there's no apostrophe in *Department of Veterans Affairs* or *Farmers Insurance.*

Keep in mind that this guidance is general and fails to account for every specific situation. For instance, King's Cross refers to an inner-city area of London, which is famously home of the London King's Cross railway station, with its many longer-distance trains. (Harry Potter fans also know King's Cross for Platform 9¾ which services Hogwarts.) Based on the advice of *The Chicago Manual of Style,* it's tempting to think that the proper noun King's Cross is spelled without an apostrophe. When unsure, always check a reputable source for proper spelling (like the official website for King's Cross).

On a related note, because attributive nouns are adjectives on their own, you often don't need a suffix like *–al* tacked on to the end of one to reinforce its adjective standing. (Notice, I didn't write *adjectival* standing because adjective is an attributive noun.)

For example, *government offices* is preferred to *governmental offices,* and *surgery department* is preferred to *surgical department.*

Eponyms

A curious case of the attributive is demonstrated by the advice that the *AMA Manual of Style* dispenses concerning eponyms. Eponyms are nouns that include the name of a person or place. The guide recommends against punctuating eponyms with an apostrophe. The *AMA Manual of Style* is the style guide of the American Medical Association, and eponyms are rampant in medicine.

According to the editors at the *AMA Manual of Style,* eponyms should be written in a nonpossessive form (without an apostrophe). Although this advice is debatable, it follows more recent trends in how experts closest to their subject matter prefer things to be written. For example, the National Down Syndrome Society argues that "Down syndrome" is right and "Down's syndrome" is wrong. After all, although English physician John Langdon Down was the first physician to formally describe this condition in a scholarly work in 1866, he doesn't *own it.*

Consider the following examples:

- Alzheimer disease (instead of Alzheimer's disease)
- the Avogadro number (instead of Avogadro's number)
- the Pascal principle (instead of Pascal's principle)
- the Tukey test (instead of Tukey's test)
- Doppler radar

Temporal or Monetary Expressions

Let's consider some examples based on the *old genitive case.* These uses have been ingrained into the English language over centuries and involve temporal or monetary expressions.

- five decades' strife
- four days' supplies
- my two cents' worth
- three years' wages

Although an argument could easily be made that the punctuated nouns in the above examples are really adjectives, and thus attributive nouns, which require no apostrophe, these examples represent steadfast conventions of usage and meaning. In other words, when you read these examples, orthography dictates that they're interpreted *four days of supplies, three years of wages, five decades of strife,* and *two cents of worth.*

Lowercase Letters and Abbreviations

Lowercase letters written alone and in abbreviations with two or more internal periods are made plural by adding an 's.

RIGHT: Make sure to dot the i's and cross the t's.

With this specific expression, according to *The Chicago Manual of Style, i* and *t* are not italicized.

RIGHT: There are three M.D.'s on the plane.

False Possessives and Other Errors

One misuse of apostrophes is in the case of *false possessives,* or noun-derived adjectives that end in an *s*. Remember that adjectives don't take apostrophes.

WRONG: I am a huge Smiths' fan; they're one of my favorite bands.

RIGHT: I am a huge Smiths fan; they're one of my favorite bands.

WRONG: My friend is a Barbados' citizen.

RIGHT: My friend is a Barbados citizen

Some writers misuse apostrophes in an attempt to make proper nouns plural.

WRONG: Deborah is always happy to see the Friedman's.

RIGHT: Deborah is always happy to see the Friedmans.

Finally, some writers show possession of a noun ending in *–y* by changing the *–y* to *–ies,* which is totally wrong.

WRONG: Here is the companies balance sheet.

RIGHT: Here is the company's balance sheet.

WRONG: Alex was worried about the surgeries risks.

RIGHT: Alex was worried about the surgery's risks.

At this point in our discussion of possessive forms, you likely understand that lots of this information is debatable. Furthermore, an explanation of every nuance of the possessive form is outside the scope of this book. I've tried to streamline some of the most important points and find common ground. If you want to learn more about finer points of usage, I suggest that you refer to the style guides—*The Chicago Manual of Style* in particular.

During the self-editing phase, you may find it useful to analyze your writing for common mistakes that many people make with possessives and correct your document accordingly.

49. Punctuating Appositives

TIP: Use commas to set off nonrestrictive appositives.

Key Points

- A nonrestrictive appositive is set off using commas because it contains information that is not essential to the meaning of the sentence.
- A restrictive appositive is necessary to the meaning of a sentence, and should not be set off using commas.

An *appositive* is the second in a dyad of paired nouns, with the two nouns written in apposition.

Many writers have difficulty deciding whether an appositive is restrictive or nonrestrictive.

A *nonrestrictive appositive* is set off using commas because it contains information that is not essential to the meaning of the sentence. If the appositive were deleted, the reader could still properly understand the resulting statement.

A *restrictive appositive* is necessary to the meaning of a sentence and should not be set off using commas.

EXAMPLE 1: Abraham Lincoln's mother, Nancy Lincoln, died when the future president was eight years old.

EXAMPLE 2: Secretariat, a Triple Crown winner, died in 1989 at age 29.

EXAMPLE 3: We Americans are a resilient people.

In Example 3, the appositive "Americans" is restrictive, because if it were deleted, the sentence wouldn't make sense. In other words, without the noun "Americans," this sentence would lose meaning; it would be unclear who "we" is referring to. Whereas, Examples 1 and 2 are nonrestrictive because the information enclosed in commas renames the subjects "Abraham Lincoln's mother" and "Secretariat," respectively.

Let's explain this concept of appositives in a different way. Imagine that Tony has only one sister and her name is Lindsay.

Tony's sister, Lindsay, plays the piano.

We would set off the appositive in commas—thus making it nonrestrictive—because Tony has only one sister. In other words, the noun phrase "Tony's sister" can only refer to one person.

Now, if Tony were to have three sisters—Jemma, Heidi, and Lindsay—"Lindsay" would become restrictive, and we wouldn't use commas to set this restrictive appositive off

Tony's sister Lindsay plays the piano.

Keep in mind that "Tony's sister" could refer to one of three people, and we need to specify whom for the sentence to make sense. We wouldn't use commas to set off essential information.

50. Question Marks

TIP: In writing, question marks are usually found only in dialogue.

Key Points

- Two areas where questions are commonly used in writing are dialogue and nut graphs (following the lede of an article).
- Don't use question marks with indirect questions, one-word interrogatives, and polite requests that are phrased as questions.
- Overuse of question marks is off-putting to your reader.

Results from corpus-based research dated from 1961 and 1991/2 done by Leech suggest that there's been a 9.5 percent increase in question-mark use in British English and a 22.2 percent increase in American English.

At least in British English, most of this rise is due to increased use of question marks in fiction as well as an increase in written dialogue. As with speech, dialogue, which represents conversation, is rich in questions. Notably in British English, there's been a decrease in the use of question marks in the press and general prose.

In British English, we've seen a dramatic increase in the number of *non-sentential questions* found in writing. In non-sentential questions there's no finite verb (for example, *Why?*, *Where?*, *Which car?*, and *Arnold?*).

In American English, there has been a dramatic rise in both non-sentential and *tag questions*.

According to *Merriam-Webster*, a tag question is defined as "a question (such as *isn't it* in 'it's fine, isn't it?') added to a statement or command (as to gain the assent of or challenge the person addressed)."

EXAMPLE: Julia is sure that Beryl is wrong, isn't she?

Typically, tag questions are too informal for most writing—even writing done for general audiences. Thus, unless you're quoting somebody, you probably won't use tag questions too often.

One common place where journalists use questions is in the nut graph of an article. The nut graph is the "nutshell" paragraph that follows the lede—typically in a feature article. The nut graph touches on the key topics of a story.

For example, if you were writing a story about the rise of populism in Europe, your lede could paint a picture of how the far-right candidate Marine Le Pen rose to take on the liberal Emmanuel Macron in France's 2017 presidential election. (Le Pen lost.) Your nut graph could then contain the following question: Does Le Pen's rise signal a wave of populism in Europe?

Please keep in mind that question marks are used only with direct questions. In other words, they are used only when it makes sense to provide an answer. Question marks aren't used with indirect questions, one-word interrogatives, and polite requests that are phrased as questions.

INDIRECT QUESTION: Howard asked whether Sue had the book.

NOT: Howard asked whether Sue had the book?

One-word interrogative: Don't ask "how."

NOT: Don't ask "how?"

POLITE REQUEST: Could you please move your bike.

NOT: Could you please move your bike?

If you didn't know that indirect questions, one-word interrogatives, and polite requests don't take question marks, be on the lookout for these constructions in your writing—particularly in dialogue. Keep in mind that although the use of question marks is on the rise in written English, they're still relatively uncommon. Typically, you'll only find question marks in dialogue (and sometimes in quotations from sources). Finally, remember that when you are writing, you are writing to provide answers, not to interrogate the reader. Overusing question marks is off-putting to your reader. In fact, many journalists have shifted away from using question marks in nut graphs for this exact reason.

51. Quotations

Tip: Spice up your writing by bisecting quotations in interesting and aesthetic ways.

Key Points

- A colon introducing a quotation is very useful when citing a written source.
- A colon is often used to introduce a block quote.
- When the source is an actual speaker, by placing the speaker first followed by a colon or comma, a writer squanders the potential of a quotation.

Many beginning writers deal with quotations in a very cursory way. They will introduce the speaker and use a colon to begin a quotation.

EXAMPLE: The great American orator Henry Clay once stated: "Government is a trust, and the officers of the government are trustees; and both the trust and the trustees are created for the benefit of the people."

Alternatively, this quotation could be written with a comma instead of a colon.

EXAMPLE: The great American orator Henry Clay once stated, "Government is a trust, and the officers of the government are trustees; and both the trust and the trustees are created for the benefit of the people."

Please note that when a comma is used to introduce a quotation, as with a colon, the first word of a complete quoted sentence is usually capitalized.

A colon introducing a quotation is useful when quoting a written source. However when the source is an actual speaker, by placing the speaker first followed by a colon or comma, a writer wastes the potential of a quotation. Quotations can be cut up in wonderful ways that add variety to your writing.

When cutting up a quotation, it's important to identify natural breaks or pauses in prose. One easy way to identify a pause is by searching for commas, semicolons, periods, and ellipses, and bisecting the quotation at these points. When splitting quotations at these natural pauses, you may need to alter punctuation for meaning. For example, a semicolon or period is changed to a comma; however, ellipses are retained.

Consider the following:

"Government is a trust, and the officers of the government are trustees," once said the great American orator Henry Clay, "and both the trust and the trustees are created for the benefit of the people."

Please note that the "and" in "and both the trust and the trustees" is not capitalized because it begins a fragment.

Breaking this quotation up at the semicolon definitely boosts its aesthetics and readability. It also proves to an editor that you know how to manage quotations in a publishable manner. When quotations are consistently presented as speaker first, a seasoned editor will immediately notice that the writer lacks experience with quotations.

Importantly, this quotation could be written with the speaker listed last.

"Government is a trust, and the officers of the government are trustees; and both the trust and the trustees are created for the benefit of the people," once said the great American orator Henry Clay.

Now, let's look at another bisected quotation, this one with the ellipses retained.

Late Supreme Court Justice Potter Stewart famously quipped: "I shall not today attempt further to define [pornography] … But I know it when I see it; and the motion picture involved in this case is not that."

BETTER: "I shall not today attempt further to define [pornography] … But I know it when I see it," quipped late Supreme Court Justice Potter Stewart, "and the motion picture involved in this case is not that."

Please note that with quotations, brackets are used to indicate text added by the author. If you add some text to clarify a quotation, you must include this text in brackets.

You may notice that in the preceding quotation, I write "quip" instead of the more customary "wrote" or "state." I chose the verb "quip" because this quotation regarding pornography ("I know it when I see it") is considered by many to be a great American witticism.

Longer quotations that consist of two or three sentences can be broken up in-between sentences.

For example, we could break up the following quotation from Joseph Campbell after the first sentence.

American mythologist Joseph Campbell writes: "Myth is the secret opening through which the inexhaustible energies of the cosmos pour into human cultural manifestation. Religions, philosophies, arts, the social forms of primitive and historic man, prime discoveries in science and technology, the very dreams that blister sleep, boil up from the basic, magic ring of myth."

BETTER: "Myth is the secret opening through which the inexhaustible energies of the cosmos pour into human cultural manifestation," writes American mythologist Joseph Campbell. "Religions, philosophies, arts, the social forms of primitive and historic man, prime discoveries in science and technology, the very dreams that blister sleep, boil up from the basic, magic ring of myth."

If a quotation is more than four sentences long, it can be presented as a block quotation, which is not bisected in any way. A block quotation is a free-standing block of text that can be formatted differently from surrounding text and indented. Introductory sentences in block quotations end in a colon or period, and the block quotation is not enclosed in quotation marks. But quotation marks can be used within a block quotation.

Consider the following quotation from Andrew Carnegie, an American industrialist and philanthropist who died in 1919.

> While the law [of competition] may be sometimes hard for the individual, it is best for the race, because it insures the survival of the fittest in every department. We accept and welcome, therefore, as conditions to which we must accommodate ourselves, great inequality of environment, the concentration of business, industrial and commercial, in the hands of a few, and the law of competition between these, as being not only beneficial, but essential for the future progress of the race.

When presenting dialogue between characters, block quotations are always used.

In *Death of a Salesman,* Linda Loman states:

> I don't say he's a great man. Willy Loman never made a lot of money. His name was never in the paper. He's not the finest character that ever lived. But he's a human being, and a terrible thing is happening to him. So attention must be paid. He's not to be allowed to fall into his grave like an old dog. Attention, attention must be finally paid to such a person.

During the self-editing process, look to see where you can break up quotations in more lively ways. Use the speaker-first construction followed by a colon sparingly such as when introducing a quotation taken from a written text.

52.
Semicolons

TIP: There are only a few specific uses for the semicolon.

Key Points

- Semicolons can be used as a transitional elements to separate two independent clauses that are closely related in thought.
- Semicolons are used to separate items in a series that already contain commas.
- Semicolons are used to separate two independent clauses in which the second clause begins with either a conjunctive adverb or a transitional phrase.
- Semicolons can be used to demarcate segments of a sentence with a complex elliptical structure.

Like commas, semicolons are pauses. When read aloud, the pause of a semicolon is slightly longer than that of a comma but shorter than that of a period, or full stop.

There are only four uses for a semicolon. Before you use a semicolon, consider whether you are using a semicolon for one of the following four reasons.

First, semicolons can be used as a transitional element to separate two independent clauses that are closely related in thought.

Leon tipped the waiter an extra $50; he was extremely pleased with the service.

Of note, if this semicolon were replaced with a comma, the resulting construction would be the very incorrect *comma splice.*

> WRONG: Leon tipped the waiter an extra $50, he was extremely pleased with the service.

Alternatively, the semicolon could be replaced by a colon.

Leon tipped the waiter an extra $50: He was extremely pleased with the service.

Corpus-based research done by Leech suggests that the use of a colon instead of a semicolon in contexts where either will do is rising. Specifically, colons are becoming more common in written texts, and semicolons are becoming less common.

Second, semicolons can be used to separate items in a series that already contain commas.

> EXAMPLE: Agnes decorated the table with small American flags; red, white, and blue streamers; posters; and glitter.

> EXAMPLE: Sharon has lived in Detroit, Michigan; Phoenix, Arizona; and Ithaca, New York.

Third, semicolons are used to separate two independent clauses in which the second clause begins with either a conjunctive adverb, such as *however, thus*, or *nevertheless*, or a transitional phrase, such as *for example* or *for instance.*

EXAMPLE: Javier likes several types of cakes and pies; however, he doesn't like cheesecake.

EXAMPLE: Jackson always gives this employees sizeable holiday bonuses; for example, one Christmas he gave each of his employees $3,000.

Fourth, semicolons can be used to demarcate segments of a sentence with a complex elliptical structure.

EXAMPLE: In a March 2017 election for Hong Kong's fourth chief executive—determined by election committee—Carrie Lam received 777 votes; John Tsang, 365 votes; and Woo Kwok-hing, 21 votes.

According to Leech, use of the semicolon is in steep decline. Although still frequent in formal and academic texts, it is much less common in press and fiction. This trend could be because there is now less need to break up complex sentences for clarity. Alternatively, this trend could be because of the increased informality of many documents.

53. Slashes

TIP: Recast your prose to avoid using the slash.

Key Points

- The slash serves as a crutch for inexperienced writers.
- Avoid the slash in scientific or academic writing.

The slash (/) has become a crutch for many inexperienced writers. It's a punctuation symbol with versatile—yet ill-advised—uses.

The slash goes by many names including the following:

- forward slash
- oblique stroke
- shill

- slant
- solidus
- virgule

When writing for an academic publication, it's always best to look for an alternative to using a slash, even if the alternative requires writing more words. Same goes when writing for a reputable publication or publishing on your own platform. Believe me, use of the slash isn't going to impress anybody—especially a prospective editor whom you hope to work with. Moreover, the slash may confuse some readers with its disparate uses.

To best understand the slash, let's consider some of its many uses and better alternatives.

Better Alternatives to the Slash

Different style guides express different levels of tolerance for the slash. Interestingly, *The Chicago Manual of Style* is permissive with regard to use of the slash. Nevertheless, even with the many uses permitted by the Chicago Manual, clearer alternatives exist.

First, the slash is a symbol used to mean *and* or *or*; it is also used to mean *and* and *or.* With all these possible meanings, confusion inevitably arises. With all such uses, it's best to spell out your meaning more clearly and recast the slash. In other words, while writing or self-editing, ask yourself do you mean *and*, do you mean *or*, or do you mean both *and and or*.

Put another way, the slash is used to link alternatives with the intention of having the reader evaluate each alternative in turn. By placing the onus on the reader, use of the slash often invites inaccurate inference. Remember that it's your job to make things crystal clear for your readers.

INADVISABLE: Hamza will work the day/night shift.

BETTER: Hamza will work the day or the night shift.

INCREDIBLY UNCLEAR: At the dinner, you can choose chicken/fish.

BETTER: At the dinner, you can choose chicken or fish.

Second, the slash is used to designate a compound element.

INADVISABLE: Dr. Azar is an obstetrician/gynecologist.

BETTER: Dr. Azar is an obstetrician-gynecologist.

OR: Dr. Azar is an obstetrician and gynecologist.

When a slash is used to mean *and*, a more formal alternative is the Latin *cum*, which means "combined with" or "plus." Because *cum* is a Latin (foreign) word with a meaning that may be unfamiliar to many, you can elect to italicize this word.

INADVISABLE: Because Andy is a busy freelancer who works at home, his small bedroom/office is cluttered.

OKAY: Because Andy is a busy freelancer who works at home, his small bedroom-*cum*-office is cluttered.

Third, the slash is used to contrast two elements.

INADVISABLE: The Cornell/Harvard hockey rivalry peaks with a regular–season game at Cornell's Lynah Rink.

BETTER: The Cornell–Harvard hockey rivalry peaks with a regular–season game at Cornell's Lynah Rink.

Of note, a en dash (or short dash) is used to separate the compound adjective in "Cornell–Harvard hockey rivalry," as well as the compound adjective in "regular–season game."

Fourth, the slash is used to separate origins from destinations.

OKAY: Jasper went online to score a cheap fare on the New York/Los Angeles flight.

BETTER: Jasper went online to score a cheap fare on the New York–Los Angeles flight.

OR: Jasper went online to score a cheap fare on the New York-to-Los Angeles flight.

Fifth, the slash is used in place of per.

OKAY: Nia types 65 words/minute.

OR: Nia types 65 words a minute.

OR: Nia types 65 words per minute.

Although "per" sounds like jargon, it's okay to use in certain circumstances.

Sixth, the slash is used by some writers in *and/or* constructions, which although efficient, are probably best recast.

Inadvisable: Rita plans to major in economics and/or psychology.

BETTER: Rita plans to major in economics or psychology.

BETTER: Rita plans to major in economics and psychology.

BETTER: Rita plans to major in either economics or psychology, or both.

Seventh, a much maligned use of the slash involves *he/she* constructions, or, even worse, *s/he* constructions.

INADVISABLE: Give the usher your ticket, and he/she will escort you to your seat.

TERRIBLE: Give the usher your ticket, and s/he will escort you to your seat.

BETTER: Give the usher your ticket, and the usher will escort you to your seat.

OKAY: Give the usher your ticket, and he will escort you to your seat.

OKAY: Give the usher your ticket, and she will escort you to your seat.

In your writing, when choosing either *he* or *she* as a pronoun, remember to alternate uses to limit bias.

Acceptable Uses of the Slash

So far, we've looked at scenarios in which a slash can be avoided. In a few instances, however, a slash either can or needs to be used.

You can use slashes with dates, such as 6/25/2018.You can also use slashes to indicate a time period spanning two years such as 1994/95. On a related note, en dashes can also be used for dates, for example, 6–25–2018 or 1994–5. (If wondering, Geoffrey Leech writes "1991/2" in *Change in Contemporary English*, and I try to retain exact wording when quoting written sources.)

Another more obvious use of the slash is in fractions with a numerator and denominator such as ⅓ (one-third). Similarly, slashes can be used to indicate the division symbol, for example, 10/5 = 2.

Slashes are fine when used with certain units of measurement, such as 5 mg/mL or 100 m/s. With units of measurement, the slash means *per.*

Although rarely encountered, slashes can be used to separate compound words that already contain hyphens.

EXAMPLE: Eddy, who is an options trader, likes high-risk/high-reward investments.

In regular text, slashes can be used to separate two or more lines of poetry, wth a space before each slash.

Slashes are used with Internet addresses such as https://www.hud.gov/. (Notice that when an Internet address is the last word in the sentence it's followed by terminal punctuation such as a period.)

Finally, some expressions have taken on a clear meaning independent of the slash.

EXAMPLE: The convenience store is open 24/7.

EXAMPLE: Dora took the course pass/fail.

Part V: Organization

54. Headers

Tip: Headers help organize your writing.

Key Points

- Be consistent in how you format headers.
- Headers shouldn't be flashy. They just need to be distinct from surrounding text.
- Sometimes it's easier to figure out where headings can be placed in an article or document during the self-editing phase—after you've already written the piece.

Headers, also called headings, subdivide the text of an article, story, or document into moieties, which are more easily digested by the reader. Headers provide additional structure, and flow thematically with the title, subtitle, introduction (lede and nut graph), and conclusion (kicker).

Headers should be distinct from surrounding text; however, there's no reason to get too conspicuous or flamboyant with them. Headers only need to appear separate from surrounding text. For instance in HTML, headers are typically defined with <h3> tags that may slightly increase the font size of the header or make the text a bit bolder than text found in paragraphs. There's no need to add additional styling such as italics and underlining. Headers should draw about as much attention as a barber pole outside a barber shop—not a neon sign on the Las Vegas strip.

When writing for print, in addition to giving headers their own line, either bolding a header or slightly increasing the font size is often enough to make headers distinct from surrounding text.

Within sections demarcated by headings, subheads are completely acceptable and can facilitate meaning and proffer more organization. In other words, headers separate text into sections and these sections can be further divided by subheads into smaller sections.

With academic articles and texts, first-order headings, second-order headings, and third-order headings follow suggested style conventions. For instance, the *Publication of Manual of the American Psychology Association* offers guidance on heading levels.

In your own writing and editing, you have some latitude with respect to headings. For example, a first-order heading may simply be indicated using slightly larger font; whereas, a second-order heading (subhead) may be indicated using italics. Just be consistent with how you present these headings. In other words, if your first-order headings are bolded and your second-order headings are italicized, make sure that all first-order headings in a document are bolded, and all second-order headings in a document are italicized.

Keep in mind that even shorter documents can benefit from the prudent placement of headers.

Sometimes it's easier to figure out where headings can be placed in an article or document during the self-editing phase—after you've already written the piece. Here are some tips when coming up with headings:

- Similar to headlines and titles, with headings, right-branching headings tend to work best, especially for Internet audiences. In other words, place the subject (key term) and predicate first. Doing so helps with search-engine optimization (SEO).
- When possible, use proper nouns and other keywords to construct headings.
- Keep headings short.
- Prefer active verbs when constructing headings.
- Depending on the style of the intended publication, headings can be written in either title or sentence case. Remember to be consistent and use either title case or sentence case but not both.
- Consider hooks and angles when coming up with headings.

Let's consider the following blog posting from Psychology Today titled "The True Cost of a Tattoo." First, consider this blog posting without headings.

The True Cost of a Tattoo

Apparently, placing a tattoo in a visible area has both economic and social consequences. In particular, research suggests that a visible tattoo can affect employment opportunities.

Tattoos have been associated with society's out-groups and fringe elements, including bikers, prisoners, circus performers, gang members, and punk rockers. These individuals (or groups) have historically used tattoos to symbolize various things, such as rejection of mainstream society, physical strength, aggression, body ownership, affiliation with a group, and religious beliefs. Despite such personal intentions, however, research suggests that people with tattoos are not more aggressive, rebellious, and so forth.

In recent years, lots of people from all walks of life have been getting tattoos, and in a general sense, body modifications like tattoos have gained wider acceptance among members of the general public. Nearly 36 percent of Americans between 18 and 25 have at least one tattoo, with many Americans wearing more than one tattoo. Despite more and more people getting inked, discrimination against tattoos—in particular, those that are situated in visible areas like the face, neck, and wrist—is alive and well.

Dishearteningly, many people view those with tattoos as lacking good judgment, deviant, sexually promiscuous, self-destructive, dependent on drugs, dangerous, uneducated, and having low self-worth. Furthermore, research also shows that women with tattoos are viewed worse than men with tattoos—a slight that is doubly discriminatory.

It should probably come as no surprise that people with visible tattoos are discriminated against in the labor market. Notably, various other aspects of physical appearance have been shown to influence hiring, firing, and promotion—including height, subjective assessments of beauty, a person's natural features, grooming, and clothing choices. Potential employers either have a direct preference for certain characteristics or associate such characteristics with productivity.

Here are some research findings from various studies that indicate discrimination against people with visible tattoos:

- Miller, Nicols, and Eure have shown that employees view colleagues with facial tattoos and piercings as less suitable for work that requires interaction with a customer.
- According to Swanger, 87 percent of surveyed employers in the hospitality industry report that visible body modification is negatively perceived.
- Ligos found that 77 percent of managers believe that salespeople with visible tattoos have a harder time making sales ("closing") than do those without visible tattoos.
- Brallier and colleagues found that restaurant mangers prefer to hire people without visible tattoos.
- In an IZA (Institute for the Study of Labor) discussion paper, researchers suggest that employment status of those with visible tattoos is more vulnerable. In other words, although a person who has a job and then gets a visible tattoo may not lose a job outright,

> if this person were to lose a job for whatever reason in the future, it may be harder to get rehired somewhere else.

It seems that a lot of the data concerning visible tattoos and employment opportunities point to management's trepidation to place a salesperson with a visible tattoo in contact with a client for fear of lost sales.

As consumers, we can take these findings to heart and look within ourselves to examine whether we discriminate others based on the presence of visible tattoos. After all, the research shows that the person selling the watch, car, or candy bar is likely to be equally qualified in all respects to any other salesperson without a hand tattoo, neck tattoo, face tattoo, or so forth.

With luck, as more people get visible tattoos, less discrimination will exist. Maybe more people will realize that getting a tattoo, whether readily apparent or not, is merely a form of expression and definitely no reason to deny employment or employment opportunities.

Ironically, because only a minority of people who get tattoos actually get visible ones, it's possible that managers with non-visible tattoos themselves could discriminate against prospective employees with visible tattoos—a pretty hypocritical reality to be sure.

Now, let's go back and add headings with clarity of message, ease of comprehension, and SEO in mind.

The True Cost of a Tattoo

Apparently, placing a tattoo in a visible area has both economic and social consequences. In particular, research suggests that a visible tattoo can affect employment opportunities.

Tattoo History

Tattoos have been associated with society's out-groups and fringe elements, including bikers, prisoners, circus performers, gang members, and punk rockers. These individuals (or groups) have historically used tattoos to symbolize various things, such as rejection of mainstream society, physical strength, aggression, body ownership, affiliation with a group, and religious beliefs. Despite such personal intentions, however, research suggests that people with tattoos are not more aggressive, rebellious, and so forth.

In recent years, lots of people from all walks of life have been getting tattoos, and in a general sense, body modifications like tattoos have gained wider acceptance among members of the general public. Nearly 36 percent of Americans between 18 and 25 have at least one tattoo, with many Americans wearing more than one tattoo. Despite more and more people getting inked, discrimination against tattoos—in particular, those that are situated in visible areas like the face, neck, and wrist—is alive and well.

Tattoo Misconceptions

Dishearteningly, many people view those with tattoos as lacking good judgment, deviant, sexually promiscuous, self-destructive, dependent on drugs, dangerous, uneducated, and having low self-worth. Furthermore, research also shows that women with tattoos are viewed worse than men with tattoos—a slight that is doubly discriminatory.

It should probably come as no surprise that people with visible tattoos are discriminated against in the labor market. Notably, various other aspects of physical appearance have been shown to influence hiring, firing, and promotion—including height, subjective assessments of beauty, a person's natural features, grooming, and clothing choices. Potential employers either have a direct preference for certain characteristics or associate such characteristics with productivity.

Tattoo Research

Here are some research findings from various studies that indicate discrimination against people with visible tattoos:

- Miller, Nicols, and Eure have shown that employees view colleagues with facial tattoos and piercings as less suitable for work that requires interaction with a customer.
- According to Swanger, 87 percent of surveyed employers in the hospitality industry report that visible body modification is negatively perceived.
- Ligos found that 77 percent of managers believe that salespeople with visible tattoos have a harder time making sales ("closing") than do those without visible tattoos.
- Brallier and colleagues found that restaurant mangers prefer to hire people without visible tattoos.
- In an IZA (Institute for the Study of Labor) discussion paper, researchers suggest that employment status of those with visible tattoos is more vulnerable. In other words, although a person who has a job and then gets a visible tattoo may not lose a job outright, if this person were to lose a job for whatever reason in the future, it may be harder to get rehired somewhere else.

Bottom Line

It seems that a lot of the data concerning visible tattoos and employment opportunities point to management's trepidation to place a salesperson with a visible tattoo in contact with a client for fear of lost sales.

As consumers, we can take these findings to heart and look within ourselves to examine whether we discriminate others based on the presence of visible tattoos. After all, the research shows that the person selling the watch, car, or candy bar is likely to be equally qualified in all respects to any other salesperson without a hand tattoo, neck tattoo, face tattoo, or so forth.

With luck, as more people get visible tattoos, less discrimination will exist. Maybe more people will realize that getting a tattoo, whether readily apparent or not, is merely a form of expression and definitely no reason to deny employment or employment opportunities.

Ironically, because only a minority of people who get tattoos actually get visible ones, it's possible that managers with non-visible tattoos themselves could discriminate against prospective employees with visible tattoos—a pretty hypocritical reality to be sure.

---

55. Lists

TIP: Consistency is key with list items.

Key Points

- If you capitalize the first word of at least one list item, all list items should be capitalized.
- If you choose to end one list item with a comma or semicolon, each list item should end with a comma or semicolon, respectively, with the last list item ending in a period.
- When at least one list item is written as an independent clause, all list items should be written as independent clauses.
- A sentence ending in a colon is typically used to introduce a displayed list.
- Use numbered lists when list items are sequential.

It's nearly impossible to properly write a long article or other nonfiction document without using lists. Lists help organize your writing and help the reader better understand your message. Remember, a list is a sentence written with optimal organization in mind.

Two types of lists are used when writing: *run-on* (also called *run-in*) lists and *displayed lists* (also called *vertical lists*). With run-on lists, the list items are incorporated into the continuous prose of the document and are thus directly part of a paragraph. Run-on lists are useful when the list items are short—think single words, proper nouns (names), or short phrases. Displayed lists are formatted separately from the surrounding prose, and the items in these lists can be either numbered or bulleted.

Numbered list items are used when sequential order is important. For example, steps in a process are numbered. Numbered lists can also be used to emphasize priority. Note that items in a bulleted list can be organized alphabetically, by importance, by geography, and so forth. Ordering list items can help present information in a logical fashion.

The construction of lists, especially displayed lists, tends to confuse writers. Many writers are unsure whether to capitalize the first letter in each list item and whether to end list items with a period, comma, or semicolon. Ultimately, guidance regarding such issues varies, and when writing on your own, you have lots of options when listing out items; all you really need to be concerned with is consistency.

Put another way, if you choose to end one list item with a comma or semicolon, each list item should end with a comma or semicolon, respectively, with the last list item ending in a period. (When list items contain internal punctuation like commas, then use semicolons.) Furthermore, if each list item is a phrase, you can choose whether to capitalize the first word in each list item or leave these words in lower case—just be consistent. Finally, if at least one item in a list is written as an independent clause (with initial capitalization and a terminal period), each list item should be written as an independent clause. Consistent use of punctuation and capitalization with list items is a type of parallelism and bolsters continuity. Notably, many online publishers prefer *up style* and begin list items with capital letters. Ostensibly, capitalized list items aid with online readability.

An independent clause followed by a colon (akin to a topic sentence) is usually used to introduce a list. Alternatively, this topic sentence can be followed by a period. Colons are used to introduce lists after expressions like *as follows* or *the following*. When a fragment is used to introduce a list, and the list items complete the sentence, no colon or period is used.

Okay, so we've looked at some guidance regarding list usage. Now, let's look at some specific examples of lists to better illustrate these points.

Ronald Reagan had five children including: Maureen Elizabeth Reagan,

Michael Edward Reagan, Christine Reagan, Patti Davis, and Ronald Prescott Reagan.

Because the items in this list are names in a series, a run-on list works here. The items in this run-on list are listed according to birth date, with Maureen Reagan born first and Ronald Prescott Reagan born last.

Now, let's consider the following list with each item being a phrase.

Ronald Reagan had five children including: Maureen Elizabeth Reagan, born in 1941; Michael Edward Reagan, born in 1945; Christine Reagan, born in 1947; Patti Davis, born in 1952; and Ronald Prescott Reagan, born in 1958.

Here, a run-on list would work because the items are short. Additionally, because each item is internally punctuated with a comma, semicolons are used at the end of each list item.

Because there is internal punctuation in each list item, an em dash can also be used to introduce the run-on list. (An em dash can also be used to introduce a run-on list in which list items are emphasized.)

Ronald Reagan had five children—Maureen Elizabeth Reagan, born in 1941; Michael Edward Reagan, born in 1945; Christine Reagan, born in 1947; Patti Davis, born in 1952; and Ronald Prescott Reagan, born in 1958.

Alternatively, this run-on list could be written as a displayed list.

Ronald Reagan had five children.

- Maureen Elizabeth Reagan, born in 1941;
- Michael Edward Reagan, born in 1945;
- Christine Reagan, born in 1947;
- Patti Davis Reagan, born in 1952;
- Ronald Prescott Reagan, born in 1958.

Now, let's look at a list where each list item is an independent clause, and the list is introduced by a colon.

Ronald Reagan had five children including the following people:

- Maureen Reagan was born in 1941 to Ronald Reagan's first wife, Jane Wyman.
- Michael Edward Reagan was adopted by Jane Wyman and Ronald Reagan in 1945.
- Christine Reagan was born to Jane Wyman and Ronald Reagan in 1947; she died shortly after birth.
- Patti Davis was born to Nancy Davis Reagan, Ronald Reagan's second wife and the former first lady, in 1952.
- Ronald Prescott Reagan was born in 1958 to Nancy and Ronald Reagan.

You'll notice that because each list item is its own independent clause, each item is written with initial capitalization and a period.

Next, let's consider a numbered list in which order is important. When backing the car out of the garage, you must do the following:

1. Open the garage door.
2. Situate yourself behind the wheel.
3. Buckle your seatbelt.
4. Check the rearview mirror.
5. Shift the car into reverse.
6. Release the brake.
7. Gently back the car out onto the driveway.
8. Close the garage door.

The order of these steps is important, which is why this list is numbered. In other words, if you were to close the garage door (Step 8) before you rolled the car out onto the driveway (Step 7), you would wreck your car and the garage door.

When possible, limit the number of list items to between 5 and 10. If you need to list more items or the list is particularly long, consider an alternative means of organization such as a table.

Importantly, with lists, it's best that list items be limited to one order. In other words, a list in which list items contain sublists should be avoided whenever possible. This organization can become confusing and often indicates more global issues with organization.

When self-editing, keep the concepts described here in mind and fix your lists accordingly.

56. Paragraphs

TIP: With general audiences, shorter paragraphs help with comprehension.

Key Points

- Topic sentences summarize meaning and usually begin paragraphs.
- In print publications, most paragraphs are between three and eight sentences.

- For the web, paragraphs between two and four sentences are oftentimes preferred.
- Scrutinize long paragraphs.

A porterhouse steak is a big piece of meat which can weigh up to 40 ounces. It's cut from the thick end of a sirloin. It is essentially a combination of filet mignon and New York strip—tender like filet and tasty like strip. When people go to fancy steakhouses like Ruth's Chris or Peter Luger, they often order porterhouse steaks. It's a generous cut of beef which could easily feed two people.

To eat a porterhouse steak, you need to first carve it into morsels, mouthfuls that are savored. No human would pick up a steak and begin gnawing away. Doing so would probably ruin the experience of enjoying a remarkable cut of meat and could even be dangerous … People choke on meat all the time.

Similarly no matter how well written, no article or other document can be presented as a single block of prose without paragraphs or breaks. Without such breaks rending comprehensible bits, any writing would be a jumbled mess.

Like the sentence itself, the paragraph is a unit of meaning. A paragraph conveys a thought or action and is typically detailed using a group of sentences. This thought is summarized as a topic sentence which usually begins—but can be located elsewhere in—a paragraph. Sometimes two sentences that are very closely related in meaning can make for a topic sentence. Furthermore, topic sentences are linked in thought with the paragraph before.

Paragraphs need to flow from one to the next. There needs to be cohesion between one paragraph and the next. Paragraphs drive the narrative. A paragraph taken out of context is like removing a link from a chain.

According Pulitzer Prize–winning journalist and long-time writing teacher Donald Murray, the paragraph has points of emphasis. The greatest point of emphasis is at the end. The next greatest point of emphasis is at the beginning. The point of least emphasis is in the middle. According to Murray, keeping these points of emphasis in mind will help you clarify the writing process.

The length of a paragraph in sentences varies based on context and audience. Most paragraphs are between three and eight sentences. Newspapers often use one- or two-sentence paragraphs (the inverted pyramid). Short paragraphs are more immediate and visually appealing than are longer ones. Academic writing is different, with longer paragraphs giving more attention to the topic. Moreover, many academics are wary of using shorter paragraphs for fear of appearing cursory in their analysis. Finally, some publishers prefer that each paragraph be no longer than five or six sentences. With general audiences, longer paragraphs should always be scrutinized.

The first word of each paragraph can either be indented or written without an indent (blocked format). With *blocked format*, the first word of each paragraph is flush with the left-hand margin. Online writing is often presented in block format, and indents are used with print publishing.

A fundamental skill that any writer should possess is an understanding of where to break continuous prose into separate paragraphs. One useful way to check onscreen where to best place paragraph breaks is to remove all the paragraph breaks in a selection and then look for potential paragraph breaks. Think about it this way: Paragraphs are visual units that break up a piece of writing. By combining these units, you can identify where breaks should go.

Consider this blog posting with all paragraph breaks removed.

> Surprisingly, little research has been done on the health effects of crying. In popular media, crying is promoted as healthful and cathartic. But is it? The results are mixed. In a literature review titled "Adult Crying," Vingerhotes and co-authors bring up some interesting points regarding what we do know about crying. When people are asked to recount how they felt after crying, most people state that they felt better after crying; however in laboratory studies, people often feel worse after crying. This immediate effect on affect may be because crying results in sympathetic (fight-or-flight) overstimulation. In other words, the physical act of crying doesn't result in relief; instead, people feel better *after having cried*. From a physical perspective, there is little support for the notion that crying promotes recovery or homeostasis. First, crying has either no effect on or increases heart rate. Second, crying doesn't result in the shedding of toxic metabolic products; instead, crying decreases levels of secretory IgA, which is a first-line immunological defense. Third, crying doesn't affect levels of pituitary hormones or cortisol. The immediate benefits of crying likely lie in the way that crying "softens" the environment. When people cry, others become more comforting and empathetic. Thus by crying, we are able to convey personal needs and desires. In other words, and as you can likely attest to, when someone else cries, you feel sympathy for this person, and you are more inclined to comfort and help this person. But why do some people deliberately engage in crying behaviors? For example, why do some people watch sad movies only to cry after the movie is done? People who engage in deliberate crying behaviors possibly do so because the world seems more positive after negative-mood induction.

Now, read this blog posting with the paragraph breaks intact.

> Surprisingly, little research has been done on the health effects of crying. In popular media, crying is promoted as healthful and cathartic. But is it? The results are mixed. In a literature review titled "Adult Crying," Vingerhotes and co-authors bring up some interesting points regarding what we do know about crying.
>
> When people are asked to recount how they felt after crying, most people state that they felt better after crying; however in laboratory studies, people often feel worse after crying. This immediate effect on affect may be because crying results in sympathetic (fight-or-flight) overstimulation. In other words, the physical act of crying doesn't result in relief; instead, people feel better *after having cried*.
>
> From a physical perspective, there is little support for the notion that crying

> promotes recovery or homeostasis. First, crying has either no effect on or increases heart rate. Second, crying doesn't result in the shedding of toxic metabolic products; instead, crying decreases levels of secretory IgA, which is a first-line immunological defense. Third, crying doesn't affect levels of pituitary hormones or cortisol.
>
> The immediate benefits of crying likely lie in the way that crying "softens" the environment. When people cry, others become more comforting and empathetic. Thus by crying, we are able to convey personal needs and desires. In other words, and as you can likely attest to, when someone else cries, you likely feel sympathy for this person, and you are more inclined to comfort and help this person.
>
> But why do some people deliberately engage in crying behaviors? For example, why do some people watch sad movies only to cry after the movie is done? People who engage in deliberate crying behaviors possibly do so because the world seems more positive after negative-mood induction.

With the paragraph breaks removed, this blog posting is hardly readable. The paragraph breaks give the article meaning. Let's consider where the paragraph breaks are in this article about crying.

First, although a topic sentence can be embedded within a paragraph—except for the lede—each paragraph in the preceding selection begins with a topic sentence.

Second, it's expected that the introduction (lede) and conclusion (kicker) be broken up into at least one paragraph, both of which are. The lede is the first paragraph, and the kicker is the last paragraph.

Third, the third paragraph in this blog posting is a run-on list with each of the items in the list written with the transitions *first*, *second*, and *third*, and *fourth*. Lists—whether run-on or displayed—get their own paragraphs. Similarly, quotations can also get their own paragraphs.

When writing for the Internet, paragraphs are often best limited to between two and four sentences. Research shows that shorter paragraphs are easier for online readers—who are often scanners—to comprehend. Consequently, some Internet writers choose to break paragraphs at transitions, words such as *furthermore*, *additionally*, and *however*.

Consider the following paragraph from the preceding blog posting:

> From a physical perspective, there is little support for the notion that crying promotes recovery or homeostasis. First, crying either has no effect on or increases heart rate. Second, crying doesn't result in the shedding of toxic metabolic products; instead, crying decreases levels of secretory IgA, which is a first-line immunological defense. Third, crying doesn't affect levels of pituitary hormones or cortisol.

Alternatively, this paragraph could be written as the following four one-sentence paragraphs. Breaking this paragraph up into four sentences aids with comprehension by the online reader.

> From a physical perspective, there is little support for the notion that crying promotes recovery or homeostasis.
>
> First, crying either has no effect on or increases heart rate.

> Second, crying doesn't result in the shedding of toxic metabolic products; instead, crying decreases levels of secretory IgA which is a first-line immunological defense.
> Third, crying doesn't affect levels of pituitary hormones or cortisol.

When checking your own work, try removing the paragraph breaks from a short selection (between 250 and 400 words), and then carefully consider where paragraph breaks should be placed to facilitate meaning. If you have trouble breaking up the text into paragraphs after removing the breaks, you may need clearer topic sentences, which are more easily identifiable. Alternatively, you may need to better clarify your transitions and transitional elements.

On a final note, if the sentences, paragraphs, or sections of your article or other document flow together and follow a narrative thread, there's little need for *signposting*. Signposts are phrases that refer to other parts of the document, such as "in Paragraph 11" or "in Chapter 6." Although some cross-referencing may be needed in long documents, it's best to avoid frequent or long signposts, which indicate overarching issues with organization.

57. Sentence Length

TIP: Evaluate whether long sentences can be broken up.

Key Points

- If a sentence is longer than 20 words, you may want to consider reducing its length in some way.
- Variations in sentence length can effect tempo.

Nobody should endeavor to write a long and complicated sentence. A long and complicated sentence doesn't sound fancy.... It sounds complicated. With nonfiction writing, the purpose of your words should be to inspire thought in the brain, not confusion on the page. Every sentence should represent a key point, and this idea should be concise.

So what is the perfect sentence length? A rule of thumb is that sentences should be fewer than 20 words long. This guidance is particularly salient with respect to Internet content; research shows that online readers prefer shorter sentences and short paragraphs.

But does this mean that a good sentence can't exceed 20 words? No, absolutely not! This advice merely suggests that if a sentence is longer than 20 words, you may want to consider reducing its length in some way—especially during the self-editing phase during which longer sentences in your writing can be targeted. Keep in mind that when breaking up long sentences, endeavor to retain your intended meaning.

There are a number of ways that you can break up a longer sentence into two.

Two coordinate clauses, or closely related independent clauses—each with a subject and predicate—can form a sentence. These independent clauses are linked by a coordinate conjunction (*and*, *but*, *or*, *for*, *nor*, *so*, **or** *yet*). Sometimes by linking two independent clauses, you create an unwieldy monster of a sentence. These sentences can easily be chopped into two.

EXAMPLE: Before boarding the airplane, Willy used the bathroom next to the food court near the terminal, and then he bought a foot-long Subway sandwich as well as two cookies, all of which he planned to share with his son who was hungry and demanded food.

BETTER: Before boarding the airplane, Willy used the bathroom next to the food court near the terminal. He then bought a foot-long Subway sandwich as well as two cookies, all of which he planned to share with his son who was hungry and demanded food.

Even broken up, the second sentence is still greater than 20 words, which is fine.

Another place to break up long sentences is before a conjunctive adverb joining two independent clause (for example, *thus*, *therefore*, *nevertheless*, *moreover*, *however*, **or** *indeed*).

LONG: During the winter, Emily usually keeps plenty of firewood in her backyard so that she can fuel her fire pit and stay warm when relaxing on her patio; nevertheless, if you can't find firewood in Elizabeth's backyard, you can ask her neighbor Oliver for some.

BETTER: During the winter, Emily usually keeps plenty of firewood in her backyard so that she can fuel her fire pit and stay warm when relaxing on her patio. Nevertheless, if you can't find firewood in Elizabeth's backyard, you can ask her neighbor Oliver for some.

In *The Elements of Style*, Strunk and White recommend not beginning a sentence with the conjunctive adverb *however* when the intended meaning is *nevertheless*, and instead only beginning a sentence with *however* when the intended meaning is *in whatever way* or *to whatever extent*. This advice is a bit arcane and often ignored by modern writers.

Sentences with complex compound predicates are also often good candidates for separation.

EXAMPLE: In her older age, after her husband died, Yvette would spend every Sunday serving homeless women at the shelter downtown, and would always show up before all the other volunteers at 6 a.m. sharp.

BETTER: In her older age, after her husband died, Yvette would spend every Sunday serving homeless women at the shelter downtown. She would always show up before all the other volunteers at 6 a.m. sharp.

With complicated combinations of phrases and clauses, try breaking up the sentence for clarity.

LONG: In the aftermath of her upset loss to Donald Trump in the 2016 election, Hillary Clinton placed blame squarely on FBI Director James Comey, thus denying accountability and minimizing any mistakes she may have made during the campaign, including her lack of focus on key states like Michigan, Wisconsin, and Pennsylvania.

BETTER: In the aftermath of her upset loss to Donald Trump in the 2016 election, Hillary Clinton placed blame squarely on FBI Director James Comey. Clinton thus denied accountability and minimized any mistakes she may have made during the campaign, including her lack of focus on key states like Michigan, Wisconsin, and Pennsylvania.

When a modifier is particularly long or could function well as its own sentence, two sentences can readily be extracted from one.

LONG: In the 2016 election—which was a historic election, in part, because it marked the first time a woman had ever run for president of the United States—Donald Trump, former host of the reality show *The Apprentice*, beat Hillary Clinton, who was a U.S. senator and Secretary of State, as well as a former First Lady.

BETTER: In the 2016 election, Donald Trump, former host of the reality show *The Apprentice*, beat Hillary Clinton, who was a U.S. senator and Secretary of State, as well as a former First Lady. The election was historic, in part, because it marked the first time a woman has ever run for president of the United States,

Finally, experienced writers will sometimes vary sentence length to effect tempo. For instance, short sentences can break up runs of longer sentences. These shorter sentences can be used to emphasize meaning or as visual relief—it can be hard for readers to digest a string of long sentences. Whereas, longer sentences can be used to convey certain emotions, such as monotony, pain, and frustration. On a related note, some writers like to vary paragraph length to effect tempo, too.

58. Tables

TIP: Use tables when presenting a large amounts of data.

Key Points

- Tables allow for the display of complex relationships.
- Tables accurately support what's written in the text.
- Tables must be able to stand alone without referring back to the text.

When writing articles and other documents, tables are useful at presenting large amounts of data. Tables consist of (vertical) columns and (horizontal) rows. (If you have trouble remembering the difference between columns and rows, visualize the columns of a building, which are vertical.)

Tables allow complex relationships to be displayed; they summarize, condense, and organize information. The use of tables reflects advanced levels of expertise described by Bloom's Taxonomy: knowledge, comprehension, application, analysis, synthesis, and evaluation (listed in ascending order). They also allow for comparisons to be drawn among data, as well as saving on space and adding visual appeal to a piece.

When self-publishing, here are some general tips taken from various sources that may help develop your own tables:

- Don't abbreviate terms in column or row headings—spell abbreviated terms out. However, abbreviated terms can be used in the body of a table as long as they're spelled out in the footnotes.
- Abbreviations like *e.g.* and *i.e.* can be used in tables.
- The first word in every table entry should be capitalized.
- Punctuate all table entries in a consistent manner.
- Numerals—not spelled out numbers—are usually used for table entries, as well as in the title.
- Write the title of a table as a descriptive phrase in title case.

Please note that the body of a table presents the actual data showcased and can contain numerals, text, and symbols.

Remember that when using a table, the information in the table must accurately reflect what's in the text and vice versa. Tables are used to support what is written in the text. Moreover, tables must be able to stand on their own without referring back to information in the text.

59. Titles and Headlines

TIP: Invest time in crafting engaging and informative titles and headlines.

Key Points

- When coming up with titles, write out several and choose one.
- Prefer simple titles to obscure ones.
- Titles are usually written in title case.
- Headlines are a specific type of title.

Titles

Good titles are even harder to write than good articles. This assertion may sound strange; however, most experienced writers will likely agree. The title is supposed to catch the essence or a book, journal article, blog posting, or so forth in a conspicuous fashion; whereas, the body of the document itself has hundreds or thousands of words to convey its essence.

Titles are important because they serve as overtures to entire documents. Think about it: How many times have you read a title and passed on reading a book or online article? If you're like most readers, you skim countless more titles than you read actual documents. You can quickly tell from a title whether it's worth your time to invest attention in the article itself.

At big publications, editors often help with titles and headlines. A writer, however, is encouraged to make suggestions. When self-publishing, title creation is a writer's responsibility.

Here are some functions of a good title:

- Good titles reflect the voice of the work.
- Good titles speak to an audience—either general or specialized.

- Good titles establish the subject of the document.
- Good titles focus on the topic.
- Good titles deliver an entire message.
- Good titles relate to the piece in a logical fashion.
- Good titles grab the reader's attention.
- Good titles hint at the angle of the piece.

Here are some characteristics of a good title.

- clever
- direct
- energetic
- funny
- honest
- interesting
- lively
- pointed
- short
- simple
- sophisticated
- unique

Please note that some of these characteristics are mutually exclusive. For example, sophisticated titles are not simple. Thus, a good title will not possess all of these listed attributes.

Here are some tips when coming up with a good title:

- Write titles after you have written the document; doing so will give you better perspective.
- Write many titles and choose one.
- For online articles and blog postings, choose keywords from the body and incorporate these keywords into your title. In addition to establishing a subject, keywords in the title boost search-engine optimization (SEO) value. Try to keep titles between 27 and 70 characters long.
- When creating a title, write longer titles and cut down on words used.
- Use specific nouns and verbs in the title.
- If a title almost seems right, try changing a word or two.
- Consider the unexpected when writing a title.
- Always prefer simple and engaging to more obscure titles, even if the obscure title is more clever, witty, cheeky, snarky, or humorous. Keep in mind that readers must readily understand the meaning of a title.

- It's best to limit punctuation used. If necessary, you can use a colon to create a *double title.* For example, Malcolm Gladwell's book titled *Blink: The Power of Thinking Without Thinking* has a double title. You can also use a question mark when the title takes the form of a question.
- To increase engagement, when coming up with a title, draw inspiration from the hook and angle of a piece.

Titles are typically written in title case. The following list contains guidance regarding the use of title case and is taken from *The Associated Press Stylebook.* This guidance applies to titles of books, plays, online articles, and so forth.

- Capitalize the first and last word in a title.
- Capitalize all major words, including nouns, verbs, pronouns, adjectives, and adverbs.
- Capitalize all words that are four letters or more.
- Don't capitalize minor words that are three letters or fewer, including conjunctions, articles, and prepositions.

There are two main approaches to capitalization in titles of books, magazine articles, and so forth. With *headline style,* the first and last words of a title or subtitle are capitalized. Additionally, all interior words are capitalized except for articles, coordinate conjunctions, prepositions, and some scientific terms written without capitalization. With headline style, subtitles are mostly introduced using colons, but sometimes em dashes are used. With *sentence style* (sentence case), in addition to proper nouns, proper adjectives and the word *I,* only the first word of a title or subtitle is capitalized.

Consider the following example of an article title and subtitle written in headline style.

Alarm Fatigue: The Danger of Missed Hospital Alarms

In addition to titles, articles published online also frequently have subtitles. Subtitles function as second titles and provide additional information. Subtitles further explain the content of an article. Moreover, subtitles can provide interesting detail that entices the reader to keep on reading. Subtitles are mostly introduced using colons, but sometimes em dashes are used.

Subtitles in articles can also be written in sentence case when the subtitle reads more like a sentence than it does a title. For instance, let's imagine that the aforementioned "alarm fatigue" article had a different subtitle: "Nurses are inundated with alarms each shift."

This subtitle looks more like a sentence and less like a second title; thus, sentence case can be used.

Headlines

Some people use the words *headline* and *title* interchangeably. To be sure, these concepts overlap. Furthermore, in content managements systems (CMSs), both headlines and titles are defined using the same header <h1> tags. However, headlines and titles are different.

Headlines refer to specific types of titles. Headlines are found at the head of newspaper or magazine articles, as well as on magazine covers and are usually set in larger type. They are also found on the landing pages of digital publications, in Internet search results, on newsfeeds, and so forth. No hyphenation is used with headlines, and headlines are typically written in the present tense, even if the event has already occurred.

The AP Stylebook provides the following style guidance regarding headlines:

- Headlines should be written in sentence case, with only the first word and proper nouns capitalized.
- Only single quotation marks—not double quotation marks—should be used in headlines.
- Numerals should be used in place of numbers in headlines.

This guidance isn't followed by all publications, and some publications use title case with headlines.

Much of the preceding guidance regarding titles also applies to headlines; headlines should be crisp, accurate, and concise. Furthermore, headlines should be topical and readily understood.

Here is some additional guidance regarding headlines (and, by extension, titles):

- Headlines are typically right branching with the subject and verb coming first. Because subjects are typically keywords, when a headline appears online, using right-branching constructions can boost SEO. Of note, this guidance also can apply to titles.
- The headline should not repeat exact phrasing found in the body of the article.
- Headlines that appear online or on covers of print publications are typically presented without any context; thus, these headlines should be as specific and comprehensible as possible.
- Headlines can include elements of alliteration, assonance, and wordplay.
- Headlines can be presented as a question or informative phrase.
- An effort should be made to minimize punctuation in headlines. No terminal punctuation should be used at the end of an informa-

tive phrase; however, headlines that take the form of a question should end in a question mark. (Online advertisers sometimes use pipes [|] as punctuation in ad headlines.)

- Similar to a double title, a headline that contains a colon is called a *double headline*. For instance, a Yahoo Sports article titled "Aaron Hernandez trial: Fiancée shows her loyalty with a new last name" is a double headline. This article details how now-deceased NFL star Aaron Hernandez, who was convicted of murder and was already in prison serving a life sentence, now faced two more murder charges. Furthermore, his fiancée, who remained with Hernandez after his conviction, took the stand with an additional surname: Shayanna Jenkins-Hernandez.
- When introducing a "how-to" or service piece, consider using "how to" in the headline. For example, "How to apply sunscreen" could be the headline for an article describing best practices when applying sun protection.
- Headlines can include the following words: *your, best, worst, future, secret, new, will, how, why, discover, announcing, now, results,* and *top*.
- Avoid negatives in headlines. For instance, prefer the word "fat-free" to "contains no fat."
- Readers like numbers; thus, a headline with numbers can draw a reader in. For instance, "10 ways to identify health scams" hints at a list, and readers like lists. In fact, articles that have a body that takes the form of a list are called listicles. Listicles are so popular among online readers that certain online publications, such as Listverse, have leveraged this trend.

Headlines are often followed by decks. The *deck* refers to a short article summary that follows the headline. The deck is one or more lines of text that is placed between the headline and body of the article. *The Wall Street Journal* is famous for its use of decks.

Every year ACES: The Society for Editing sponsors a contest to choose the best headlines among the nation's top print and digital publications. Let's take a look at two winners from 2015.

HEADLINE: They feed their lust, then bite the dust

DECK: It's afterlife instead of afterglow for males of rare marsupial species

This article from the *Dallas Morning News* describes how a small mammal called the antechinus becomes so stressed out after nonstop mating that it dies.

HEADLINE: Egg prices soar as disease ravages hen populaton

DECK: Get ready to shell our more

This headline was printed in the *Star-Ledger.*

PART VI: ONLINE PUBLICATION

60.
Header Tags
Titles, Subtitles, and Subheads

TIP: Header tags boost SEO value.

Key Points

- Header (heading) tags are arranged in a top-down hierarchy from <h1> to <h6>.
- Headlines and titles are displayed using <h1> tags.
- Subtitles are displayed using <h2> tags.
- Headings are displayed using <h3> tags.
- In terms of search-engine optimization (SEO) value, <h1> and <h2> tags carry the most weight.
- It's best to place keywords as close to the beginning of a heading tag as possible

With respect to online publication, titles, subtitles, and headings (headers) serve three purposes:

- They improve user experience and provide information for the reader.
- They engage the reader.
- They boost the search-engine optimization (SEO) value of a website, blog posting, or article.

Search engines, such as Google, use web crawlers and indexing programs to analyze the content of a page and figure out how these pages link together. When analyzing a web page, these software programs are most interested in the HTML text for the page.

According to *The Art of SEO: Mastering Search Engine Optimization,* HTML (Hypertext Markup Language) is defined as follows:

> The main markup language for the creation of web pages, used to mark up web content and display it in a formatted manner. HTML defines how data is structured and informs the web browser how the page is to be displayed. It's up to the web browser software (e.g., Microsoft Internet Explorer or Mozilla Firefox) to render the HTML source.

Although not mentioned in the preceding definition, Google Chrome is currently the most popular web browser.

Technically, HTML is not a programming language and is instead a subset of SGML (Standard Generalized Markup Language). It's static in nature and codes for page titles, paragraphs, lines, lists, phrases, colors, character data, and so forth. If interested in looking at the HTML source code for any web page, you can choose to view the source code onscreen.

Harnessing the power of HTML will help boost whatever online content that you're creating. Remember that SEO is defined as efforts to maximize exposure for a website and increasing the number of visitors by achieving a high rank on a (Google's) search engine results page (SERP).

The CSS (Cascade Styling Sheets) complements HTML; CSS is a mechanism that enables publishers to control the layout and design of a website, including background and visual effects. Notably, CSS has no SEO value.

In sum, by making the best use of HTML heading tags for titles, subtitles, and headings, you can boost the SEO value of a website or online article and attract more readers by having your online content place more prominently in search engine results.

Heading tags are arranged in a top-down hierarchy from <h1> to <h6>, with <h1> tags displaying the largest font size and <h6> tags displaying the smallest. The headline of a page or title of an article or blog posting is marked using an <h1> tag, a subtitle is marked using an <h2> tag, and subheads get <h3> tags. Google, which is the big player in search, probably cares most about <h1> and <h2> tags. (I write "probably" because Google is reticent about how it performs search. Most of what we know about how Google does search is based on limited information provided by the company itself.)

If you're using WordPress or other user-friendly content management systems, you typically don't have to worry about manipulating source code. Instead, I present this information about <h1> to <h6> tags to explain the importance of titles, subtitles, and headings in terms of SEO.

When coming up with titles, subtitles, and headings, keywords should be at the forefront of your mind. It's best to place these keywords as close to the beginning of the tag as possible. For example, British singer-songwriter Adele is known for her playful onstage presence. If you were writing about some of her funniest onstage antics, such as twerking in a 2016 concert in

London, her name should be written first in the title. As is the case with any proper noun, Adele is the main keyword in any search for her.

Title: <hl>Adele's Cheekiest Onstage Moments</hl>

Of note, when publishing to the Internet, titles are usually written in title case.

The key term *Adele* should also be placed at the beginning of the subtitle.

Subtitle: <h2>Adele tells dirty jokes, cusses, and twerks onstage</h2>

When subtitles are formed as sentences, they can be written in sentence case (with no period at the end).

Now, a subhead may detail one of these cheeky moments. Perhaps when she swore an estimated 33 times while performing at the Glastonbury Festival. She joked that the BBC had to warn her about her "potty mouth" before performing.

Subhead: <h3>Adele's Potty Mouth</h3>

In addition to using key terms in titles and subtitles, you want to keep these titles and subtitles descriptive, short, and simple (fewer than 70 characters). Other headings should be short and simple, too. For more general guidance on titles, subtitles, and headings, please see the relevant portions of this book.

61. Keywords

Tip: Keywords boost SEO when used judiciously.

Key Points

- Two types of keywords are *head terms* and *long-tail keywords.*
- Long-tail keywords represent a special opportunity for content developers.
- Keywords can be placed in titles, headings, the first paragraph of an article, or in the anchor text of links.

It's the dream of every publisher of online content to rise to the top of Google's search engine results page (SERP). (Google dominates search and controls a majority search-engine market share.) To ascend to the top of organic search engine results, search engine optimization (SEO) is needed. According to SEO-software developer Moz, "Search engine optimization (SEO) is the practice of increasing the quantity and quality of traffic to your website through organic search engine results." Of note, organic search results are search results that are not paid for.

Search Terms and Keywords

Search begins with a *search query.* In an ideal world, exact keywords would be typed into a search engine to generate SERP. In reality, however, search queries or search terms that are typed into the search box usually only approximate the meaning of keywords.

According to Google: "Understanding the meaning of your search is crucial to returning good answers. So to find pages with relevant information, our first step is to analyze what the words in your search query mean. We build language models to try to decipher what strings of words we should look up in the index. This involves steps as seemingly simple as interpreting spelling mistakes, and extends to trying to understand the type of query you've entered by applying some of the latest research on natural language understanding.... We also try to understand what category of information you are looking for. Is it a very specific search or a broad query?"

Based on the search terms entered, Google checks its cyclopean index of webpages for relevant keywords. Thus, the appropriate use of keywords is a valuable component of SEO.

Head Terms vs. Long-Tail Keywords

Two types of keywords exist. Head keywords, or *head terms,* are popular keywords with high search volumes (greater than 50,000 searches a month). *Long-tail keywords* are more specific and are searched for far less (between 500 and 5,000 times a month). Typically, head terms contain fewer words and long-tail keywords contain more words.

Let's imagine that you were writing an article about protein shakes. Here are head keywords generated by Google for the search term "protein shake":

- best protein shake
- protein powder
- protein shake powder
- protein shakes
- whey protein shake

Now, here are some long-tail keywords:

- protein shakes for muscle gain
- homemade protein shakes
- protein shakes recipes for weight loss
- peanut butter protein shake

It's really hard to ascend SERP with a head term—the competition is fierce. However, long-tail keywords offer more tangible opportunities to rise to the top of search. Whereas a listicle detailing the five best protein shakes will probably get buried in search results, a limpid article on homemade peanut butter protein shakes could garner a top spot.

On a historical note, in 2006, Chris Anderson wrote a *New York Times* best seller titled *The Long Tail: Why the Future of Business Is Selling Less of More.* In the book, Anderson explains that, when taken together, products in low demand can sum to a substantial market share. According to Anderson, the secrets to a thriving long-tail business are to make everything available and help consumers find all this stuff. This principle was later extended to Internet marketing in the form of long-tail keywords, which cater to niche users.

Where to Stick Keywords

With respect to SEO, here are some particularly important places to stick keywords in web content:

- titles
- headings
- in the first few lines or paragraph
- anchor text of links

It's best to use keywords judiciously, in a fashion that flows with the content. Using too many keywords results in *keyword stuffing*. Keyword stuffing is penalized by Google search.

Google can still recognize articles or other types of web content that don't use keywords that exactly match search queries. Google has evolved, and now it can guess a user's intent and curate articles accordingly by utilizing *semantic SEO*. Thus, although you should always endeavor to use keywords and phrases that accurately reflect user queries, you shouldn't feel compelled to stick in keywords when doing so sounds forced. Remember that Google can still do a good job at inferring meaning.

Google Trends is a good place to search for relevant keywords to include in and link from in your content. Here is how the Google News Lab describes Google Trends:

"Trends data is an unbiased sample of our Google search data. It's anonymized (no one is personally identified), categorized (determining the topic for a search query) and aggregated (grouped together). This allows us to measure interest in a particular topic across search, from around the globe, right down to city-level geography. You can do it, too—the free data explorer on Google Trends allows you to search for a particular topic on Google or a specific set of search terms. Use the tool and you can see search interest in a topic or search term over time, where it's most-searched, or what else people search for in connection with it."

62. Links

Tip: Linking to outside content can improve your content.

Key Points

- Links to outside sources will help your readers learn more about the topics that you're writing about.
- Links help you curate good content and boost its credibility.
- Outbound links are modestly associated with improved search-engine optimization (SEO).

If you're self-publishing your own content online, links to outside sources are important and serve several purposes.

It's likely that, to a limited extent, external linking to quality content helps optimize whatever content that you're writing. Search engine optimization (SEO) will help your content show up higher on a search engine results page (SERP)—most importantly, in Google SERP.

Historically, there have been two schools of thought on linking to outside content.

The first school of thought is competitive: Outbound links to other competing sites hurt SEO by elevating the competition in search rankings and potentially notifying Google of other, better sites. Furthermore, linking to a competitive site adds no value to one's own site and directs value to a competitor. It's best to keep the "juice" in-house.

The second school of thought is that outbound links to high-quality, authoritative websites boost the authority of a website and add contextual signals to content, which helps Google with search and improves SEO. Moreover, linking to other competitive websites engenders good faith, and competitors can respond in kind. In other words, outbound links encourage inbound links (backlinks) from competitors, and inbound links have special SEO cachet.

Many SEO specialists are in favor of judiciously linking to outside content. In fact, limited data suggest that there is a modest positive correlation between external links on a page and search ranking. In 2016, the marketing firm Reboot published results of a study analyzing whether there was a positive association between outgoing links of a website and rankings in search. Reboots online Managing Director Shai Aharony concludes:

> The main thing to take away from this test is that although we don't know and have not proved how powerful outgoing links are in the grand scheme of things, we have proved they do have a positive impact if used correctly. More importantly, we disproved the old myth of PageRank retention which in my opinion [Reboot Online Managing Director Shai Aharony] has done nothing but harm to the internet as a whole as webmasters try to keep the 'link juice' in house slowly eroding the building blocks of the web.

There are other reasons to link to outside content.

First, links to outside content will help your readers learn more about the topics that you're writing about.

Second, by linking to visual media, such as video or alternative story forms like charts and infographics, you provide you readers with a richer experience.

Third, links help you curate good content and boost the credibility of what you're writing.

Fourth, links can limit liability and help curb the risk of copyright infringement by leading to the source material that you're quoting or talking about.

Here are some tips on choosing anchor text to link to outside content.

- Choose anchor text that logically flows into the link.
- Link descriptive keywords to content that also uses these keywords.

- Link to reputable outside content on high-quality websites.
- Link to primary sources such as journal articles.
- Choose to open your link in a new window.
- Provide a link at least every 200 words.
- Never link a whole sentence or long string of words. Make sure that a link doesn't contain anchor text that "wraps" to a second line of text.
- Avoid using italics, boldface, commas, or periods in anchored text.

What are some examples of high-quality websites? If you are reporting about medicine, for instance, you could link to content at the National Institute of Health (NIH) or the Centers for Disease Control (CDC). Often, U.S. government (.gov) and university (.edu) websites are reputable. Furthermore, large nonprofit organizations (.org), including the March of Dimes or American Cancer Society, are also good sites to link certain medical content.

Certain anchor text is perfect for linking and the flow is absolutely logical. For example, imagine you were writing about delayed gratification and cite the "hot-and-cool" system, which is a framework proposed by psychologists Walter Mischel and Janet Metcalfe to explain why willpower succeeds or fails in humans. If you want to link back to the original 1999 article explaining this hypothesized framework, you could choose the anchor text "hot-and-cool system" and link back to the DOI of the original article: http://dx.doi.org/10.1037/0033–295X.106.1.3. Importantly, the DOI or Digital Object Identifier is a persistent and unique digital identifier for a published article or study. Because the DOI never changes, if available, it's the best link for a published digital object.

In case you're interested, the hot-and-cool system of delayed gratification is rooted in Mischel's famous "Marshmallow Test," a "replication-crisis" study involving marshmallows, preschoolers, and delayed gratification. The results of these experiments were originally published in 1972. According to the American Psychological Association, "If this framework were a cartoon, the cool system would be the angel on your shoulder and the hot system, the devil."

It's always best to link to primary sources whenever possible, such as peer-reviewed journal articles and statistical data. When writing original web content, you should limit your links to secondary sources—such as articles found on news sites—to a minimum.

Curtail linking to other content that you've written, and only do so when the content is absolutely relevant. Google will penalize content that contains unrelated or promotional links—especially if these links are directed back toward your website, blog, or so forth.

63.
Meta Descriptions

TIP: Write meta descriptions with the reader in mind.

Key Points

- Because meta descriptions have no search-engine optimization (SEO) value, they should always be written with only the reader in mind.
- Meta descriptions are short descriptions, which should run about 20 words (fewer than 160 characters).
- Don't stuff meta descriptions with keywords.

Metadata are data used to describe other data. With respect to websites, metadata provide information about the page that is not actually written on the page. Instead, *meta descriptions* are summaries pulled by search engines while curating information about the webpage on which an article, blog posting, or so forth is published. These summaries are displayed under blue links on the search engine results page (SERP).

Because meta descriptions have no search-engine optimization (SEO) value, they should always be written with the reader in mind. Although it's a good idea to list some keywords in the meta description, there's no need to list the keyword first in these descriptions. All these descriptions do is provide information to the reader. A useful tip about writing meta descriptions: Write these descriptions as you would write out the angle for an article or other document. Meta descriptions are similar to angles.

Meta descriptions are short descriptions that should run about 20 words (fewer than 160 characters). Let's imagine, for instance, we were writing an article about the unusual number of prominent celebrity musicians who died in 2016. The meta description may read as follows.

What a tragic and troubling year for music fans everywhere! David Bowie, Prince, and George Michael all died in 2016.

Tags are HTML-speak for hidden instructions used by the web browser to format and display content. In HTML, the meta description would be written using the following tags:

```
<head>
<meta name = “description” content = “What a tragic and troubling
    year for music fans everywhere! David Bowie, Prince, and George
    Michael all died in 2016.”>
</head>
```

When publishing online, you typically don’t have to worry about code. Meta descriptions can be added to a WordPress blog using plugins such as Yoast SEO. Moreover, content management systems (CMSs) have fields that can be populated with meta descriptions.

In addition to meta descriptions, *meta keywords* also provide information about the website. However, because meta keywords were exploited early on—a black-hat SEO practice called *keyword stuffing*—they are of no SEO importance now. You can forget about them altogether, and if the content management system that you’re using asks you for them, you can leave these fields blank. Put another way, there’s no need to populate fields asking for meta keywords.

In recent years, Google has rolled out algorithm changes (including Google Panda, Google Penguin, and various updates) to help improve user experience and display high-quality sites higher in search results. The exact details of these algorithm changes are proprietary, and—as with any company—it’s not incumbent on Google to be completely transparent in its business practices and strategies. We do know that it’s getting much harder to game Google search results and manipulate an outcome—something content farms did ad lib in the years before the algorithm changes. Gone are the days of keyword stuffing, meta tag stuffing, duplicate content, unnatural backlinks, spamdexing, and other black-hat SEO practices. On a final note, whereas black-hat SEO practices are aggressive techniques and strategies that focus on manipulating search engine results and defying rules and regulations, white-hat SEO practices are geared toward the human user and follow the rules and guidelines of a search engine.

---

64. Photos

Tip: Photos make online content more engaging.

Key Points

- Most online readers are scanners and skip around to photos and other engaging visual elements, which are enticing. Photos help draw a reader in.
- A picture should have only one clear message.
- In almost all cases, horizontal—as opposed to vertical—pictures are best.
- Make sure that you have purchased rights to any royalty-free images that you plan to use.

The EyeTrack Studies done by the Poynter Institute, a journalism think tank, examined how readers interact with digital media and how people read and absorb news. Here are some findings:

- On average, online readers complete 77 percent of any story that they choose to read. Whereas, readers of print media complete 63 percent of any story that they choose to read.
- Whereas, the majority of readers of print media are methodical and systematic in their approach to reading content, the majority of online readers tend to scan and skip around—jumping from headlines to photos to headers and paragraphs. Moreover, online readers are drawn to alternative story forms, such as fact boxes, charticles, and timelines.
- After about 78 seconds, an online reader will decide to keep on reading an article or stop altogether (referred to as the bailout point).

Taken together, this research is encouraging for those of us who write online articles and content. These results indicate that online readers are even more engaged by online content than print content (broadsheets and tabloids). However, online readers tend to scan and skip around looking for pieces of highest interest, and if they aren't intrigued after about a minute, they'll bail out and stop reading.

To keep readers interested, the folks at Poynter suggest that writers incorporate into their stories *gold coins* that maintain reader interest. These gold coins often take the form of appealing photos or graphics.

After you've written your article, blog posting, or other online document, it's a good idea to find intriguing photos to complement your piece. You may also want to place photos throughout your piece to keep the reader interested. These pictures can serve as gold coins, which punctuate your prose. After all, nobody wants to read several straight paragraphs of prose without visual relief. And because online readers are typically scanners, they'll skip ahead and be daunted or discouraged by lines and lines of unbroken body copy.

Broadly, photographs can be evaluated using three factors: technical quality, composition, and message.

Here are some general tips to consider when choosing appropriate photos to complement your online work:

- Pick images that are vivid, colorful, and bright.
- Pick images in which the subject and other important parts are in focus.
- Pick images that are topical and illustrate the story that you are telling. Make sure that each photograph has only one clear message.
- Pick images that demonstrate strong *composition*. Composition refers to the arrangement of visual elements, either people or objects, in a picture. This arrangement should be balanced and visually pleasing. To achieve strong and simple composition, for instance, the principal subject can fill most of the picture.
- Consider choosing images that are inspirational, authentic, relatable, warm, and colorful.
- Consider choosing images that show point of view, or the vantage at which somebody or something is observed.
- Make sure that the photo has one center of interest. For instance, if you're using a photo of a woman breastfeeding, and breastfeeding is the topic of the corresponding article, you don't want a cat playing with a curtain in the background.
- Action should move into the screen or page and not out of it. For instance, a dancer should be facing (dancing) into the computer screen and not out of it.
- Prefer images with natural light. Make sure the photos that you use have proper exposure (aren't over- or underexposed).
- Consider choosing images with pleasing shapes and patterns. Also, prefer photos with strong lines, triangles, diagonals, S-shapes, and curves to achieve simple and notable composition.
- Choose photos in which people are doing something and engaged in an activity. For example, a picture of a fireman fighting a fire is more engaging than a picture of a fireman sitting around the station waiting for a call.
- Choose photos in which important details are clear. For instance, if including a photo of a specific individual, make sure the individual's face is clearly recognizable. Remember that readers like images of people where the faces are large enough that expressions can be recognized.

- Typically, try to avoid using ID photos, passport photos, and mug shots. (A mug shot is useful when a story is about crime.)
- In small group photos, all faces and expressions should be recognizable (no more than five people).
- When showing a group of objects, limit the number to no more than five so that the details are recognizable. For instance, a photo of five flowering shrubs will likely still demonstrate details of the flowers; whereas, a picture of 20 flowering shrubs will fail to show as much detail.
- If you want to show a crowd, consider a very large crowd with thousands of people to reinforce the message and look impressive. Similarly, depending on the message, you could show thousands of animals in migrations, hundreds of cars on a lot, or so forth.
- Choose pictures that represent diversity of race, age, sex, and gender.
- Make sure that the message of the image is easy to understand, and the subjects are identifiable.
- Make sure that the details included in the photo are relevant and don't clutter an image. For instance, an action shot of a lumberjack wielding a felling axe or electric chainsaw is a relevant detail if you're writing about the logging industry. However, a lumberjack standing in front of a display of potato chips at a convenience store is an irrelevant detail.
- Choose pictures that display enough contrast between the subject and background, as well as the background and the web page. For instance, a white background will bleed into a white web page.
- Avoid photos with text that is already superimposed.
- Avoid photos that are too busy and distract the reader.
- Avoid unrealistic images. Choose images that are true to life.
- Compare the photo that you use with photos that other authors and editors have used when writing similar articles or when writing for similar publications.
- With an inanimate object, such as a car or a bed, the image probably looks best when it's centered. But images of people often look more dynamic and interesting when the subject is slightly off-center. In art and film, artists use the "rule of thirds" when setting up compositions that are off-center yet visually pleasing. (Google the "rule of thirds" for more on this topic.)
- The shape of the picture should fit the shape of the subject. Empty space is wasted space.
- Limit the space between people, which can end up looking like dead space and occupying the middle of the photo. One reason why professional photographers encourage people to get close

together is that any space between people appears larger in a photo.

- With landscape photos, consider adding some foreground elements to give the background depth.
- Try to keep both sides as well as the top and bottom of a picture balanced. One side shouldn't be busy with the other side barren.
- When using your own photos, consider cropping the pictures in Photoshop to remove empty space, remove distracting details, add emphasis, or otherwise improve composition. Photoshop can also be used "straighten" a picture out.
- Make sure that the photo that you use has a pleasing shape. In most instances, prefer horizontal to vertical photos.
- Rectangular photos are more pleasing than square photos. Rectangular photos should not be narrow (taller than they are wide) or shallow (much wider than they are tall).
- The subject of a picture should be centered vertically and far enough away from the camera.

Here are some more technical details regarding photo selection:

- Always pick a maximum-quality JPEG. Good images are between 1500 and 2500 pixels wide.
- Make sure that you have displayed proper credit info. Credit info typically contains the name of the photographer and the name of the royalty-free stock photography provider from which you've purchased rights to the photo. For example, the credit may read "iStock.com/Artist's Member Name" if you're purchasing photos for editorial use from iStock by Getty Images. Typically, whatever photo service that you use will detail how to credit photos for editorial use in the section of the website containing frequently asked questions (FAQs).
- When naming an image, provide a descriptive image file name and descriptive alt text ("alt tag"). The file name is displayed once you roll over the image. The descriptive alt text is embedded in the HTML of the website and is read by screen readers for the benefit of users with visual impairment. When using a blogging platform or content management system (CMS), you populate fields with this information after uploading the picture that you plan to use. For instance, don't name a picture "image-1" if you're posting a picture of the ballet dancer Misty Copeland. Instead use a descriptive image file name such as "Misty-Copeland." The alt text may read "Misty Copeland performs at the American Ballet Theatre"—without terminal punctuation.

- You should only use alphanumeric text, hyphens, and underscores with file names. Special characters, such as hashtags and brackets, should be avoided.
- Most of the time when using stock photography, you don't need a caption. However, if you do need to use a caption because people won't understand the picture without one, limit the caption to one or two lines at most. Clearly identify and explain what is relevant in the picture. If you are identifying people, provide their names using phrases like "from left to right" or "clockwise from the top." Make sure that a caption is to the point and doesn't explain any unnecessary details.

Please make sure that you have purchased rights to any royalty-free pictures that you plan to use. Remember that using photos without permission is piracy, a form of theft. When using pictures in an article or blog posting, you should purchase royalty-free pictures for editorial use. (You don't need extended use for editorial work. Extended use is commercial.) The prices of pictures and plans vary. Examples of photo sites that sell royalty-free photos are 123RF, Shutterstock, Adobe Stock, and iStock.

If you don't want to purchase pictures, there are some places you can score images for free, including the New York Public Library Digital Collections and the Met Museum Art Collection. Furthermore, you can find some images that are free to use on Wikimedia Commons and Google. However, always check for the following when looking for free images:

- usage rights
- licensing conditions
- creative commons license
- whether the photo can be modified
- how the photo should be attributed

If an image is open source, it is freely available for use and can be edited or modified.

To be on the safe side, if you're searching Wikimedia Commons or Google and find an image that is watermarked or appears to be a stock photo, it's best to avoid using it for fear of copyright infringement.

Finally depending on your need, if you're writing for an established publication, you can also request media or press kits, which contain promotional photos and information. Press kits are public-relations tools made available for music, television, film, product launches, company launches, mergers, and so forth. For example, if you are writing about entertainment, such as a movie or television, you can request a (link to a) media kit from a studio that includes photos, cast bios, and so forth.

65. Taxonomy

Tip: The taxonomy of a website or blog should be as simple as it can be.

Key Points

- Even if the content on a website is great, if it's poorly organized, your reader will navigate away.
- Categories, subcategories, and tags are taxonomic divisions in WordPress blogs.
- The exercise of card sorting can help you determine a taxonomy for your website or blog.

All websites and blogs have taxonomies or systems of classification. If you're publishing content on your own, it's important to carefully consider the website's topical hierarchy. You want to create a structure and flow that follows this topical hierarchy. Furthermore, a well-organized website with logical relationships and links between subjects contributes to search engine optimization (SEO). Even if the content on a website is great, if it's poorly organized, your reader will navigate to another website and forget your site forever.

On a related note, *bounce rate* refers to the percentage of users who navigate away from a site after viewing only one page. Google Analytics expert Avinash Kaushik famously defined bounce rate as "I came, I puked, I left." The lower the bounce rate, the better. Ideally, the bounce rate of a site should be under 40 percent, with bounce rates around 50 percent being average.

WordPress is the biggest content management system (CMS) online, and most blogs are hosted on WordPress. Moreover, WordPress hosts many big-brand websites, including those of BBC America, the New Yorker, and TechCrunch. In WordPress, categories, subcategories, and tags comprise taxonomy.

Categories are like the chapters listed in a book's table of contents. Categories help the user figure out what the website or blog is about. For instance, a category can comprise a larger group of blog postings or articles.

Categories can be further divided into subcategories. *Subcategories* are like sections in a chapter.

Tags are the most granular taxonomic division. Tags describe specific details of your website or blog and are like index words in a book. Tags are similar to keywords in that they're short and descriptive. However, tags usually carry little weight in terms of SEO.

The taxonomy of a website or blog should be as simple as it can be. Although there is no "right" number of categories, subcategories, and tags, it's best to limit the number of top-level categories that you create and instead use subcategories and tags to further classify your content. The categories that you create should have lasting value and set up a more static framework for your website or blog. Moreover, categories, subcategories, and tags should reflect reader *ontology*. Oxford dictionaries define ontology as follows: "A set of concepts and categories in a subject area or domain that shows their properties and the relations between them." In other terms, the categories, subcategories, and tags that you create to organize content on a blog or website should lay out logical relationships for your readers.

Let's imagine that you're a fitness coach and have decided to create a WordPress blog about various sports and fitness activities that you believe are fun and can help people get in shape. We'll call this blog *Fitness Fun*. Here are some potential top-level categories that serve primarily to organize your content:

Categories for Fitness Fun
Swimming
Aerobics
Martial Arts
Yoga
Cycling

We can further divide these categories into subcategories related to specific fields of interest. For example, the category martial arts may be subcategorized as follows:

Boxing
Kickboxing
Tae kwon do
Jiujitsu

Now, if you were to develop content specifically relating to one of these subcategories, you could use tags to help identify this content for a reader. For instance, perhaps you're writing about different belt tests for tae kwon do beginners, you might tag this content with descriptors, such as *white belt*, *yellow belt*, and *orange belt*.

With respect to the content that you create, taxonomy is more of an existential concern. If you're writing for a big publication, you won't have to worry about taxonomy at all—these issues are handled by the publisher. However, when publishing your own content—as with a WordPress blog—organization is something that you always have to think about.

When developing taxonomy for your website or blog, one useful tool is *card sorting*. With card sorting, you write down all the categories and subcategories that you plan to use on separate index cards. You then ask some friends or acquaintances to organize these cards in an order that makes sense. You can also ask them whether the terms that you use make sense or sound obscure or confusing, thus checking for intended meaning. In addition to your own sensibility, others can help you develop logical flow. Taken together, this information can help you with site taxonomy.

Part VII: Global Considerations

66. Angles and Hooks

Tip: With every nonfiction document that you write, be able to articulate the angle and the hook.

Key Points

- The *angle* is the emphasis of an article or—by extension—the document.
- The *hook* refers to the appeal of an article or—by extension—the document.

Journalism exists as a domain separate from the rest of nonfiction. However, journalism draws on many of the principles of general prose and academic writing. In kind, certain principles that guide journalism can be applied to the creation of not only writing for general audiences and academic writing but also other types of documents, such as business communications, grants, website content, and electronic communications.

Angle

In journalism, the *angle* is the emphasis of the article. The angle holds the piece together, and data, research, quotation support, and expert input are used to support the angle and flesh out the article.

For instance, if you were writing a service piece on phishing, which is defined by *Merriam-Webster* as "a scam by which an e-mail user is duped into revealing personal or confidential information which the scammer can use illicitly," the angle of the piece may focus on how easy it is for anyone—not just the gullible—to get scammed by phishers.

Hook

In journalism, the *hook* is what makes the article interesting and newsworthy. It's what draws a reader in. The hook is kind of like an article's gimmick. On a related note, hooks (and angles) can serve as inspirations for titles, as well as headings. Remember that hooks draw readers in.

Many articles posted on news sites and printed in magazines and newspapers follow *trends*. The hooks—and angles—of these articles leverage these trends. Trends are defined as quantifiable changes in social, economic, scientific, or popular phenomenon. Trends usually begin as observations or individual anecdotes and are later tracked. Fads are different from trends because they don't have staying power.

During the holiday season of 2016, for instance, Hatchimals, a type of plush toy that hatches from an egg was a fad, which followed the more general trend of "it" toys that make their way to market every holiday season. These "it" toys become so coveted that parents go to great personal and financial lengths to procure them.

With regard to the proposed piece on phishing, phishing follows the more general trend of virtual identity theft that has become a big problem in the Digital Age.

Here are some other examples of trends:

- cloud computing
- genital cosmetic surgery
- home brewing
- Internet memes
- Internet of Things (IoT)
- selfies
- transportation network companies like Uber and Lyft

Examples of Angles and Hooks

To illustrate the more general relevance of an angle, let's look at the "angle" of arguably two of the most important texts in human history: the New Testament and the Quran.

John 3:16 could be considered the "angle" of the Bible, especially for evangelical Christians.

"For God so loved the world, that he gave his only begotten Son, that whosoever believeth in him should not perish, but have everlasting life."

The Quran, which is revered as the word of God by Muslims, also has an "angle." This angle focuses on how the text is infallible, which is of central importance to Muslims. Here's verse 2 from *Surah Al-Baqarah* (The Cow):

"This is the book; in it is guidance sure, without doubt. To those who fear God."

(Chapters of the Quran are referred to as *Surahs.*)

Now, let's look at the angle and hook of a more quotidian document: the business proposal.

Business proposals are used by sellers to attract buyers or investors. The *objectives* section of a business proposal typically presents the "opportunity" and the objectives for addressing this opportunity. The objectives section is akin to the "angle" of a business proposal.

For instance, let's consider a business proposal for a new Laundromat in a small town of 7,000 residents with no other Landromats. The objectives section or "angle" of the proposal may emphasize to investors the opportunity to open a Laundromat in a small town with no other competition.

The *benefits* section of a business proposal can be considered its "hook." The benefits section explains the return on investment to a potential investor. In the case of the Laundromat, the benefits section or hook may project exactly how much money investors could expect to make in return for a requested investment.

During the self-editing phase, carefully consider whether the document that you're preparing has an angle and a hook. Can you articulate the angle, or emphasis, in one or two sentences? Can you clearly identify the hook, or appeal, to the reader? If you're having trouble conveying either the angle or the hook, then you need to carefully consider your approach to the document, its organization, and its wording.

67. Audience

TIP: Write for your audience.

Key Points

- Your audience has expectations.
- Always be thinking about your audience.

- Generalizations can yield insights about your audience.
- If interested—and entrepreneurial—you can always create your own audience.

Who has an audience? An entertainer has an audience.

Many writers pay little heed to the fact that like musicians, actors, and dancers, they, too, are entertainers. There's some entertainment value in even the most formal of documents. For instance, the entertainment value of a research paper may be its astuteness as expressed in the discussion section.

When writing for a general audience, the entertainment value is pronounced. Whether it's the tempo of the prose or vividness of the imagery and examples, the writer has plenty of tools to entertain the audience with. More generally, a writer's voice tends to entertain the audience.

William Zinsser, a writer, editor, critic and instructor of much acclaim, devoted a chapter of his book *On Writing Well* to "The Audience."

Here's what he advises:

"'Who am I writing for?' It's a fundamental question, and it has a fundamental answer: You are writing for yourself. Don't try to visualize the great mass audience. There is no such audience—every reader is a different person. Don't try to guess what sort of thing editors want to publish or what you think the country is in a mood to read. Editors and readers don't know what they want to read until they read it. Besides, they're always looking for something new."

Unless you're writing for yourself and are satisfied with the possible prospect of being an audience of one, I respectfully disagree with this idea for many reasons.

First, you write for your audience foremost. Your audience has expectations. When a reader clicks on article from *The Onion*, they expect to laugh. If somebody surfs on over to CNN's website, they expect real news, not fake news that aims to mislead and misinform. If you're reading this book, then you want to learn how to self-edit your work so that it's ready for publication. Writers fulfill such expectations to the best of their ability.

Second, although no two people are the same, audience members do share commonalities. For example, you can expect a general audience member to know who Arnold Schwarzenegger is. But how about *Le Pétomane*, a professional flatulist (farter) who entertained French audiences around the beginning of the twentieth century. Save for some French people and Francophiles, should I ever mention *Le Pétomane* (real name Joseph Pujol), I need to explain who he is.

Third, guessing at what the reader or your editor—who serves as a proxy for reader interest—wants to read is *exactly* what you should be doing. A common complaint among writers who have failed in their attempts at pitching a publication or create a following for their online writing is that they were somehow screwed.... The reader, editor, or world doesn't *understand* them. In fact, more often than not these "screwed" writers have failed to understand the intended audience. Even the most well-crafted pitch or article will not succeed if it fails to appeal or engage the appropriate audience.

Keep in mind that editors depend on writers to spot *trends*. A trend is a measurable change (either increase or decrease) in a social, an economic, or a scientific phenomenon. Unlike a fad, which is short-lived—think fidget spinners or leisure suits—a trend has staying power and can endure. Examples of trends include reality television, cancer immunotherapy, and house flipping. Such topics have been covered extensively because people want to read about this stuff.

To be fair, William Zinsser was a luminary, and lots of his advice is evergreen and spot on. Furthermore, he recommends that all writers master the craft and style of writing in the interest of the reader. However, times have changed and technology has made media consumption increasingly fragmented. Present-day professional writers face the realities of trend analysis, search-engine optimization (SEO), and bespoke content, which is content created on behalf of a client. Now more than ever, we should first be writing for the audience and second for ourselves. Good writers are typically gratified when the audience is satisfied.

Identifying Your Audience

While writing, you should always be thinking about your audience. While self-editing, you should always be thinking about your audience. Never forget your audience. You should revise your writing with audience in mind. Moreover, the concept of audience also touches on more global concerns such as tone and style.

Here are some questions to ask yourself about your audience:

- Who will read your document? Is this document intended for a general or specialist audience?
- How much background information does your reader already know about the topic?
- Will the reader scan the document or read it carefully? Will the reader skip to certain sections?
- Is the document intended for one-time use, lifelong reference, or something in-between?
- What will this document do for your reader? What is your reader interested in?

- Why will the reader want to read your document?
- What will help your reader?
- What will surprise your reader?
- What will your reader be excited to share with friends?
- What coherences need to be presented to your reader to give an authoritative understanding? (In the field of journalism, *coherences* are options that provide the reader with a full picture.)
- What is the reader's main concern when reading your document?
- How many different audiences, or groups of readers, do you plan to appeal to? Are you writing for a general audience, a specialist audience, or both?
- How do other authors write for this audience? If you're writing an article for a publication, how does your document compare with others?
- What are some demographics of your audience?

Here is some advice concerning audience from science editor and educator Barbara Gastel. This passage is excerpted from a 2015 article published in the *AMWA Journal* titled "Editing and Proofreading Your Own Work."

"[C]onsider suitability for the *audience*. Is a journal article for generalists or specialists? Will a proposal be reviewed by scientists or by a community board? What do prospective readers of a brochure know and care about? What about the native language(s) of the readers? Consider whether to modify aspects of the text to suit your audience. Also consider whether any content should be revised accordingly."

Generalizations

In life, it's never a good idea to stereotype. A stereotype is an unfair belief about a group of people based on neither evidence nor personal experience.

But to survive, sometimes we need to make *generalizations*. Generalizations are made based on our past experiences or previous observations; they're general conclusions. For example, if you see—and hear—a rattlesnake in your backyard, for instance, and you've never seen one before, you probably won't pet it. You know based on a small amount of information that you've acquired during the course of a lifetime that rattlesnakes are deadly.

When identifying your audience, generalizations can be helpful. Big publications endeavor to know the demographics of their readership, including age, gender, location, and income. Furthermore, Google has made it easy to assess demographics and user interests using tools like Google Analytics. Demographic information, analytics, focus groups, and more help big publications make generalizations about what their readers want.

Writers often need to make good-natured and common-sense generalizations about the audience to succeed. These generalizations are not discriminatory; they're based on experience and insight. They help the writer assess and cater to the reader. Here are some generalizations to think about when writing for specific audiences:

- Engineers are comfortable with diagrams and blueprints.
- Accountants understand tables of financial figures.
- Human resource managers like photos of people.
- Scientists appreciate charts, graphs, and figures.
- Librarians are prolific readers.
- Physicians have an encyclopedic knowledge of medical terms.

Please keep in mind that these generalizations don't apply to everyone. But based on our shared understanding and experiences, they seem to make sense. If anything, they can provide food for thought when thinking about your audience.

Assessing your audience can be an exercise in expediency. Put another way, you'll need to pull out all the stops when there may be a paucity of information regarding your reader, even if that means sometimes thinking in generalized terms.

Creating Your Own Audience

As was initially mentioned, if you're writing by yourself and willing to take the risk of being your only reader or, more realistically, catering to a smaller audience, you can write without an audience in mind. You can *create* your own audience. There is an entrepreneurial side of writing that has paid handsomely for those who have been typically well prepared … and lucky.

These successful entrepreneurs tap into what rhetorician Edwin Black calls the *second persona*. Instead of presenting to an existing audience, the entrepreneur creates an audience. We've seen this second persona manifest as a substantial far-right or alt-right readership, which was originally exploited by Internet publishers like Andrew Breitbart. His early roasting of liberal figures set the foundation for the ultraconservative Breitbart News we know today.

Breitbart serves a massive audience of alt-right readers that is composed of younger white nationalists, white supremacists, extreme libertarians, and neo–Nazis. Many of these younger white nationalists extol white identity and decry their perceived attrition of white political and economic power. They also fear for the fate of white culture as a result of factors including immigration and multiculturalism.

Breitbart is widely regarded as a racist, misogynist, and xenophobic publication.

According to a 2017 study in the *Columbia Journalism Review*, Benkler and co-authors write that Breitbart is the "center of a distinct right-wing media ecosystem, surrounded by Fox News, the Daily Caller, the Gateway Pundit, the Washington Examiner, Infowars, Conservative Treehouse, and Truthfeed."

Another, less divisive, entrepreneurial venture that has found its own audience is *Scary Mommy,* which grew from an online chronicle of founder and stay-at-home mother Jill Smokler's kids to a parenting-multimedia empire with millions of readers.

68. Hedging

Tip: Hedge words help when writing about science.

Key Points

- In most contexts, it's best to be specific and concrete with your words.
- Because few things are absolutely certain in science, it often benefits the careful writer to hedge and use somewhat evasive or insecure language when writing about science.

As stated in *The Elements of Style,* "The surest way to arouse and hold the reader's attention is by being specific, definite, and concrete."

When you write, you want to get to point efficiently, You don't want to write in circles. After all, the shortest distance between two points is a straight line, and the most meaningful distance between two ideas is a modicum of words.

Example: I know that I observed the boy remove a candy bar from the retail establishment without explicit permission.

Better: I saw the boy steal a candy bar from the store.

Strunk and White also call out auxiliaries and conditionals as constructions that represent evasive and insecure language.

EXAMPLE: Sheila would be considered one of the highest-achieving students in her class.

BETTER: Sheila is a top student in her class.

When writing about science, however, it's often a good idea to hedge, or qualify statements using guarded language. In science, it's nearly impossible to prove something conclusively, and in the words of Strunk and White, science entails "real uncertainty." It takes only one exception to undermine either an *axiom* (an established rule, principle, or proposition) or a *theory* (a well-substantiated unifying explanation). Keep in mind that findings in science are usually probabilistic not binary.

In 1686, for instance, Sir Isaac Newton debuted his laws of motion as axioms, or truths. These laws were deterministic: Based on the exact positions and velocities of all particles at any given time, it's possible to calculate the positions and velocities of these particles at another point in time (either past or future).

Newton's laws worked well for a couple of hundred years and did a good job of explaining the positions and velocities of everyday objects like falling apples. (Newtonian mechanics even got us to the moon.) By the late nineteenth century, however, scientists observed that Newton's laws didn't describe the motion of subatomic particles. Thus, scientists needed a new general theory: quantum mechanics. Quantum mechanics requires us to abandon the idea that the trajectories of particles are precisely defined as traveling through time and space.

In a 2005 article published in *Physics Education*, Ogborn and Taylor write that "Newton was obliged to give his laws of motion as fundamental axioms. But today we know that the quantum world is fundamental, and Newton's laws can be seen as consequences of fundamental quantum laws."

The paradigm shift that occurred between Newton's discoveries and the elucidation of quantum mechanics is one example of how science is always evolving. For good measure, let's take a look at another major paradigm shift: the cholesterol-diet-CHD hypothesis.

For decades, cardiologists ascribed to the idea that elevated levels of cholesterol in the blood secondary to a diet rich in cholesterol and animal fats led to CHD. In CHD, plaques build up in the coronary arteries, which supply oxygen to the heart. At face value, this hypothesis seemed to make sense, and physicians everywhere were treating people with cholesterol-lowering medications (statins) in the hope of mitigating coronary heart disease. An emerging body of evidence, however, has subverted this thinking. Nowadays, it's unclear whether a diet rich in cholesterol and saturated fats leads to an increase of cholesterol levels in the blood. It's also unclear whether lowering cholesterol levels in the blood prevents most types of heart disease.

Because few things are absolutely certain in science, it often benefits the careful writer to hedge and use somewhat evasive or insecure language when writing about science. For example, results form a double-blind, randomized, placebo-controlled clinical trial, which is the gold standard of clinical research, don't "prove" anything. Instead, these results "suggest" or "indicate" support for certain hypotheses, or possible explanations.

EXAMPLE: Results from clinical trials ~~prove~~ that Drug X is an effective treatment for heart disease.

BETTER: Results from clinical trials *suggest* that Drug X is an effective treatment for heart disease.

On a related note, causal—or cause-and-effect—relationships in science are elusive. Although two variables may be associated, correlated, or linked, proving that one variable causes another requires a different approach.

Recent research indicates, for example, that there are significant disparities in life expectancy among Americans living in different counties throughout the United States. People living in certain communities in California and Colorado tend to live much longer than those who live in places like West Virginia and South Dakota.

This research suggests that there is an association between where a person lives and how long they will live. Physical location, however, doesn't *cause* an extended lifespan. People who live in certain counties in California or Colorado don't live longer because there's something special about the geography in California or Colorado. Instead, residents of communities in these states typically make more money, keep better tabs on their health, exercise more, smoke less, drink less alcohol, and so forth. The careful science writer would never write that living in California or Colorado *causes* longer life spans, but rather that living in these states *is correlated with*, *is associated with*, or *predicts* longer life spans.

When writing about science, the prudent use of core modals can also help the writer hedge against making absolute statements. For instance, if a person were to donate $50 million toward the construction of a library at a university, the library *will* get built. However, that same $50 million earmarked for cancer research *could* result in a breakthrough in cancer treatment. The truth is that you never really know what will happen with science—no matter how much money you throw at it—and this reality is doubly true with a field like cancer research where progress is often fragmented and diffuse.

Ultimately, when writing about science, it's good to consider using the following hedge words:

- associated with (instead of causes)
- could (instead of can)
- may (instead of can)
- hypothesize (instead of theorized)
- linked (instead of caused)
- indicate (instead of prove)
- suggest (instead of prove)

69.
Humanism and Unbiased Language

TIP: Think carefully about how to refer to disability, race, gender, and age.

Key Points

- Strive to write in a humanistic fashion without bias.
- Both the *AMA Manual of Style* and *Publication Manual of the American Psychological Association* are excellent resources with respect to unbiased language.
- Refer to the *GLAAD Media Reference Guide* when writing about sexual orientation and gender.

One definition of *humanism* is devotion to human welfare. As a writer, you should endeavor to write in a humanistic fashion that informs and engages your reader without bias or offense. Always remember that words carry weight and, when used improperly, contribute to bias and stigma.

The American Medical Association (AMA) and the American Psychological Association (APA) offer detailed style guidance on race, sexuality, gender, disease, disability, and age. It would behoove anybody interested in learning about the specifics of humanistic language to consult the *AMA Manual of Style* or the *Publication Manual of the American Psychological Association*. In addition to these printed texts, this information is available on the websites of these organizations. Furthermore, the *GLAAD Media Reference Guide* is available online and "is intended to be used by journalists reporting for mainstream media outlets and by creators in entertainment media who want to tell LGBTQ people's stories fairly and accurately."

Overall, when writing about race, sexuality, gender, disease, and disability, it's a good idea to assess your writing with humanism in mind and revise accordingly.

First, ask yourself whether it's absolutely necessary to refer to gender, race, or so forth. If referring to specific characterizations adds nothing to your description and will likely appear conspicuous and subtly biased, then forego characterization. For instance, if you are quoting a mechanic on the price of brake pads for a story that you're doing on common forms of car maintenance, there's likely no reason to mention this person's race, appearance, or sexuality.

Second, it's always a good idea to prefer specific depictions to general ones. If you were writing about the culture of Guatemala, let's say, it's best to refer to it as Guatemalan culture rather than Hispanic culture. The term Hispanic fails to capture vast differences present among various countries and groups.

Third, avoid labeling people. By labeling an individual, this person loses individuality and is reduced to one characteristic. For instance, calling someone a *paraplegic* implies that this person is chiefly viewed in terms of disability. Instead, in addition to being a person *with paraplegia*, the individual may be a mother, father, daughter, son, teacher, mentor, professional, basketball player, or so forth.

It's beyond the scope of this text to delve into every example of misguided word usage with respect to humanistic language. (Sadly, the media is rife with examples.) Instead, let's examine the principles underlying humanistic style concerns. By understanding the thinking behind the recommendations, you will likely appreciate why we should make certain choices when referring to concepts that need to be treated with empathy, humanism, and sensitivity.

Race and Ethnicity

According to *Merriam-Webster*, race refers to "a category of humankind that shares certain distinctive physical traits." Whereas, ethnicity refers to "a particular ethnic affiliation or group," with ethnic referring to "large groups of people classed according to common racial, national, tribal, religious, linguistic, or cultural origin or background."

Race and ethnicity are cultural constructs, or concepts that humans created to separate people into categories. These characterizations are often monolithic, inaccurate, and flawed. Nevertheless, they can be useful. In medical practice and research, for instance, certain diseases or conditions present more frequently in people belonging to certain races. Prostate cancer is most frequent among blacks, and cystic fibrosis is most common among whites. These distinctions can help with diagnosis so they serve a purpose.

Race and ethnicity can also be a useful construct in the social sciences. For instance, in *Talking Back, Talking Black,* linguist John McWhorter describes the form, structure, and development of Black English, and makes the case that Black English is a legitimate dialect.

Here are some acceptable ways to refer to race and ethnicity:

- White (or white)
- Black (or black)
- African American
- Latino
- Hispanic
- Chicano
- Asian American
- Native American
- American Indian
- First Nations or Inuit people (indigenous peoples of Canada)

As is generally the case when using humanistic language, it's always best to be specific in your choice of racial or ethnic descriptor. For instance, *Japanese American* or *Chinese American* is often preferable to *Asian American.* (Don't use the word *Oriental* to refer to people.)

According to the *AMA Manual of Style,* it's best to avoid hyphenation when referring to race. Furthermore, some experts recommend that certain terms describing racial and ethnic identity be capitalized because they are proper nouns and adjectives and not colors per se. The American Psychological Association (APA) capitalizes *White* and *Black*; whereas, the American Medical Association (AMA) doesn't. Notably, the AMA advises against using *Hispanic* and *Latino* as nouns and recommends that—with certain qualifications—terms like white and black be left in descriptions of study participants who are white or black.

According to the APA, the use of the word *minority* to refer to races and ethnic groups other than White "may be viewed pejoratively because minority is usually equated with being less than, oppressed, and deficient in comparison with the majority (i.e., Whites). Use a modifier (such as ethnic or racial) when using the word minority. When possible, use the actual name of the group or groups to which you are referring."

According to the AMA—but not the APA—it's best to avoid the term *non-white,* which is a nonspecific label of convenience, and prefer *multiracial* instead.

The APA brings up an interesting point regarding balance and race terminology:

"Unparallel designations (e.g., African Americans and Whites; Asian Americans and Black Americans) should be avoided because one group is described by color while the other group is described by cultural heritage."

Sexuality

Sexual orientation should not be referred to as *sexual preference.* Sexual orientation is not a voluntary choice.

According to the AMA, the term *lesbian* can be used as a noun; *gay man* (not *gays*) can also be used as a noun. However, *heterosexual* and *homosexual* should be used only as adjectives. In other words, refer to a *gay man* as a *homosexual man* and not a *homosexual.* Similarly, *bisexual men* and *bisexual women* shouldn't be referred to as *bisexuals.*

A member of a couple, either homosexual or heterosexual, can be referred to as *partner, life partner* or *companion.* Other acceptable terms are *same-sex marriage* and *same-sex couple.*

According to GLAAD, avoid terms like *gay lifestyle, homosexual lifestyle,* and *transgender lifestyle.* Please keep in mind that LGBTQ (lesbian, gay, bisexual, transgender, and queer) people live a variety of different lifestyles. Similarly, there is no such thing as a "straight" lifestyle.

Gender

According to the *AMA Manual of Style:*

"Sex refers to the biological characteristics of males and females. Gender includes more than sex and serves as a cultural indicator of a person's personal and social identity."

Sex is assigned at birth based on the appearance of external anatomy. More generally, a person's sex is based on anatomy, genetics, physiology, and secondary sexual characteristics.

Gender can be further divided into *gender identity* and *gender expression.*

According to GLAAD, the term *gender identity* refers to the following:

"A person's internal, deeply held sense of their gender. For transgender people, their own internal gender identity does not match the sex they were assigned at birth. Most people have a gender identity of man or woman (or boy or girl). For some people, their gender identity does not fit neatly into one of those two choices.... Unlike gender expression ... gender identity is not visible to others."

The term *gender expression* refers to the following:

"External manifestations of gender, expressed through a person's name, pronouns, clothing, haircut, behavior, voice, and/or body characteristics. Society identifies these cues as masculine and feminine, although what is considered masculine or feminine changes over time and varies by culture. Typically, transgender people seek to align their gender expression with their gender identity, rather than the sex they were assigned at birth."

All members of society automatically assign gender to others. We refer to people as men, women, boys, and girls without their input. We expect people to use certain bathrooms and play on certain sports teams based on these imposed categorizations. The individual has little say in how gender is interpreted.

The bias to see gender as binary (male or female), immutable, and essential is called *cisgenderism*. (Cisgender refers to a person whose gender corresponds with their sex assigned at birth.) It's a form of discrimination that fails to conceptualize that much like sexuality, gender lies on a spectrum.

You should always refer to people in a manner concordant with their desires. A person has the right to choose appropriate personal pronouns and names. If a person was assigned the male sex at birth and chooses to be identified with the personal pronouns *she* and *her*, then that's her choice. Similarly, a person who was assigned to the female sex at birth should be referred to as *he* and *him* based on personal preference. Moreover, some people prefer being referred to as *they* and *them*, which is also appropriate based on preference.

Because we lack non-binary gender pronouns, some people prefer to use *they*, *them*, and *their* as singular, gender-neutral pronouns. In fact, the AP Stylebook was updated in 2017 to accommodate this specific usage for people who don't identify as he or she.

"They, them, their—In most cases, a plural pronoun should agree in number with the antecedent: The children love the books their uncle gave them. They/them/their is acceptable in limited cases as a singular and-or gender-neutral pronoun, when alternative wording is overly awkward or clumsy. However, rewording usually is possible and always is preferable. Clarity is a top priority; gender-neutral use of a singular they is unfamiliar to many readers. We do not use other gender-neutral pronouns such as xe or ze…

In stories about people who identify as neither male nor female or ask not to be referred to as he/she/him/her: Use the person's name in place of a pronoun, or otherwise reword the sentence, whenever possible. If they/them/their use is essential, explain in the text that the person prefers a gender-neutral pronoun. Be sure that the phrasing does not imply more than one person."

Of note, in 2017, *The Chicago Manual of Style* also suggested the usage of *they* for people who identify neither as male nor female.

According to GLAAD, *transsexual* is a dated term and *transgender* is preferred. Transgender is "an umbrella term for people whose gender identity and/or gender expression differs from what is typically associated with the sex they were assigned at birth."

Gender dysphoria is a condition where a person's experienced gender is different from the gender assigned at birth. This incongruence leads to distress and discomfort, and often people with gender dysphoria take steps to transition, such as dressing differently, changing names and pronouns, seeking hormone therapy, or undergoing sex reassignment surgery or gender confirmation surgery. (Refrain from calling such surgery a "sex change.")

According to GLAAD: "Use 'transition' to describe the process of transitioning from male to female or female to male. Use the terms 'gender confirmation surgery' or 'sex reassignment surgery' to describe medical procedures that are part of the transition process. Avoid using the terms 'post-op' and 'pre-op.' One can transition from one sex to the other without having such surgery."

For more specific information concerning gender terminology, I encourage you to refer to the *GLAAD Media Reference Guide,* which can be accessed online.

Disability and Disease

Although unintentional, a common mistake many writers make is to refer to disability inappropriately. Many writers tend to inappropriately label people with disabilities and disease. Instead of labeling, it's best to use person-first constructions.

WRONG: Sophia is an epileptic.

BETTER: Sophia is with epilepsy.

WRONG: After being thrown from a horse in 1995, Christopher Reeve, who famously played Superman, became a quadriplegic.

BETTER: After being thrown from a horse in 1995, Christopher Reeve, who famously played Superman, developed quadriplegia.

WRONG: American professional football player Jay Cutler is a diabetic.

BETTER: American professional football player Jay Cutler is with diabetes.

With scientific writing, labeling groups is sometimes acceptable. For example, if members of an experimental group are diagnosed with diabetes, then this group could be called the *diabetes group*. You can also refer to patients with diabetes as *diabetes patients*.

Please remember that the term *patient* is clinical and refers to people being treated in either an inpatient or outpatient health-care facility. You should refer to people as *people* outside of a medical context.

WRONG: Jamie was told that Randy and his wife, Clea, are cardiac patients who exercise regularly.

BETTER: Jamie was told that Randy and his wife, Clea, are people with heart disease who exercise regularly.

Keep in mind that a *patient* is person who is examined and treated; whereas, a *case* is something that's evaluated, documented, and reported. A *case* isn't human.

WRONG: The case was diagnosed as early-stage Alzheimer disease.

BETTER: The patient was diagnosed with early-stage Alzheimer disease.

Finally, it's probably best to avoid the term *subject* when referring to participants in a research study. For more than 100 years, the term subject has been part of the jargon of experimental psychology, and the APA still permits its usage. Nevertheless, the AMA recognizes the use of subject as impersonal—and possibly derogatory—and recommends using the term *participant* instead. After all, participants in a study are an integral part of the research and participate of their own free will; they aren't subservient subjects.

AVOID: There were originally 5,209 subjects in the Framingham Heart Study, which began in 1948 and continues to this day.

BETTER: There were originally 5,209 *participants* in the Framingham Heart Study, which began in 1948 and continues to this day.

Please don't confuse the terms *handicap* and *disability*. According to Barbara Gastel in the *Health Writer's Handbook:*

"A disability is a condition that interferes with one or more major life activities, such as walking, hearing, breathing, or learning. In contrast, a handicap is something that is a barrier to a person with a disability. For example, a man whose legs are paralyzed has a disability, not a handicap. However, stairs may be a handicap to him, as may the attitude of some employers."

You should also avoid referring to people with disease and disability as follows: *afflicted, suffering from, maimed, stricken with, disabled, retarded, mentally ill, victim, wheelchair bound,* and *confined to a wheelchair*. These terms are emotionally charged and can be considered patronizing.

WRONG: Penelope is a mentally ill person.

BETTER: Penelope is a person with mental illness.

Wrong: Olaf has been a victim of osteoarthritis ever since he was 65.

Better: Olaf was diagnosed with osteoarthritis when he was 65.

Furthermore, avoid euphemisms when describing disabilities, such as *special* or *physically challenged.*

Age

Generally, discrimination based on age—either young or old—is called ageism. Adultism is a type of ageism that discounts children and adolescents. When the term *elderly* is used as a noun, it implies an ageist stereotype. Instead, write *elderly people, older people, older adults, older population,* and so forth.

Instead of using imprecise language to describe age, it's best to specify age whenever possible.

EXAMPLE: Marcy is an old woman.

BETTER: Marcy is 85 years old.

EXAMPLE: Lorenzo is a young boy.

BETTER: Lorenzo is five years old.

Editorializing

Avoid editorializing when describing disability, medical conditions, and disease. For instance, researchers have noticed that autism and gender dysphoria tend to co-occur in some children. (To be fair, this relationship is quite murky.) In an attempt to show empathy, a person may write something like "it must be doubly difficult for parents and children to deal with both gender dysphoria and autism, two chronic conditions with complicated treatments." However, unless you have these two conditions or are a parent to a child with these two conditions, you are just making an assumption about how "difficult" things are. This assumption can ring hollow and insincere.

70. Identification

TIP: Identify concepts that the reader may not know about.

Key Points

- Provide concise explanations for specialized concepts or jargon.
- With in-text references to articles or studies, provide just enough information such that the reader can find the article if so desired.
- With online writing, links help with identification and provide additional information.

When writing for a general audience, you don't want to introduce concepts that may be foreign without a brief accompanying explanation as well as examples if pertinent. Remember that even very informed people don't know everything. A nuclear physicist may be unaware, for instance, of who won the Heisman Trophy—an annual award given to the college football player voted most outstanding. Similarly, a Heisman Trophy winner may know little about nuclear fission, a process by which the nucleus of an atom is split to create energy.

Many general-interest publications prefer that prose be written at a high-school reading level. Extending this recommendation further, it's also a good idea to imagine that you're writing for a person with a general knowledge of the world, and potentially new concepts should be explained in general terms. You don't want to take too much for granted with a general audience.

While composing clear, cohesive, comprehensible, concise, and correct prose (the 5 Cs), you want to proactively seek out specialized concepts or jargon and provide succinct explanations and examples.

EXAMPLE: New technology is making fracking more profitable.

The term *fracking* is jargon for hydraulic fracturing, an industrial process that breaks apart rock deep underground to release oil and gas. Fracking is an issue of concern to environmentalists because we know little about its potential repercussions for the environment. Although many people know about fracking, it's still a specialized concept and thus jargon. When writing for a general audience, we should concisely identify what fracking is when first mentioning the term.

BETTER: New technology is making fracking, a controversial industrial process used to extract fossil fuels, more profitable.

You'll notice that the added nonessential element not only defines fracking but also adds meaning to the entire sentence.

EXAMPLE: As of April 2016, fracking was practiced in 21 states.

In this next sentence, it's a good to provide examples of the states in which fracking occurs. Examples illustrate the widespread practice of fracking and enable the reader to visualize the geographical diversity of this practice, which extends well past the Texas oilfields of yore.

As of April 2016, fracking was practiced in 21 states, including Texas, Colorado, California, and Michigan.

A special case of identification involves the attribution of in-text references to articles, books, and other sources. Resist the temptation to provide too much identifying information when referring to another source. For example, if referring to a journal article, the most you usually need to do is mention the date, author, and either the publication title or the article title. You want to provide enough information so that an interested reader can find the article that you're referring to based on the information that you provide.

Consider the following in-text identification of an article.

> In an important—yet somewhat understated—2015 study published in the journal *Cognitive Development,* researchers discovered that young children are more likely to anthropomorphize attachment objects with humanlike features (faces). A child is more likely to attribute mental states, such as happiness, love, or loneliness, to their one-and-only teddy bear to which they are emotionally attached than to another preferred teddy bear that they merely like and play with. Furthermore, these researchers showed that children don't anthropomorphize objects without faces such as blankets.

Alternatively, the study could be identified as such:

> In an important—yet somewhat understated—2015 study published in the journal *Cognitive Development,* Gjersoe and co-authors discovered that young children are more likely to anthropomorphize attachment objects with humanlike features (faces). A child is more likely to attribute mental states, such as happiness, love or loneliness, to their one-and-only teddy bear to which they are emotionally attached than to another preferred teddy bear that they merely like and play with. Furthermore, these researchers showed that children don't anthropomorphize objects without faces such as blankets.

When publishing online, linking keywords to relevant web sites or documents can also help with identification. For instance, in the preceding example about fracking, the keyword "fracking" could be linked to ProPublica's coverage of this issue. ProPublica is a Pulitzer Prize–winning investigative newsroom that acts in the public interest. Linking keywords to outside content might also boost search engine optimization (SEO), which refers to tactics used to boost website traffic. (Notice how I identified both ProPublica and SEO because not everyone knows what these things refer to.)

71.
Narrative
Beginnings, Middles and Ends

TIP: Everything that you write has a beginning, a middle, and an end.

Key Points

- Good ledes share common characteristics.
- Every paragraph should move the reader toward a clearer understanding of the meaning of the entire document.
- A good ending offers closure and fulfillment.

When self-editing your work, an important question to ask yourself is whether you've established a story that people can understand and follow. All documents tell stories with beginnings, middles, and ends.

Stories or narratives run like a thread through all types of documents. Consider the following guidance from Pulitzer Prize–winning journalist and long-time writing instructor, Don Murray.

"All writing, poetry, fiction, drama and all the varieties of nonfiction—personal essay and impersonal essay, argument, description and exposition, research report, scholarly journal article, business memo, CIA account, proposal, biography and autobiography, textbook, thesis, and dissertation—are all narrative. The reader moves forward according to an emotional or intellectual chronology or both. We are all storytellers."

Even scientific articles that cover original research using the IMRAD structure (introduction, methods, results, and discussion) tell stories—albeit in a predictable fashion.

Murray was an interesting fellow and had many admirers. (He died in 2006.) During his lifetime, he was a high school dropout, sausage maker, grocery clerk, paratrooper, military police officer, and English professor. His own life was just as interesting as the stories he wove. Although he wasn't big into what we now think of as "evidence-based" teaching and eschewed traditional grammar, he did spend a lot of time thinking about the writing process. He was introspective and analyzed his own writing skill in detail.

According to Murray: "In life and in narrative, we know that a clock is ticking, that time is moving forward, that every event is marked by time: the present is becoming the past as the future is becoming the present. The reader knows this and is discomforted and confused when the narrative goes against what I call natural time. Readers will not recognize the problem, they will just stop reading.... As much as possible our stories should move forward in natural time.... Readers' problems—or discomforts—may simply be that information is not being delivered in the order it would be experience in life.... The excellent writer anticipates the readers' need for information. Timing is everything."

William Strong, who wrote the work *Coaching Writing,* offers the following advice concerning narrative: "The organization enhances the central idea or story line. The order, the structure, or the presentation is compelling and moves the reader through the text.... Relevant anecdotes and details enrich the central theme or story line."

In this quotation, Strong points out that anecdotes can fuel the story line and help the writer travel from beginning to middle to end. Anecdotes are interesting little stories that provide minor narrative diversions and keep things interesting.

Beginnings

Although all stories begin with a beginning, as far as journalists, and more generally article writers, are concerned, it's usually not a good idea to just start at the beginning. (The narrative lede, which is described briefly below, is an exception.) Instead you start with a *lede* (also spelled lead) that is interesting and draws your reader in.

Ledes are the beginnings of articles. Good ledes share certain characteristics.

- The lede promises an engaging story that the rest of the article delivers on.
- The lede reflects the angle of the piece.
- The lede is simple, clear, and concise.
- The lede is immediate and gets the reader ready for the story. You don't want to bury your lede in verbosity.
- The lede is interesting and provides a hook that is relevant and draws the reader in.

- The lede puts the writer's voice on display and sets the tone for the rest of the story.

Hooks

Hooks are especially important when writing articles or other types of documents intended for more general audiences. They attract the reader to your narrative. To a large extent, writing is entertaining in addition to being informative. Remember that the writer is not only an informer but also a performer.

The Zika virus outbreak gripped the attention of the world in 2015. Countless pregnant women who had been infected with the Zika virus went on to have babies with severe birth defects and brain abnormalities. In the months following the Zika outbreak, the story of Zika had been reported in nearly every conceivable capacity. It became harder to find an original hook to draw a reader in.

Then in early 2017, the CDC published research that quantified the risk of Zika birth defects. Using population-based data, researchers figured out that American women who had been infected with the virus while pregnant were 20 times more likely to have children with birth defects. Never before had we understood the impact of the disease on birth defects in numerical terms, and this research served as a hook that breathed new life into service articles detailing how the pregnant reader could protect herself from the Zika virus.

Types of Ledes

Here are some different types of ledes:

- Quotation ledes begin with a brief, interesting, and topical quotation.
- Scenario ledes use narrative elements to describe a place of particular importance to the story.
- Narrative ledes begin at a chronological beginning.
- Anecdotal ledes begin with an anecdote or interesting story.
- First-person anecdotal ledes begin with a relevant anecdote that involves the writer. Service and celebrity pieces often begin with first-person ledes.
- Opinion ledes begin opinion pieces or editorials.
- Prescriptive ledes begin with a call to action.
- Paradoxical ledes begin in a counterintuitive fashion.
- Shock ledes shock the reader, such as with salacious or horrific details.

- Transformative ledes use transformative explanations to present counterintuitive information.

A full discussion of the many types of ledes is outside the scope of this book. If interested in learning more, I wrote a book titled *The Complete Guide to Article Writing: How to Write Successful Articles for Online and Print Markets* (Writer's Digest Books) that details not only ledes but all elements of article writing and journalism. (In the book I explain transformative ledes—something I developed—in more detail. These ledes are very useful for science writers.) Nevertheless, let's detail one type of lede that's particularly pervasive: the summary lede.

Summary ledes touch on the 5 Ws (who, what, where, why, and when) and 1 H (how). They are useful when writing about complex subjects or emerging stories. For instance, when the Zika virus first gripped Brazil and spread north all the way to Mexico and the Caribbean, many people were understandably distressed. Summary ledes helped summarize what we knew about Zika during this incipient period.

Relevance of Ledes

This book provides self-editing guidance that applies to not only article writing but all types of writing. I mention ledes because even if you aren't writing an article, it's good to mull over the wide-ranging applicability of an engaging introduction. Anything you write should draw the reader in before the body of your work is presented. If your beginning isn't engaging, then you've likely failed the reader.

Now consider this gem from Robert Flesch's long-out-of-print *How to write, speak and think more effectively.* Flesch was a mid-twentieth century author and readability expert, who championed the use of plain English in writing.

"It's simple to show readers what to read and what to skip. Newspapers do it by starting most stories with summary leads, by putting summary headlines on top of these leads and by using the front page as a quick summary of the paper itself. The reader gets the gist of each story and of the day's news at a glance; if he needs just the bare information, he can skip the rest.... The same can be done with letters, memos, and reports. They should start with summary lead sentences and paragraphs.... Leads should give readers the main point and nothing *but* the main point; heads and subheads should summarize the leads."

On a related note, in feature articles, nut graphs follow ledes and contribute to narrative. The nut graph is the "nutshell" paragraph, which touches on the key topics of a story.

Middles

After the lede or introduction, your story or narrative begins in earnest. Depending on what type of document that you're writing, middles, or bodies of documents, can be arranged in various structures.

One way to think of each paragraph in your story is as an image that documents your progression to an end. According to Strong:

"It may be useful to visualize paragraphs as frames. Within each paragraph frame, a series of images, ideas, or sentences can be arranged and layered for desired effects. Of course, boundaries of frames can also change, for example, when a writer divides a paragraph into parts or when sentences are deleted, reordered, or expanded."

Murray compares the progression through story to a trail. The writer starts with an abundance of information and research. The writer finds order in the chaos, and along the way informs, explains, entertains, and persuades using voice. A writer's voice is the glue that holds the document together.

Keep in mind that every trail has diversions and digressions. The traveler needs pit stops for nourishment and replenishment. These pit stops often come in the form of interesting little stories or mini-narratives. In more formal writing, there's little room for digression. But in articles, books, and other writing meant for a general audience, anecdotes are a wonderful addition, and they sustain the flow of the work.

The writer should write with meaning in mind and work to develop, explore, and refine this meaning. Every paragraph should move the reader toward a clearer understanding of the meaning of the entire document.

Ends

Really good writers have a sense of how a document ends even before they begin writing. They've done enough footwork researching that they can see the trail meandering toward the destination in the distance. Research shows that readers most often remember the ending best, which makes sense because endings are not only last but also most poignant. A good ending offers closure and fulfillment. It's a reward for the reader who has invested time in your words.

For formal and academic documents, conclusions are often summations. However, when writing entertaining and informative pieces for general audiences—such as feature articles—the conclusion can be as deft as the lede. Here are some typical conclusions, or kickers, used by article writers:

- The kicker can look toward the future.
- The kicker can expand on the lede.

- The kicker can provide perspective—perhaps explain the importance of the piece to the reader.
- The kicker can end with a quotation. Remember that any quotation used, especially those used at the end of a piece, should be salient and express an idea or perspective that is best presented in someone else's words.

72. Paraphrasing

Tip: Paraphrase, don't plagiarize.

Key Points

- With paraphrasing, you take the essential ideas expressed by another writer and put them into your own words.
- Paraphrasing limits the need for quoted text and allows you to write in your own voice.

The nonfiction writing that you do needs to be verifiable. Verifiable writing can be traced back to a (preferably primary) source. However, the information that you include in your writing shouldn't be copied directly from the source—this would be plagiarizing. Instead, *paraphrasing* becomes a necessity.

With paraphrasing, you take the essential ideas expressed by another writer and put them into your own words. A good way to paraphrase is to reread the passage which you are drawing from a couple of times—truly comprehend it—and then without looking at the passage, use your own words to describe relevant points. You can then check your writing against the original source to make sure that it expresses the same essential ideas but in a novel fashion. Inevitably, a few of the words that you write will be the same as the original source, but whenever possible, find your own words to express meaning.

Paraphrasing is crucial because it limits your use of excess quotations—especially from passages that are more garden-variety. Paraphrasing also allows you to use our own voice. When you paraphrase, you want to change the vocabulary and syntax as much as possible. Simply transposing elements or changing tenses while retaining syntax and vocabulary of the source material is a dishonest practice called *patchwriting.*

Now, let's look at paraphrasing in action.

Here is a passage from an article titled "Contrition in the Courtroom: Do Apologies Affect Adjudication?" by Rachlinski and co-authors:

"Because judges decide many civil cases based on pretrial motions, preside over many civil settlement conferences, resolve about half of all civil cases that proceed to trial, and impose virtually all criminal sentences, trial judges are probably the most critical actor in the legal system with regards to the potential influence of apologies."

Here is the paraphrased text:

If you stop and think about it, judges shoulder a huge responsibility and represent the public interest in staggering ways. For instance, judges oversee civil settlements, decide approximately half of all civil cases that go to trial, and impose nearly all criminal sentencing. Moreover, trial judges are often in receipt of apologies by offending parties and have the ability to attach value to contrition. Judges can weigh their decisions in light of contrition.

73. Prescriptive vs. Descriptive

TIP: Unless a prescriptive approach is logical, prefer a descriptive approach to language and writing.

Key Points

- Prescriptivists are quick to appraise change and either assign it preference or eschew its use.
- Descriptivists merely record change and accept diversity in language.

Central to all published writing is the push-pull dynamic between prescriptive and descriptive practices: the poles that influence spelling, idiom, and word usage in fundamental ways.

Language is in constant flux. Many changes that occur are almost imperceptible and dispersed over an ambit of disciplines and fields. Some changes are more pervasive and recorded, researched, and debated.

In the face of change, we have two options. We can judge a change's merits—claiming that the change is "right" or "wrong." Or, we can accept such change as merely different and document it as such without passing judgment; we can accept a choice of forms in different contexts.

Prescriptivists are quick to appraise change and either assign it preference or eschew its use. Contrarily, descriptivists merely record change and accept diversity.

In the sixteenth and seventeenth centuries, those who commentated on language espoused a descriptive approach. The tides changed in the eighteenth, later nineteenth, and early twentieth centuries with a shift toward the prescriptive. With the emergence of modern linguistics in the twentieth century, descriptive approaches were once again on the rise.

Currently, the preference for descriptive approaches to writing and language is in part attributable to two phenomena. First, in academics, there's been a shift toward more egalitarian, universal, and democratic systems of thought. Second, the influence of corpus linguistics on grammar and style has been indelible—with scholars much more interested with patterns of word usage and trends rather than more abstract concepts such as right and wrong. In other words, many experts are now much more interested in how things are different than whether things are "correct" or "incorrect."

The difference between descriptive and prescriptive approaches is apparent in the style guides and the dictionaries that we commonly use. You can usually tell whether a dictionary or style guide is descriptive or prescriptive in nature based on length: It takes fewer words to prescribe usage.

For instance, *The Elements of Style*, which was originally published several decades ago, is highly prescriptive and a mere 43 pages long. Whereas, *The Chicago Manual of Style,* which is regularly updated, is more descriptive in nature, and tips the scales at more than 1,000 pages. Similarly, *Webster's New World College Dictionary,* which is a favorite of the AP Stylebook and used in news rooms everywhere, is a prescriptive text that's more than 10 times shorter in length than the descriptive *Oxford English Dictionary.* The unabridged version of the *Oxford English Dictionary* was published in 1989 and comprises 20 volumes!

Beginning writers often wonder what is "correct" or what is "incorrect." They are left unsatisfied with the reality that answers are more nuanced. In reality, a balance between descriptive and prescriptive approaches is evident in many of the decisions that professional writers and editors make. The informed writer recognizes variants and prefers certain alternatives based on logic, evidence, and style preferences; whereas, prescribed variants that make no logical sense have been relegated to the category of shibboleth or stylistic fetishism.

Let's consider two examples of word usage variants. The first supports a more descriptive stance and the second a more prescriptive stance. Both of these stances are based on logical arguments.

Due To

For three centuries, many writers took exception to the use of *due to* as a compound preposition. Most notably in 1926, Fowler argued that *due to* should act as either a participle or adjective affixed to a noun—not a notion pulled from a sentence or clause.

Furthermore, as described in Follett's *Modern American Usage:*

"Everybody agrees that an effect is *due to* a cause. Hence, a disease is *due to* an infection, exhaustion *due to* overwork, success or failure *due to* aptitude or inaptitude, and so on. One thing is *due to* another thing. In such uses, *due* is an adjective modifying the nouns *disease*, *exhaustion*, *success*, or *failure*."

Accordingly, the following two iterations would be considered incorrect:

We exited due to a fire in the building.

Due to a fire in the building, we exited.

In these two examples, *due to* is used as a prepositional phrase and its meaning depends on the entire sentence.

However, the following would be correct:

Our exit was due to the fire in the building.

Here, "due to" is an adjective that describes a cause-and-effect relationship: The fire caused the exit.

The problem with this prescription is that even when used at the head of a clause or sentence, the meaning of *due to* is still clear to modern-day readers.... No reader will be led astray. Writers have embraced the use of *due to* in more versatile contexts. Even the speech writer for the Queen has used *due to* in a fashion contrary to Fowler's recommendation.

In reality, *due to* has been used as a prepositional phrase ever since the late nineteenth century, with the Oxford Dictionary first recording such use in 1897. As with *due to*, the prepositional use of *owing to* was disputed in the eighteenth century before later finding acceptance.

In *The Careful Writer*, Theodore Bernstein, one of the twentieth century's most prolific prescriptivists, writes that "there can be little doubt that *due to* used as a prepositional phrase will ultimately become thoroughly established in the language."

Significant

When writing for a general audience, the words *significant*, *substantial, important, appreciable, notable,* and *remarkable* are often used synonymously. However, when writing about scientific research—as in a peer-reviewed journal article—the term *significant* is used to mean statistical significance, or the likelihood that a relationship involving two or more variables is caused by something other than random chance.

In light of the widespread notion of statistical significance in science, when writing articles or documents detailing scientific studies, there's always the off chance that the synonymous usage of *significant* and *substantial* or so forth could confuse the reader.

> UNCLEAR: There was significant participant attrition in the clinical trial—early on, 20 of 100 participants dropped out of the study.

> BETTER: There was substantial participant attrition in the clinical trial—early on, 20 of 100 participants dropped out of the study.

On a related note, *nonsignificant* is a scientific term that refers to a lack of statistical significance; whereas, *insignificant* means "unimportant" or "meaningless."

Ultimately, the binary tendency of writers to claim that certain propositions are either right or wrong is a cultural habit rooted in a system of logic handed down to us by the Greeks. According to the Greeks, if two propositions contradict each other, then one statement must be wrong. Instead of thinking in terms of right and wrong, as a writer and editor, it's infinitely more useful—and realistic—to think of *what is* and *what isn't*. Moreover, when choosing your words, imagine *what is* and choose the best alternative.

---

74. Sources

TIP: Use primary sources for research.

Key Points

- The facts you use must be verifiable.
- Primary sources inform your writing, and secondary sources inspire your writing.
- Attribute the sources of your information.

When writing an article or document, you should make sure that your writing is verifiable. The facts that you present should be able to be traced back to reputable primary or, if necessary, secondary sources.

When writing for online audiences, it's often a good idea to judiciously link to the sources that you use—especially when you're writing about specific facts, figures, or findings. Links to original sources provide your reader with an avenue to learn more.

Primary Sources vs. Secondary Sources

To keep your writing original and insightful, it's best to mostly use primary sources. Primary sources include the following:

- abstracts
- breaking news
- expert accounts and interviews
- information taken from social media
- journal articles
- press releases
- questionnaires
- raw data (statistics)
- speeches
- surveys
- transcripts
- white papers

Unlike primary sources, secondary sources are processed and pass through an intermediary. With a secondary source, an author, a group of authors, or a publication has analyzed and interpreted facts and events on behalf of the reader. Here are some examples of secondary sources:

- blog postings
- books
- magazine articles
- news analyses
- online articles

- podcasts
- radio shows
- television shows

If access is an issue, then you may need to use a secondary source. For instance, if you're writing a blog posting about the president's position on Syria, then you may need to find secondary sources in which the president was interviewed about the topic and quote that article because you won't be able to access the president's thoughts otherwise.

Secondary sources are useful when providing inspiration for your writing. When President Trump announced his budget blueprint for Fiscal Year 2018, for instance, the blueprint proposed massive cuts to many agencies including the National Institutes of Health (NIH), which funds cancer and other disease research. Many people found these suggested cuts perturbing, and many secondary news sources, including newspapers and news websites, analyzed the potential cuts. These secondary-source stories and news analyses can serve as fantastic inspiration for an original story, but they shouldn't be used as sources for information about the actual budget. Trump's proposed budget is available online, and anybody who is writing an article or document about the budget should pull relevant information from the budget itself, which is a primary source.

Now, let's consider another example.

Alternate-day fasting is touted by some as an alternative to the continuous calorie restriction of regular diets. With alternate-day fasting, "fasting" days are followed by "feast" days. For instance, one day a person may consume 25 percent of suggested caloric requirements and the next day that person would consume 125 percent of caloric requirements; whereas, with a calorie-restriction diet, a person would consume 25 percent fewer calories every day.

Let's imagine, after reading an article about alternate-day fasting on a website, you were inspired to write a blog posting examining the drawbacks of this practice. This secondary source draws information about alternate-day fasting from a recent *JAMA* (the *Journal of the American Medical Association*) article. The authors of the *JAMA* study suggest that alternate-day fasting is no more effective than continuous calorie restriction, and that people find it more difficult to drastically cut calories every other day than to moderately reduce calories every day. Even if you may have been inspired by this secondary source, don't use it directly to write your blog posting. Instead, find the original *JAMA* article referred to in the article and use this instead. Of note, secondary-source treatments of articles are derivative, and you'll find a lot more concrete and comprehensive information in the primary source itself.

Please note that some online publications pull together *aggregate stories,* which are stories devoid of original reporting. These aggregate stories are written using secondary sources—often articles from various reputable news organizations. Aggregate stories are highly derivative and bad journalism.

Attribution

When writing for general audiences, it's rare that you'll need to include actual references and citations. All you need to do is attribute the sources of your information.

Attribution is important for many reasons. Proper attribution helps verify your writing and bolsters its transparency. If you attribute the information that you use, readers will not need to question the source. They will trust your voice and find your writing more credible. Furthermore, attribution can slow the tempo of a piece.

On a related note, cross-referencing attributions is often useful when researching an article. Although a secondary source, such as a newspaper or magazine article, makes for weak verification, attributed primary sources in these articles can be very helpful in your writing.

Some good places to provide attribution include the following:

- when your reader would likely want to know the source
- when directly or indirectly quoting a source
- when outside opinions or commentary are used
- when the veracity of facts is questionable
- when what is being cited is controversial

There are a number of ways to provide attribution to a source in your work. In every instance, you should endeavor to provide enough information for the reader to find the original source of your claims, if so inclined. Moreover, it's a good idea to link to sources whenever possible.

Be careful not to attribute in excess. After some time, information enters the public domain and becomes common knowledge and no longer needs to be traced back to a source. For instance, everyone knows that Elvis Presley lived in mansion called Graceland, and this fact would not have to be attributed.

Here are two ways to provide attribution to the *JAMA* article on alternate-day fasting that was discussed in the preceding example.

EXAMPLE: In a 2017 article titled the "Effect of Alternate-Day Fasting on Weight Loss, Weight Maintenance, and Cardioprotection Among

Metabolically Healthy Obese Adults," Trepanowski and co-authors found that it's more difficult for dieters to adhere to an alternate-day fasting regimen than to daily caloric restriction.

EXAMPLE: In a 2017 *JAMA* study, Trepanowski and colleagues found that it's more difficult for dieters to adhere to an alternate-day fasting regimen than to daily caloric restriction.

Finally, it's important to know that Google search has evolved to become more discriminatory of source material. Google can distinguish high-quality content written using primary sources, such as journal articles and expert input. One useful way to increase the search-engine optimization (SEO) value of your content is to judiciously quote primary sources.

75. Tone

TIP: When writing for a general audience, consider using a personal tone.

Key Points

- The term *tone* refers to the manner in which a document expresses meaning, feeling, or attitude.
- Style, voice, and tone often conflate.
- Metaphor, contractions, conciseness, and personal pronouns help establish a personal tone.
- Avoid the temptation to make yourself a focal point of your writing

Style, voice, and tone are related concepts. With respect to writing, these terms have been defined differently.

Much of this book deals with style. Style refers to widely accepted conventions of writing. Depending on audience, different style guides have been developed, such as *The Associated Press Stylebook* and *The Chicago Manual of Style*.

Writers for specific publications tend to conform to conventions of style dictated by the publication. For this reason, articles in the *New York Times*, a publication that has its own style guide, appear more similar to each other than to articles appearing in *People*, *Science News*, or *The Daily Beast*.

Tone to the manner in which a document expresses meaning, feeling, or attitude. Tone can run the gamut, from the highly personal opinion piece or blog posting to the more impersonal article, business proposal, or instruction manual.

Voice is the distinct fashion in which a writer pieces together words. Although voice can be coached or inspired, it can't be taught per se. Successful writers cultivate their own voices after years of writing and study. Think about popular writers—such as J.K. Rowling, Michael Crichton, or John Grisham—each has a unique voice which engages the audience.

The Conflation of Style, Voice, and Tone

Style, voice, and tone often tend to run together, so much so that it's hard to tell where one concept begins and another ends. For example, consider the first few lines from *Pimp,* written by Iceberg Slim.

"Dawn was breaking as the big Hog scooted through the streets. My five whores were chattering like drunk magpies. I smelled the stink that only a street whore has after a long, busy night. The inside of my nose was raw. It happens when you're a pig for snorting cocaine."

Iceberg Slim (Robert Beck) was a one-time pimp who turned to writing after his release from prison. His first novel, the autobiographical *Pimp,* was published in 1967, during the Civil Rights Movement. It was a huge commercial success and read widely by African American audiences. (Unfortunately, this book was never promoted in the mainstream media and among general audiences thus limiting its wider exposure.) He was so influential that both Ice Cube and Ice-T named themselves in his honor.

Although Iceberg Slim is one of the most influential African American writers of all time, and although he had some formal education, he was never formally trained as a writer. His voice, tone, and style tend to blend into a unique mix. So special was his gritty language that *Pimp* has its own glossary, which was requested by his publisher for meaning. For instance, in the preceding excerpt from *Pimp,* the term "Hog" refers to a Cadillac.

Iceberg Slim's conflation of tone, style, and voice had huge, yet divisive, cultural import. In a podcast interview, Justin Gifford, who wrote *Street Poison: The Biography of Iceberg Slim,* summarized the contribution of Iceberg Slim as follows:

"Some people read that book [*Pimp*] and think 'I could really make my own art out of this,' and that's where you get gangsta rap and street fiction and the comedy of Chris Rock and Dave Chappelle. And then you have other people who read that book and say 'I can do this better than Iceberg Slim; I'm going to take these lessons, and I'm going to become a pimp myself.' And so, the book has a really divided influence and impact on the culture in which we live."

Personal Tone

Without any outside directive, such as style preferences required by a publisher, by default, when writing for a general audience, you should try to write in a friendly, conversational, engaging, and accessible tone. No matter how smart your reader, you will always succeed when writing in plain English.

Of course, plain and simple has its place. This tone may not work with more formal academic, research, or business documents. Nevertheless, even in these registers, a more personal tone can be appreciated. For example, researchers have often used the passive voice to disguise their own input to sound more clinical and detached.

EXAMPLE: The study participants were administered questionnaires.

However, this preference for the passive voice has eroded, and now many researchers take a more personal tone when writing scholarly articles, using the active voice instead.

EXAMPLE: We administered questionnaires to the study participants.

The proliferation of the personal tone is well demonstrated in advertising. Advertisers have a limited amount of time and space to convince us to buy something. They have to convince us that we have a need or desire for an item or service, even if this need or desire doesn't originally exist. Advertisers are salespeople first and foremost. And in some alternative reality, if door-to-door salespeople were cheaper to employ than advertisers, many advertisers would be out of a job.

In 1992, Gatorade aired a commercial with a highly personalized tone, which featured basketball player nonpareil, Michael Jorda (sorry LeBron). In the montage, Jordan flew through the air, dunked, played basketball with children, and goofed around. The tagline of the commercial was "Be like Mike. Drink Gatorade."

This commercial perfectly captured the cultural zeitgeist. At the time, Michael Jordan was at the height of his fame and would go on to win an astounding six NBA National Championships with the Chicago Bulls. Children and adults everywhere imagined that they could play basketball like Michael Jordan, a man who seemed unfettered by the laws of gravity.

Tone: Metaphor

Writing in a personal tone also depends on the metaphors that you use. You want the metaphors that you use to resonate with the reader and mean something without sounding sentimental or cheesy.

Amid the tumult of the Financial Crisis of 2007 and 2008, many people became particularly concerned with economics, and with good reason. With major market indices getting slammed, people on the verge of retirement who had more than $200,000 saved up saw their 401(k)s tumble nearly 25 percent. Instead of lying on a chaise lounge in Boca Raton, some retirees were looking for work at Walmart. Because people were so interested in what was going on with the market, and because what was consuming the market—subprime and credit default swaps—was complicated, we saw lots of plain-word metaphors presented.

- The Financial Crisis resulted from a perfect storm.
- The economy was a critically ill patient on a gurney.
- The economy was a broken-down car.
- Warren Buffett called the Crisis an "economic Pearl Harbor," a sound bite and chyron that gained lots of traction in the media.

None of these metaphors are perfect. Metaphors are always substitutions, and with transference, some meaning is lost to ensure that the reader receives most of the message in relatable terms. For instance, comparing the economy with a perfect storm implies that we can do little to slow the destruction, when in fact the U.S. and other governments essentially bought their way out of the Financial Crisis. However, people were scared and filled with consternation like no time in modern history; they were looking for answers. With their tone and framing, financial metaphors helped answer some of these questions.

Tone: Contractions

Another strategy to make your tone more personal involves the usage of contractions, such as *you've, they've,* and *it's.*

The best writers write as they speak. They transcribe the thoughts sounded in their minds. By nature, people think in contractions. Because the use of contractions dominates communication among all people, when permissible, it's a good idea to use such relatable language in your writing.

Keep in mind that scientific writing is different from literature or informal writing. Both the *AMA Manual of Style* and *Publication Manual of the American Psychological Association* recommend that contractions be spelled out in formal writing.

Tone: Conciseness

A good way to keep your tone personal is by using short words and concise phrases. Except for with verbs and nouns—where it can be a good idea to use words that most precisely capture meaning despite length—even if the topic is complicated, it's best to keep all other parts of speech as simple as possible. It's also best to limit the use of adverbs and adjectives in your writing. Remember that adverbs and adjectives can make your writing unwieldy.

FORMAL, WORDY, AND STILTED: Our organization dispatched your person a missive expatiating our stipulations.

PERSONAL AND SHORT: We sent you a letter detailing our conditions.

Tone: Personal Pronouns

The pronoun *you* is probably the most versatile choice when conveying a personal tone. For instance, in service pieces, such as how-to articles the writer is writing directly for the reader and giving guidance. Use of *you* not only makes things personal but also directs the reader. Even though the pronoun *I* or *we* may have less place in a service article, the pronoun *you* is integral to keep things sounding believable.

On February 28, 1571, a 38-year-old French nobleman named Michel de Montaigne changed the tone of writing forever. He began writing about himself, which before had been considered taboo and insufferably egocentric. Montagne's *Essays* astonished the world and showed everyone it was okay to write about yourself; it was okay to use the pronouns *I, we, me,* and *my.*

"Because I found I had nothing else to write about," explains Montaigne, "I presented myself as a subject. When I wrote of anything else, I wandered and lost the way."

In the wake of Montagne's revelation, the world saw every celebration of the self from Walt Whitman's *Leaves of Grass* to Tucker Max's *I Hope They Serve Beer in Hell.* However, even when writing in a personal tone, the pendulum has most recently seemed to swing away from the use of certain self-referential personal pronouns like *I, me, my,* and *we*—even with online publication.

Nowadays, Internet publishers are interested in keeping things as evergreen as possible and reaping as many income-generating clicks as possible. In their attempts to maximize profits, many of these publishers have moved away from a preference for first-person accounts, marked by pronoun usage *I, me, my* and even *we,* and are instead requesting that pieces be written without these personal pronouns.

More generally, these publications are requesting that writers avoid self-referential pronouns. Apparently, using the personal pronouns *I, me, my,* and *we* somehow detracts from the universality of a document.

Of course, the more personal *I, me, my,* and *we* will always have their place in personal essays, personal statements, cover letters, and opinion pieces. However, even in blog postings and online feature articles, which were once packed with self-referential pronouns and first-person ledes, it's becoming trendier for writers to avoid *I* and only use the pronoun *you* judiciously and as needed. Moreover, much like the use of generic singular pronouns, if possible, it sounds better to clump your use of *you*s together. Reading a *you* once every few sentences—or randomly distributed throughout the length of an article—can appear disconcerting.

Ultimately, unless what you're writing requires that you explicitly focus on yourself, then it's best to avoid pronouns like *I* and *me.* Keep in mind that you are just one person, with one person's worldview and one person's attitudes and biases; yet, you are writing for many people who are in many ways different from you.

In medicine, physicians have known for some time that communicating personal anecdotes while advising the patient detracts from the interaction. In fact, physicians are encouraged to avoid discussing personal recollections with patients. Patients don't want to hear about the physician's stories. Instead, patients want to hear about themselves and what they need to do for their health. An interaction can still be personal without the physician concentrating on personal experiences.

Many beginning writers are obsessed with memoir and want to use words like *I* and *me* often. Keep in mind, however, that although lots of people have interesting life stories, only a limited number of memoirs have become best sellers. Many successful professional writers realize that there's professional longevity in shifting the focus away from oneself and instead focusing on the reader. A writer who only writes about oneself becomes a one-trick pony. And audiences eventually bore of even the most entertaining tricks. Although focusing on yourself is both tempting and easy, in many situations, it's unwise.

Although field and context specific, in a podcast interview with NPR's *On the Media* aired in December 2016, CNN Chief Washington Correspondent Jake Tapper offers advice that can extend to writing.

"As a general notion, my opinions about political events of the day are not as important as the opinions of … Benjamin Netanyahu [or] Hillary Clinton. Those are world actors, and what they say is much more important than what I say.… Making myself the center of attention … that undercuts the journalism."

By unnecessarily injecting yourself into the narrative, you lose objectivity and risk grandstanding. On a related note, *editorializing*, which involves a writer inserting opinion when reporting facts, can also undermine your message.

During the self-editing phase, it's always a good idea to take a few moments and ask yourself whether you would—in real life—speak to a member of your audience in the same manner that you've written. If the answer is no, the advice in this chapter will help you.

Appendix I: Understanding Editing

Editing isn't merely a natural talent that defies explanation. There's nothing magical about editing. Sure, the best editors do have a proclivity for the practice. But, the best editors also spend years honing their skills and studying the nuances of the English language. They learn not only what style conventions are generally accepted but also what mistakes are most commonly made, so as to target these common slips efficiently. Ultimately, all this hard work leads to acumen, and it's this acumen that separates good editors from great ones.

To become a great self-editor, it's important to grasp what editing actually means and how editors approach the documents of others. It's also important to appreciate that editing occurs at *levels* and that there are different *types* of editing. These levels and types of editing target different concerns in a document. An awareness of what editing is will put the more focused practice of self-editing—which is expatiated in this book—in context and perspective.

The Roles of an Editor

A good editor is invisible to the reader.

Probably one of the hardest temptations for novice editors to resist is the desire to introduce correct errors into a document. The editor is not the writer, or principal creator of content, and should rather endeavor to preserve the author's voice and meaning whenever possible. In other words, editors shouldn't fix things that aren't broken. Even if a *commission* improves a piece, it's not the editor's place to introduce the unnecessary. Moreover, when in doubt, an editor should err on the side of *omission,* or doing nothing.

Copyeditors who are employed by publications serve three stakeholders:

- the author
- the audience
- the publisher (publication)

The copyeditor helps develop a document that's free of errors, resonates and engages the reader, and meets the needs of a publication. To this end, the copyeditor works with a publisher's editorial team ("editorial") and a document's author.

Sometimes, juggling the needs of all three stakeholders can be tricky. For example, editorial may have a vested interest in covering topics that appeal to their readers as well as their advertisers. Editorial often employs copyeditors to help meet this goal. Nevertheless, when editing for a general audience in a general-interest journalism publication, just like the writer, the copyeditor must keep in mind that the coverage must remain *transparent, verifiable,* and *coherent* and flag or fix any transgressions. Veritably, the duty of a substantive copyeditor often extends well past mechanical or content concerns and is necessarily global.

Transparency means that there are no conflicts of interest, or, if there are, these conflicts are disclosed to the readers. For example, if a subscription-based, general-interest publication were to commission a piece solely praising an advertiser's product (say a new sports car), and this article is budgeted in with all the others that the publication runs, this biased article would lack transparency. This article shouldn't be passed off as journalism. (In these cases, big publications will often explicitly label such bespoke or branded content.)

Verification refers to the general journalistic (and nonfiction) practice of using demonstrable facts to support claims. These facts are often taken from *primary sources,* such as journal articles or interviews with human sources, and more sparingly from *secondary sources* like reputable news coverage. In the case of this book, I used multifarious tertiary sources, such as dictionaries, textbooks, and style guides—all of which can be found in the bibliography—to develop the writing, publication, and self-editing principles detailed herein.

In journalistic terms, *coherence* refers to the practice of providing the readers with robust and comprehensive options when learning about a topic. By providing the "whole story," a writer of any document illumines the reader and helps the reader draw conclusions. For instance, when reviewing a gamut of sports cars for a general readership, it's important to realize that different sports cars meet different uses and desires. Thus, any coherent review of sports cars would look at several different types and not focus on only a few select ones.

Macro-editing vs. Micro-editing

In broad strokes, editing can be categorized as either *macroediting* or *microediting.*

With macro-editing, the editor is concerned most about communication and whether the message is clear to the reader. Micro-editing is more detail oriented.

Here are some macro-editing concerns:

- connecting sentences and paragraphs
- eliminating wordiness
- length
- logic
- organization
- rewriting the introduction or conclusion
- tone
- word usage

Micro-editing deals with the nitty-gritty. Typically, many micro-editing concerns are addressed in a publication's preferred style guide, house style (in-house style guide), or some combination. Sometimes publications have neither the time nor the resources to put together an entire style guide and draw up a shorter editorial style sheet instead. These publications then direct the copyeditor to refer to conventional style guides—with which every qualified editor should be familiar—for more guidance.

Here are some typical micro-editing concerns:

- abbreviations
- grammar
- punctuation
- spelling
- units of measurement
- use of italics
- spelling out numbers

The scope of macro-editing and micro-editing is different, and the typical editor either solely macroedits or solely microedits with each individual pass. For most editors, it would be difficult to comprehensively tackle big concerns like logic and consistency at the same time that they're worrying about smaller issues, such as punctuation and abbreviations.

Research suggests that about 2 percent of people can effectively multitask. The other 98 percent of people who multitask end up doing all the tasks poorly. Similarly, a very small minority of professional editors can deal with macro-editing and micro-editing at the same time. For the rest of us, it's a good idea to tackle macro-editing and micro-editing issues separately.

Different Types of Editing

In global terms, editing can be appreciated as either macro-editing or micro-editing. However, editing can be limned more specifically, too.

Mechanical editing entails making sure that a document conforms with house style or the style of the intended publication. With large publications, there is little gray area with mechanical editing, and all the necessary information that directs changes during this phase can be found in the publication's specified guides, stylebooks, and dictionaries.

Mechanical editing deals with the following:

- capitalization
- formatting citations
- hyphenation
- punctuation
- spelling
- treatment of numbers and numerals
- use of abbreviations
- use of (avoidance of) boldface type
- use of charts
- use of footnotes and endnotes
- use of graphs
- use of headings
- use of italics
- use of lists
- use of tables

When *language editing,* editors often rely on their knowledge, favorite style manuals, and preferred usage guides. While language editing, an editor will address the following:

- diction
- grammar
- idiomatic phrasing
- syntax
- usage (for example, wording that is confusing, ambiguous, or inappropriate)

With mechanical editing, an observant and meticulous approach is required to fix rote inaccuracies which can usually be recalled. Language editing is more subjective and addresses higher levels of Bloom's taxonomy, such as analysis and evaluation. Even though the practice of language editing is more subjective, the editor must be careful not to introduce personal preference or biases into a document's prose, as is always the case when editing for others.

Content editing is more substantive, and the content editor is often given permission by the publisher or author to fix internal inconsistencies, discrepancies, structural problems, and organizational problems. Content editing can involve heavy editing and rewriting. At the very least, while content editing, the editor must identify inconsistencies and discrepancies so that the writer can address them. Despite being more permissive in practice, with content editing, it's imperative that the writer's meaning is maintained by the editor. If the content editor questions the veracity of a fact, the content editor should present this concern to the author in the form of an editing comment or query (for example, using track changes).

Technically, in publication circles, *proofreading* is considered separate from editing, and proofreading and editing aren't synonymous. Copyeditors are concerned with the author's words, and proofreaders are concerned with errors introduced during formatting, typesetting, and file conversion. Nevertheless, the word "proofreading" has been co-opted to more generally refer to catching mechanical errors in spelling, punctuation, and so forth.

Levels of Editing

There are three levels of language editing and content editing: *light*, *medium*, and *heavy*. A publication's editorial coordinator will specify which level a copyeditor should edit at. As can you can probably figure, light copyediting of a document takes less time than medium copyediting, and medium copyediting takes less time than heavy copyediting.

With respect to language editing, a light edit may entail correcting incontrovertible errors in syntax, usage or grammar, while ignoring things that may not sound great but are not wrong, such as wordiness. A medium or heavy edit could flag or revise such wordiness, respectively.

With respect to content editing, a light edit may address factual inconsistencies only. A medium edit may take things a step further by examining organization and logic. And a heavy edit will fix (rewrite) problems with organization and logic.

Finally, please remember that internal consistency is key to all editing. In other words, all changes made must agree with one another.

Style Guides

Let's consider some different style guides.

The Chicago Manual of Style is typically used by book publishers.

The Associated Press Stylebook (AP Stylebook) is used by many newspapers, magazines, and online publications.

The *Publication Manual of the American Psychological Association* is used for academic writing in the social sciences, including journal articles or academic texts.

The *AMA Manual of Style* is published by the American Medical Association, which also publishes *JAMA*, or the *Journal of the American Medical Association*, and is used by medical writers and editors.

The ACS Style Guide is developed for the American Chemical Society and used when writing about chemistry.

Nowadays, many organizations not only publish hard copies of their style guides but also electronic versions for ease of use. For copyeditors (and self-editors) who often refer to these works, online access, albeit pricier, is clutch.

Please keep in mind that the use of a specific style guide can transcend the publication type. For instance, *The Chicago Manual of Style* has a broad scope, and sometimes the information that you need can only be found in this style treatise, regardless of a publication's preference to use a different style guide. *The Chicago Manual* proffers, for example, a treatment of adverb placement that rises above all other treatments and is useful to all writers. Moreover, the *AMA Manual of Style* is far better at suggesting humanistic language regarding medical conditions than any other style guide. (The AP Stylebook is now only starting to direct readers on the proper and empathetic use of medical terms.)

Appendix II: Grammar vs. Style

Both macroevolution and microevolution rely on the same four mechanisms of change: migration, mutation, genetic drift, and natural selection. Microevolution occurs on a small scale, within a single population; whereas, macroevolution transcends species. Although both macroevolution and microevolution occur, we can only observe microevolution in action. A similar dynamic exists between style and grammar, with changes in style occurring frequently but changes in grammar taking time.

Style refers to standards of writing and grammar that are, in general, considered desirable or acceptable. Style is arbitrary and rigid. Style can guide font choice, hyphenation, word choice, paragraphing, and so forth. More generally, book publishers tend to follow advice laid out in *The Chicago Manual of Style*, and newspapers, magazines, and online publications tend to follow *The Associated Press Stylebook*.

Writing in *Change in Contemporary English*, Leech defines grammar as "the vast and complex system of rules which helps us organize words into constituents, clauses and sentences." Leech goes on to point out that grammar is erroneously used "to refer to a collection of variable and disputed usages which have been selected arbitrarily in the course of almost 300 years of prescriptive thinking about good grammar and proper English." In other words, people often confuse style, which is capricious and prescriptive, with grammar, which is established and descriptive.

In *The Cambridge Guide to English Usage,* Pam Peters writes, "The deeper secrets of any language lie in its grammar, in the underlying rules and conventions by which words combine with each other. This is especially true of English, where word relationships are only occasionally marked in the forms of the words themselves. Many words can work as nouns, verbs or adjectives without showing it in their outward form.... The *grammar of the word,* as well as its particular meaning, only emerges in the phrase or clause in which it is used."

As any student of French, German, or Latin can attest, in these languages, grammar is evident in the morphology, or on the surface, of a word. Specifically, forms and inflections are indicators of grammar. Inflections refer to a change to the ending of a word that indicates number, person, gender, mood, tense, voice, and case. In English, however, syntax, or the order of words, is more telling.

Like microevolution, changes in style can be observed directly. During the past few decades, for instance, we've noticed vast changes in how publications refer to race and gender. Whereas, like with macroevolution, the emergence of grammaticalizations occur more slowly over time. There's actually a word that describes this slow evolution of language: *diachronic.* Conversely, *synchronic* refers to language as it occurs at one point in time.

Style is intrinsic to all forms of written and spoken English. Style can be formal, informal, or somewhere in-between. Effective and clear style involves the prudent use of sentences whose length and structure reflects intended meaning. Moreover, writers are often taught that a limpid, or crisp, style, employs active verbs in lieu of passive ones and abstractions in lieu of generalizations.

Style is often linked to institutions. Government institutions write in an official style. Businesses write in a commercial style. The style of legal writing is more protracted and impersonal with a penchant for passive constructions. Academic writers tend to create in the abstract. Styles inherent to a profession serve various functions including the following:

- They set up an in-group consisting of those within the profession.
- They reflect professional competence.
- They standardize language usage in reproducible ways.

Nevertheless, no matter how entrenched many of these styles seem, it's always encouraged that all writers—including those at institutions—endeavor to use plain English whenever possible. The use of plain English can help expand the appeal of writing to broader audiences.

Writing for publication, which is the focus of this book, is highly dependent on style. Many publications have their own house styles or defer to stylebooks such as *The Associated Press Stylebook* or *The Chicago Manual of Style*. These style guides cover spelling, punctuation, word choice, and word usage. House styles also espouse prescriptive choices that make writing appeal to readers in a lively, engaging, aesthetic, and comprehensible manner.

The diachronic aspects of grammar development can be contrasted with the synchronic aspects of style. Just because we observe changes in how words are written and used during the course of our lifetimes, does not mean that grammar changes. Instead, we're observing changes in style, rhetoric, phonetics, and lexicon. In fact, the "new" changes that we see in style often have grammatical precedence.

"The grammar, seen as the system of rules and options underlying usage, has been very stable for the past few centuries," writes Leech. "What might have changed, though, are stylistic conventions or expectations of formality."

Typically, grammatical innovations begin as spoken and spread to writing. This process is moderated by sociohistorical factors. During the past two centuries, there have been few such innovations. Furthermore, for something to stop being grammatical, it would have to fall into complete disuse, which is also rare. Ultimately, because grammar is descriptive and explains what could, many variations, which are viewed as poor and improper usage by style purists, are grammatical.

Corpus Linguistics

A *corpus* (plural corpora) is a systematic collection of naturally occurring written or spoken texts. These texts are sampled systematically using defined criteria and are thus scientific. Corpora are analyzed using computer programs to assess frequencies and occurrences of linguistic and, potentially, grammatical change.

For instance, the Brown Corpus (named after Brown University) was the first general corpus of texts that could be read by computer. It consists of about 1 million words drawn from 500 American edited texts published in 1961. More descriptively, the Brown Corpus is also called the Standard Corpus of Present-Day American English.

Different corpora have different foci. There are corpora representing language as whole, historical English, spoken English, regional variations of English, and English written by learners of the language. For example, the British National Corpus (or Bank of English) is a general, reference corpus which represents different types of spoken and written British English. Another example: The London-Lund Corpus of Spoken English represents spoken language.

In addition to formal analysis of corpora, linguists and other researchers can assess linguistic change based on their own anecdotal experiences, the experiences of others, and random sampling. Of note, a search of usage frequency on Google would comprise a random sampling.

Grammar vs. Style: Specific Examples

To best consider how truly different style and grammar are, here's a list of grammatical trends:

- Use of *same as*, *like*, and *immediately* as conjunctions. EXAMPLE: Zain will become a teacher, like Lindsay became a teacher.
- Placement of frequency adverbs before auxiliary verbs instead of between the auxiliary verb and main verb. EXAMPLE: Holly always has taken the high road.
- Omission of the definite article in noun phrases consisting of a premodifying noun phrase and a proper noun. EXAMPLE: Oscar-winning actress Whoopi Goldberg took the stage.
- Decline in the use of *whom*. EXAMPLE: The football player *who* Jake likes.
- Use of *less* and not *fewer* with countable nouns. EXAMPLE: Alistair wants less guests at the party.
- Loss of *shall* as a future marker when speaking in first person.
- Formation of the possessive case with nonhuman nouns. EXAMPLE: Saeed likes the film's ending.
- Extending the progressive tense to create new constructions. EXAMPLE: The building would not be being razed had it not been for urban restructuring.
- Use of *which* in place of *that* in formal and academic contexts. EXAMPLE: Alfred Wegener's hypothesis which continents slowly drifted laid the basis for a comprehensive theory of plate tectonics.
- Emergence of auxiliary-like uses of certain lexical verbs. EXAMPLE:

Do you wanna go to the park with Cyrus? Instead of: Do you want to go to the park with Cyrus?

Many of these grammatical trends violate conventions of style. For instance, you would be hard-pressed to find an academic publication that will feel comfortable with the auxiliation "wanna." However from a grammatical perspective, "wanna" is acceptable because it represents a possibility of language.

Another grammatical construction that violates stylistic sensibilities is the use of *who* in the objective case. Any editor at any publication will likely prefer *whom* in the objective case. However, in daily vernacular, we rarely hear *whom* and instead hear *who* in relative clauses and questions, making this choice grammatical. Moreover, such usage has historical precedence in published work. Even Shakespeare used *who* in the objective case. Please note that the use of *whom* after a preposition is usually preferred. For example, "For Who the Bell Tolls" is wrong and instead is "For Whom the Bell Tolls."

Here's another example of how grammar and style differ: American editors in particular have taken exception to the use of *which* to introduce restrictive clauses. This development traces back to Fowler's 1926 work, *A Dictionary of Modern English Usage*. However, this usage is widely demonstrated in educated discourse—most notably in British usage. In fact, people have been writing *which* instead of *that* for nearly a thousand years. Ultimately, the distinction that *which* should solely be used for nonrestrictive clauses and *that* should be used for restrictive clauses is completely arbitrary and not grounded in reality. This distinction caters to a sense of aesthetics, formality, and logic that appeals to style prescriptivists even though grammar need not be logical. When editors and style experts (like those at *The Chicago Manual of Style*) cite this distinction, true grammarians recognize this claim for the shibboleth that it is. Nevertheless, because this convention is so ingrained, most American writers don't use *which* in a restrictive sense.

Most of the tips in this book deal with style, not grammar. Thus, although I prescribe the use of *whom* in the objective case, *which* for nonrestrictive clauses, and so much more, I do so only because this guidance is stylistic. It's my intention to teach you to write in a way that conforms to well-accepted style conventions because these conventions are expected by editors at major publications. I also teach you style so that the work that you produce resembles the writing of major publications. The guidance in this book is intended to help you either impress an editor with clean copy or provide your reader an experience that mirrors the writing of world-class publications. Ultimately, much of what I'm teaching you is not necessarily "right" but instead expected.

Appendix III: How Does Google Search Work?

Any concerns about search engine optimization (SEO) invariably depend on how Google—the major player in search—interprets websites.

When we use Google to search, we aren't searching the entire Internet. Instead, we're searching Google's index, or large sample, of the web. According to Google, "Crawling is the process by which Googlebot discovers new and updated pages to be added to the Google index."

The crawling process begins with spiders (or web-crawling bots such as Googlebot) which are software programs that start with a few applicable web pages—a list of web addresses from previous web crawls—and then follow the links on these pages until a large swathe of the Internet is indexed. Using search terms, Google is able to access hundreds of thousands of web pages based on the typical search query.

Google then pares down this vast amount of indexed content by asking more than 200 questions relevant to your search query. The answers to these questions determine what results are listed on the search engine results page (SERP). Examples of these questions include the following:

- How many times does the web page contain the keywords of interest?
- Do the keywords appear in the title or URL?
- Does the web page contain synonyms for the keywords of interest?
- Is the web page from a high-quality website or low-quality website (spam)?
- What is the page's PageRank? PageRank is a formula that was developed by the Larry Page and Sergey Brin, the founders of Google. PageRank calculates the importance of a web page by the number of inbound links, or links from other websites, and the importance of these links.

On a related note, for certain websites, sitemaps also play an important part of the initial web crawling process. According to Google:

"A sitemap is a file where you can list the web pages of your site to tell Google and other search engines about the organization of your site content. Search engine web crawlers like Googlebot read this file to more intelligently crawl your site. Also, your sitemap can provide valuable metadata associated with the pages you list in that sitemap: Metadata is information about a webpage, such as when the page was last updated, how often the page is changed, and the importance of the page relative to other URLs in the site."

Here are examples of sites that can benefit from sitemaps:

- large websites with new or updated content that could be overlooked by web crawlers
- websites with large amounts of archived web content that is either isolated or unlinked
- new websites with few inbound links
- websites with rich media content
- websites shown in Google News

There are a couple of salient takeaways from understanding how Google crawls the web.

First, the website that you're publishing to should have a robust internal linking structure to ensure that spiders can crawl it easily. Moreover, navigation on a site shouldn't be obfuscated or concealed—doing so makes it harder for spiders to crawl.

Second, the best sites on which to publish have a rich network of inbound links, or backlinks, which are incredibly important in getting web content recognized. It helps to have a lot of high-quality websites linking to a website. Some large publications covet inbound links so highly that they actually pay for them!

Consider the following explanation from *The Art of SEO* by Eric Enge and co-authors: "Links play a critical role in ranking. For example, consider two sites where the on-page content is equally relevant to a given topic. Perhaps they are shopping sites *Amazon.com* and the (less popular) JoesShopping Site.com (not a real site). The search engine needs a way to decide who comes out on top: Amazon or Joe. This is where links come in. Links cast the deciding vote. If more sites, and more important sites, link to Amazon, it must be more important so Amazon wins."

Appendix IV: Updating Content

Despite your most sincere intentions to write and self-edit your content, chances are that over time your message will become less timely. Although articles written in print have no way of being changed and can only be issued with updates (or retractions) in subsequent editions, online articles and documents can quickly be changed. In an effort to keep your online content *evergreen,* or timely and relevant, it's a good idea to periodically update your content.

Sometimes, writers worry that if they edit a high-traffic article, the article will suffer in search and place lower on Google SERP (search engine results page). However, this concern is unfounded. Furthermore, if the topicality of your article wanes over time, then the article will get buried in SERP regardless—with more timely and newsworthy articles by other authors and publishers pushing it lower. Updating your content helps with search engine optimization (SEO).

Here are some pointers on how to best update your content so that it remains timely, engaging, and informative.

Broken Links

Just because a link in your article worked when you originally published the piece, doesn't mean that it will still work days, months, weeks, or years later. Make sure that all your links direct the reader back to the content that you originally intended. If the link opens to either a different page or a 404 Not Found Error, then it's time to replace or expunge the link. Remember that when linking to a journal article or study, use a DOI (Digital Object Identifier) link. The DOI link is a persistent and unique digital identifier which won't change.

Concatenations

When following the news, trends, advances in research, and so forth, several events and occurrences are interconnected over time and thus form *concatenations.* When writing an article at a specific time, however, it's not only impossible to predict future events but also difficult to develop perspective with respect to most recent events. Only the passage of time will clarify things.

For example, although the Patient Protection and Affordable Care Act, or Obamacare, was signed into law by President Obama in 2010, its convoluted story didn't stop there. Obamacare continued to make news during the course of Obama's presidency and beyond. For instance in October 2013, the rollout of HealthCare.gov (the online health insurance exchange set up by the Obama administration to expand healthcare coverage) was plagued with software issues, and the resultant media fallout blighted Obama's efforts.

Moreover, President Trump tried to repeal Obamacare early in his presidency.

When updating an online article or document that involves concatenations, it's wise to summarize the events to date before delving into your points or arguments.

Dates

Be very careful with dates. If you start using expressions like "this August" or "next year," then your content will quickly become dated. It's always best to specify exact dates (for example, July 1, 2013) or the month and year (for example, July 2013). You can also use the qualifier "recent" if what you're referring to is in fact recent.

Tenses

When updating content, watch out for the tenses used. If an event is described using the future tense, but this event has already transpired when you go back to update the document, then switch from the future to the past tense.

Combine Articles

To keep your online articles better organized and more comprehensive, consider combining old articles and documents into a single published post and deindexing the excessive coverage. For instance, if on your blog, you were covering the rise of Bitcoin (a type of digital currency) between 2009 and 2017, it may be a good idea to combine articles for heartier and more evergreen coverage. Evergreen content stays relevant and interesting to the reader several months or years after it's published. Remember that regular updates make sense in the thick of coverage, but synopses tend to work better in retrospect.

The Competition

If you've written about a topic some time ago, when you go back to update this content, it's a good idea to do an Internet search to figure out how other writers have covered the subject in the interim. In fact, before you start writing, you should always look to see how other authors and publications cover the topic on which you plan to report.

Please keep in mind that an Internet search for other competing articles is not research. While researching your topics, you should always endeavor to use primary sources; whereas, news articles, feature articles, opinion articles, and so forth are secondary sources, which are one step removed from hard facts. Instead, the writing of others should serve to inspire your own writing.

Meta Titles and Descriptions

When updating old online content, sometimes titles, subtitles, meta titles, and meta descriptions can appear dated and cite information that is no longer timely or relevant. It's a good idea to update these things as needed.

Sources

Knowledge accrues over time. The best way to keep your content evergreen is to ensure that the sources that you're using are current. Updating content often requires that you continually incorporate up-to-date sources to inform your writing.

Word Count

In February 2011, Google launched the Panda update. This update focused on lowering SERP for thin, low-quality content. Many online publishers scrambled to adjust content in light of Google's new guidance. Specifically, articles or documents that were 250 words or fewer were identified by Google as being low quality and suffered in search. Thus, when updating your content, it's a good idea to make sure that the articles you write are longer than 600 words. In fact, Google seems to prefer content that's substantially longer, so, if prudent, you may want to increase the length of your content to more than 1500 words to improve SERP. Although in the real world, length fails to correlate with quality, as far as Google is concerned, length is a marker of quality. And remember that Google dominates SERP. (Honestly, how often do people use Yahoo or Bing to search for stuff?)

On a related note, Google now prefers articles that establish authority. If you're not an expert in the field that you're writing about, it's a good idea to interview experts and add their quotations to your content. Alternatively, you can pull quotations from primary sources such as journal articles, attribute the work, and cite the author.

Bibliography

"ACES Announces 2015 Headline Contest Winners." *ACES*. March 31, 2016. https://acseditors.org/news/2016/aces-announces-2015-headline-contest-winners.
Agnes, Michael, ed. *Webster's New World College Dictionary*. Fourth Edition. Cleveland: Webster's New World, 2001.
AMA Manual of Style. 10th Edition. Oxford: Oxford University Press, 2007.
American Cancer Society. https://www.cancer.org/.
Anderson, Chris. *The Long Tail: Why the Future of Business Is Selling Less of More*. Revised Edition. New York: Hachette Books, 2008.
Anson, Chris M., Robert A. Schwegler, and Marcia F. Muth. *The Longman Writer's Bible*. New York: Pearson Longman, 2006.
"The Art of the Follow-Up." *On the Media*. NPR, December 13, 2016.
The Associated Press Stylebook and Briefing on Media Law 2011. 46th Edition. New York: Basic Books, 2011.
The Associated Press Stylebook and Briefing on Media Law 2017. New York: Basic Books, 2017.
Bartlett, John. *Bartlett's Familiar Quotations*. 17th Edition. Edited by Justin Kaplan. New York: Little, Brown and Company, 2002.
"Beginner's Guide for Wordpress." *wpbeginner*. September 6, 2017. http://www.wpbeginner.com/beginners-guide/categories-vs-tags-seo-best-practices-which-one-is-better/.
Benkler, Yochai, Robert Faris, Hal Roberts, and Ethan Zuckerman. "Study: Breitbart-Led Right-Wing Media Ecosystem Altered Broader Media Agenda." *Columbia Journalism Review*. March 3, 2017.
Bernstein, Theodore M. *The Careful Writer: A Modern Guide to English Usage*. New York: Atheneum, 1973.
Bernstein, Theodore M. *Miss Thistlebottom's Hobgoblins*. New York: The Noonday Press, 1991.
Biber, Douglas, and Susan Conrad. *Register, Genre, and Style*. Cambridge: Cambridge University Press, 2009.
Biber, Douglas, Susan Conrad, and Geoffrey Leech. *Longman Student Grammar of Spoken and Written English*. London: Pearson Education ESL, 2002.
Blundell, William E. *The Art and Craft of Feature Writing*. New York: Plume, 1988.
Bly, Robert W. *The Copywriter's Handbook*. Third Edition. New York: Holt Paperbacks, 2005.
"BOP Policies." *Federal Bureau of Prisons*. https://www.bop.gov/PublicInfo/execute/policysearch?todo=query.
Brians, Paul. *Common Errors in English Usage*. 2nd Edition. Wilsonville: William, James & Co., 2009.
Buchstaller, Isabelle, and Beat Siebenhaar. *Language Variation—European Perspectives VI*. Amsterdam: John Benjamins Publishing Company, 2015.
Burchfield, R.W. *Fowler's Modern English Usage*. Revised Edition. Oxford: Oxford University Press, 2004.
Campbell, Joseph. *The Power of Myth*. New York: Anchor Books, 1991.

Campbell, Joseph. *Reflections on the Art of Living: A Joseph Campbell Companion.* Edited by Diane K. Osbon. First Edition. New York: HarperCollins Publishers, 1991.

The Chicago Manual of Style. Fifteenth Edition. Chicago: University of Chicago Press, 2003.

The Chicago Manual of Style. Sixteenth Edition. Chicago: University of Chicago Press, 2010.

Clark, Roy Peter. *Writing Tools: 50 Essential Strategies for Every Writer.* New York: Little, Brown and Company, 2006.

"Classical and Quantum Mechanics—in a Nutshell." *NIH Center for Information Technology: Office of Intramural Research.* https://cmm.cit.nih.gov/intro_simulation/node1.html.

Colorectal Cancer Trends. *CDC.* https://www.cdc.gov/cancer/colorectal/statistics/trends.htm.

Comparative Studies in Australian and New Zealand English: Grammar and Beyond. Edited by Pam Peters, Peter Collins, and Adam Smith. Amsterdam: John Benjamins Publishing, 2009.

The Convention on Cluster Munitions. http://www.clusterconvention.org/.

Corpus Linguistics. *The University of Chicago Library.* http://guides.lib.uchicago.edu/c.php?g=297174&p=1983784.

Cragan, Janet D., et al. "Baseline Prevalence of Birth Defects Associated with Congenital Zika Virus Infection." *Morbidity and Mortality Weekly Report (MMWR)* 66, no. 8 (2017): 219–222.

"Delaying Gratification." *American Psychological Association.* https://www.apa.org/helpcenter/willpower-gratification.pdf.

Denham, Kristin, and Anne Lobeck. *Linguistics for Everyone: An Introduction.* Second Edition. Boston: Wadsworth Publishing, 2012.

Dixon, R.M.W. *A Semantic Approach to English Grammar.* Second Edition. Oxford: Oxford University Press, 2005.

Dwyer-Lindgren, Laura, et al. "Inequalities in Life Expectancy Among US Counties, 1980 to 2014." *JAMA Internal Medicine* 177, no. 7 (July 2017): 1003–1011. doi:10.1001/jamainternmed.2017.0918.

Einsohn, Amy. *The Copyeditor's Handbook.* Berkeley: University of California Press, 2006.

Enge, Eric, et al. *The Art of SEO: Mastering Search Engine Optimization.* Second Edition. Sebastopol: O'Reilly, 2012.

The Essential Don Murray. Edited by Thomas Newkirk and Lisa C. Miller. Portsmouth: Boynton/Cook Publishers, 2009.

Federal Plain Language Guidelines. *plainlanguage.gov.* https://www.plainlanguage.gov/guidelines/.

Feldman, David, and Justin Gifford. "Iceberg Slim." *The David Feldman Show.* http://davidfeldmanshow.libsyn.com/website/2015/08, August 20, 2015.

Flesch, Rudolf. *How to Write, Speak and Think More Effectively.* New York: Harper & Row, 1960.

Fogerty, Mignon. "Units of Measure." QuickandDirtyTips.com. http://www.quickanddirtytips.com/education/grammar/units-of-measure.

Follett, Wilson. *Modern American Usage: A Guide.* Edited by Erik Wensberg. New York: Hill and Wang, 1998.

Freed, Richard C., Joseph D. Romano, and Shervin Freed. *Writing Winning Business Proposals.* Third Edition. New York: McGraw-Hill, 2011.

Garner, Bryan A. *A Dictionary of Modern American Usage.* Oxford: Oxford University Press, 1998.

Garner, Bryan A. *Legal Writing in Plain English.* Chicago: University of Chicago Press, 2013.

Gastel, Barbara. "Editing and Proofreading Your Own Work." *AMWA Journal* 30, no.8 (2015): 147–151.

Gastel, Barbara. *Health Writer's Handbook.* Second Edition. Ames: Blackwell Publishing, 2005.

Geiger, Timothy M., and Rocco Ricciardi. "Screening Options and Recommendations for Colorectal Cancer." *Clinics in Colon and Rectal Surgery* 22, no. 4 (2009): 209–217. doi: 10.1055/s-0029-1242460.

Gentner, Dedre. "Structure-Mapping: A Theoretical Framework for Analogy." *Cognitive Science* 7 (1983): 155–170. doi: 10.1016/S0364-0213(83)80009-3.
Gibaldi, Joseph. *MLA Handbook for Writers of Research Papers.* Sixth Edition. New York: Modern Language Association, 2003.
Gjersoe, Nathalia, Emily L. Hall, and Bruce Hood. "Children Attribute Mental Lives to Toys When They Are Emotionally Attached to Them." *Cognitive Development* 34 (2015): 28–38. doi: 10.1016/j.cogdev.2014.12.002.
GLAAD Media Reference Guide. 10th Edition. *GLAAD.* https://www.glaad.org/reference.
Gurdus, Elizabeth. "Exclusive: Apple Just Promised to Give US Manufacturing a $1 Billion Boost." CNBC, May 3, 2017. https://www.cnbc.com/2017/05/03/exclusive-apple-just-promised-to-give-us-manufacturing-a-1-billion-boost.html.
Hacker, Diana, and Nancy Sommers. *A Pocket Style Manual.* Seventh Edition. Boston: Bedford/St. Martin's, 2015.
Hooker, Lucy. "The Seven Best Metaphors for the Economy." *BBC News.* November 28, 2014. http://www.bbc.com/news/business-30208476.
"How Search Algorithms Work." *Google Search.* https://www.google.com/search/howsearchworks.
"How Search Organizes Information." *Google Search.* https://www.google.com/search/howsearchworks.
"How Search Works. Google Search." https://www.google.com/search/howsearchworks/ "How Search organizes information." Google Search.
Iggulden, Conn, and Hal Iggulden. *The Dangerous Book for Boys.* New York: Collins, 2007.
Kaushik, Avinash. *Google Analytics—Bounce Rate: The Simply Powerful Metric.* August 1, 2007. https://www.youtube.com/watch?v=ppgfjo6IIf4.
Keith, William M., and Christian O. Lundberg. *The Essential Guide to Rhetoric.* Boston: Bedford/St. Martin's, 2008.
Lakoff, George, and Mark Johnson. *Metaphors We Live By.* Chicago: University of Chicago Press, 2003.
"Learn About Sitemaps." *Google Search Console Help.* https://support.google.com/webmasters/answer/156184?hl=en.
Lee, Chelsea. "How to Capitalize and Format Reference Titles in APA Style." *American Psychological Association: APA Style Blog.* http://blog.apastyle.org/apastyle/2012/03/how-to-capitalize-and-format-reference-titles-in-apa-style.html.
Leech, Geoffrey, and Jan Svartvik. *A Communicative Grammar of English.* Third Edition. New York: Routledge, 2013.
Leech, Geoffrey, Marianne Hundt, Christian Mair, and Nicholas Smith. *Change in Contemporary English: A Grammatical Study.* Cambridge: Cambridge University Press, 2009.
Lester, Mark, and Larry Beason. *The McGraw-Hill Handbook of English Grammar and Usage.* 2nd edition. New York: McGraw-Hill Education, 2012.
Mars, Roman. "Episode 284: Hero Props: Graphic Design in Film & Television." *99% Invisible.* November 13, 2017.
McBride, Kelly. "'Patchwriting' Is More Common Than Plagiarism, Just as Dishonest." *Poynter.* September 18, 2012. https://www.poynter.org/news/patchwriting-more-common-plagiarism-just-dishonest.
McWhorter, John. *Our Magnificent Bastard Tongue: The Untold History of English.* New York: Avery, 2009.
McWhorter, John. *Talking Back, Talking Black.* New York: Bellevue Literary Press, 2017.
McWhorter, John. *Words on the Move: Why English Won't—and Can't—Sit Still (Like, Literally).* New York: Henry Holt and Company, 2016.
Merriam-Webster. https://www.merriam-webster.com/.
Merriam-Webster's Collegiate Dictionary. Eleventh Edition. Springfield: Merriam-Webster, 2008.
Merriam-Webster's Collegiate Thesauras. Springfield: Merriam-Webster, 1988.
Meta Description. *Moz.* https://moz.com/learn/seo/meta-description.

Metcalfe, Janet, and Walter Mischel. "A Hot/Cool-System Analysis of Delay of Gratification: Dynamics of Willpower." *Psychological Review* 106, no. 1 (1999): 3–19. doi: 10.1037%2F0033-295X.106.1.3.
Montagnes, Ian. *Editing and Publication: A Training Manual.* Manila: International Rice Research Institute, 1991.
"More Guidance on Building High-Quality Sites." *Google Webmaster Central Blog.* May 6, 2011. https://webmasters.googleblog.com/2011/05/more-guidance-on-building-high-quality.html.
Murray, Donald M. *A Writer Teaches Writing.* Revised Second Edition. Boston: Thomson Heinle, 2004.
New Oxford American Dictionary. Second Edition. Oxford: Oxford University Press, 2005.
The New York Times Manual of Style and Usage. New York: Three Rivers Press, 1999.
Nordquist, Richard. "Colloquialization (Language) ." *ThoughtCo.* March 6, 2017. https://www.thoughtco.com/what-is-colloquialization-1689764.
Nordquist, Richard. "What Is the Second Persona?" *ThoughtCo.* May 8, 2017. https://www.thoughtco.com/second-persona-audience-1691932.
Ogborn, Jon, and Edwin F. Taylor. "Quantum Physics Explains Newton's Laws of Motion." *Physics Education* 40, no. 1 (2005): 26–34. doi: 10.1088/0031–9120/40/1/001.
OneLook Dictionary Search. https://www.onelook.com/.
Oxford American Writer's Thesaurus. Second Edition. Oxford: Oxford University Press, 2008.
Oxford Dictionaries. https://www.oxforddictionaries.com/.
Oxford Idioms: Dictionary for Learners of English. 2nd Edition. Edited by Dilys Parkinson. Oxford: Oxford University Press, 2006.
"Paraphrase: Write It in Your Own Words." *Purdue Owl.* https://owl.english.purdue.edu/owl/owlprint/619/.
Peters, Pam. *The Cambridge Guide to English Usage.* Cambridge: Cambridge University Press, 2004.
A Pictorial Walk Through the 20th Century. *United States Department of Labor.* https://arlweb.msha.gov/century/canary/canary.asp.
Publication Manual of the American Psychological Association. Sixth Edition. Washington, D.C.: American Psychological Association, 2010.
Raskoff, Sally. "Understanding Generalizations and Stereotypes ." *Everyday Sociology.* May 14, 2012. http://www.everydaysociologyblog.com/2012/05/understanding-generalizations-and-stereotypes.html.
Rich, Frank. "The Real-Life '24' of Summer 2008." *The New York Times.* July 13, 2008.
Ricœur, Paul. *The Rule of Metaphor.* Toronto: University of Toronto Press, 1977.
Rogers, Simon. What Is Google Trends Data—and What Does It Mean? Google News Lab. *Medium.* July 1, 2016. https://medium.com/google-news-lab/what-is-google-trends-data-and-what-does-it-mean-b48f07342ee8.
Rosta, And. *English Mediopassive.* http://www.phon.ucl.ac.uk/publications/WPL/92papers/UCLWPL4%2015%20Rosta.pdf.
Saleh, Naveed. *The Complete Guide to Article Writing: How to Write Successful Articles for Online and Print Markets.* Edited by Rachel Randall. Blue Ash: Writer's Digest Books, 2013.
Saleh, Naveed. "The Effects of Crying." *Psychology Today.* August 23, 2015. https://www.psychologytoday.com/blog/the-red-light-district/201508/the-effects-crying.
Saleh, Naveed. "The True Cost of a Tattoo." *Psychology Today.* July 24, 2016. https://www.psychologytoday.com/blog/the-red-light-district/201607/the-true-cost-tattoo.
Saleh, Naveed. "Which Toys Do Children Anthropomorphize?" *Psychology Today.* December 22, 2015. https://www.psychologytoday.com/blog/the-red-light-district/201512/which-toys-do-children-anthropomorphize.
"See You in Court." *On the Media.* NPR, February 9, 2017.
SIL Glossary of Linguistic Terms. http://www.glossary.sil.org/.
Skillin, Marjorie E., and Robert M. Gay. *Words into Type.* 3rd Revised Edition. Englewood Cliffs: Prentice Hall, 1974.

Slim, Iceberg. *Pimp: The Story of My Life*. Cash Money Content, 2011.

Spiegel, Alix, Lulu Miller, and Hanna Rosin. "Reality." *Invisibilia*. NPR, June 8, 2017.

The Standard Corpus of Present-Day Edited American English (the Brown Corpus). *VARIENG: University of Helsinki*. http://www.helsinki.fi/varieng/CoRD/corpora/BROWN/.

Stilman, Anne. *Grammatically Correct*. 2nd Edition. Cincinnati: Writer's Digest Books, 2010.

Straus, Jane, Lester Kaufman, and Tom Stern. *The Blue Book of Grammar and Punctuation*. Eleventh Edition. San Francisco: Jossey-Bass, 2014.

Strong, William. *Coaching Writing*. Portsmouth: Heinemann, 2001.

Strong, William. *Sentence Combining: A Composing Book*. Third Edition. New York: McGraw-Hill, 1994.

Strong, William. *Writer's Toolbox: A Sentence Combining Workshop*. New York: McGraw-Hill, 1995.

Strunk, William, Jr., and E.B. White. *The Elements of Style*. Fourth Edition. Needham Heights: Allyn & Bacon, 2000.

Sugarman, Joseph. *The Adweek Copywriting Handbook*. Hoboken: John Wiley & Sons, 2007.

Sumner, David E., and Holly G. Miller. *Feature & Magazine Writing*. Malden: John Wiley & Sons, 2013.

Sundem, Garth. "This Is Your Brain on Multitasking." *Psychology Today*. February 24, 2012. https://www.psychologytoday.com/blog/brain-trust/201202/is-your-brain-multitasking.

To Describe or Prescribe, That Is the Question (with Apologies to Shakespeare). Oxford Dictionaries. August 22, 2011. https://blog.oxforddictionaries.com/2011/08/22/describe-or-prescribe-poll/.

Trepanowski, John F., et al. "Effect of Alternate-Day Fasting on Weight Loss, Weight Maintenance, and Cardioprotection Among Metabolically Healthy Obese Adults: A Randomized Clinical Trial." *JAMA Internal Medicine* 177, no.7 (2017): 930–938. doi: 10.1001/jamainternmed.2017.0936.

"Using Verbs." *University of Ottawa: The Writing Centre*. http://arts.uottawa.ca/writingcentre/en/hypergrammar/using-verbs.

VanDerhei, Jack. "The Impact of the Recent Financial Crisis on 401(k) Account Balances." *Employee Benefit Research Institute*. February 2009. https://www.ebri.org/publications/ib/?fa=ibDisp&content_id=4192.

Waters, Hannah. "Amazing Sea Butterflies Are the Ocean's Canary in the Coal Mine." Smithsonian.com. May 14, 2013. https://www.smithsonianmag.com/science-nature/amazing-sea-butterflies-are-the-oceans-canary-in-the-coal-mine-61813612/.

Weiner, Richard. *Webster's New World Dictionary of Media and Communications*. Revised Edition. New York: Macmillan General Reference, 1996.

Wetzel, Dan. "Aaron Hernandez Trial: Fiancée Shows Her Loyalty with a New Last Name." *Yahoo Sports*. March 30, 2017. https://sports.yahoo.com/news/aaron-hernandez-trial-fiancee-shows-her-loyalty-with-a-new-last-name-193023931.html.

"What Is a Persistent URL? What Is a DOI?" *ICPSR*. https://www.icpsr.umich.edu/icpsrweb/content/shared/ICPSR/faqs/what-is-doi.html.

Wright, Natalie A., David W. Steadman, and Christopher C. Witt. "Predictable Evolution Toward Flightlessness in Volant Island Birds." *Proceedings of the National Academy of Sciences of the United States of America* 113, no. 17 (2016): 4765–4770. doi: 10.1073/pnas.1522931113

Wydick, Richard C. *Plain English for Lawyers*. Fifth Edition. Durham: Carolina Academic Press, 2005.

The Yahoo! Style Guide: The Ultimate Sourcebook for Writing, Editing, and Creating Content for the Digital World. New York: St. Martin's Press, 2010.

Zinsser, William. *On Writing Well: The Classic Guide to Writing Nonfiction*. New York: HarperCollins, 2006.

Index